OECD Development Pathways

Multi-dimensional Review of Paraguay

VOLUME 2. IN-DEPTH ANALYSIS AND RECOMMENDATIONS

OECD

dev
DEVELOPMENT CENTRE

Please cite this publication as:
OECD (2018), *Multi-dimensional Review of Paraguay: Volume 2. In-depth Analysis and Recommendations*, OECD Development Pathways, OECD Publishing, Paris.
https://doi.org/10.1787/9789264306202-en

ISBN 978-92-64-30619-6 (print)
ISBN 978-92-64-30620-2 (pdf)

Series: OECD Development Pathways
ISSN 2308-734X (print)
ISSN 2308-7358 (online)

Photo credits: Cover design by the OECD Development Centre.

Corrigenda to OECD publications may be found on line at: *www.oecd.org/publishing/corrigenda*.

Foreword

Economic growth matters, but it is just one facet of development. Policy makers should focus their attention on ensuring that their country's development path is sustainable and that the lives of their citizens improve. This requires reconciling economic, social and environmental objectives.

OECD Development Pathways is a series that looks at multiple development objectives beyond an exclusive focus on growth. It recognises well-being as part and parcel of development and helps governments identify the main constraints to more equitable and sustainable growth by undertaking a multi-dimensional country review (MDCR). Governments trying to achieve economic, social and environmental objectives need to understand the constraints they face and develop comprehensive and well sequenced strategies for reform that take into account the complementarities and trade-offs across policies. The MDCR methodology is based on quantitative economic analysis, as well as qualitative approaches including foresight and participatory workshops that involve actors from the private and public sectors, civil society, and academia.

The MDCRs are composed of three distinct phases: initial assessment, in-depth analysis and recommendations, and from analysis to action. This approach allows for a progressive learning process about the country's specific challenges and opportunities. The Mutual Learning Group (MLG) for the MDCRs brings together policy makers responsible for designing development strategy to support the exchange of experiences on common challenges.

Paraguay initiated two OECD Reviews – a Multi-dimensional Country Review and a Public Governance Review – in 2017 as part of an effort to strengthen its ties with the OECD. This report is the second volume of the MDCR of Paraguay. It presents further analysis and detailed policy recommendations to address three key development challenges identified in Volume I of this MDCR: a fragmented social protection system, a health system facing a double burden of communicable and non-communicable disease, and an education system in need of reform. A preliminary version of this report was presented in Asunción in July 2018.

This MDCR is designed to help Paraguay formulate development strategies, and identify and support the policy reforms needed to achieve further sustainable and inclusive development, in the context of the implementation of its National Development Plan and Paraguay's commitment to the Sustainable Development Goals. A forthcoming third volume, based on the recommendations presented in this second volume, will present the necessary conditions and actions for making reform happen. These analyses support Paraguay's own development agenda towards achieving a brighter future for its citizens.

Acknowledgements

Multi-dimensional Country Reviews (MDCRs) are the result of a collaborative effort of the OECD and the country under review. Work on the second phase of the MDCR of Paraguay was carried out by the OECD Development Centre, with support from the Technical Secretariat for Economic and Social Development Planning of Paraguay (*Secretaría Técnica de Planificación del Desarrollo Económico y Social*, STP).

The review was produced under the guidance of Mario Pezzini, Director of the OECD Development Centre and Special Counsellor to the Secretary-General on Development, and the leadership of Jan Rieländer, Head of the MDCR Unit. The review was co-ordinated by Juan Ramón de Laiglesia (OECD Development Centre) and drafted by Ian Brand-Weiner, Juan Ramón de Laiglesia, and Juan Vázquez Zamora (OECD Development Centre). Deirdre Culley managed the workshop "Scenarios for the future of Paraguay" held in Asunción on 4 December 2017. The review also includes contributions made by Nathalia Montoya and Carine Viac (OECD Development Centre). Nathalia Montoya also provided excellent research assistance throughout the review.

The team is grateful for guidance and comments provided by José-Luis Álvarez-Galván, Samuel Kim, and Elizabeth Fordham of the OECD Directorate for Education and Skills, as well as by Caroline Berchet, of the OECD Directorate for Employment, Labour and Social Affairs. The team is also grateful for insightful comments provided by Riku Elovainio, Alexandre Kolev, Alexander Pick and Caroline Tassot (OECD Development Centre) as well as by those made by participants in the review session held on 26 and 27 April in Asunción and Paris. The report incorporates remarks and inputs provided during the review of the report by the Mutual Learning Group for Multi-Dimensional Country Reviews on its meeting held on 18 May 2018. The review was led by H. E. Ambassador Carlos Márcio Cozendey (Delegate of Brazil to International Organisations in Paris) and by Catalina Crane (Special representative of Colombia to the OECD).

The Multi-dimensional Country Review of Paraguay is made possible by the financial support of the European Union. The team extends its gratitude to the Delegation of the European Union to Paraguay for its support during the process, the insights of its staff into the development of Paraguay and their efforts to seek synergies between this review and other actions financed by the European Union in Paraguay. The team is also grateful to Eurosocial for the invitation to participate in the activities of the programme on Social Protection in Paraguay.

This review has greatly benefited from the support of Minister José Molinas Vega, Executive Secretary of the Technical Secretariat for Economic and Social Development Planning (STP) of Paraguay, and his staff. Jazmín Gustale (Deputy Minister of the STP), and her team have been valuable counterparts. The contributions of Gisella Dimodica, Verónica Gauto, Claudia Martínez and Marcos Martínez in ensuring the smooth interaction between the OECD team and the Paraguayan authorities were particularly helpful. The review has also benefitted from the reactivity and inputs provided by Martha Peña (Ministry of Finance), María Emilia Ayala, Verónica Bogarín, Octavio Ferreira, and

Sebastián Ortiz (Ministry of Foreign Affairs). The team extends its gratitude to the Directorate-General for Surveys, Censuses and Statistics (DGEEC) and to the Ministry of Employment, Labour and Social Security (MTESS) for providing household-level data used in this report. The following ministries, agencies and institutions provided useful inputs and contributions to the review throughout the process: the Central Bank of Paraguay (BCP), the Ministry of Agriculture and Animal Husbandry (MAG), the Ministry of Education and Culture (MEC), the Ministry of Employment, Labour and Social Security (MTESS), and its Labour Observatory, the Ministry of Finance (MH), the Ministry of Industry and Commerce (MIC), the Ministry of Justice, the Ministry of Public Health and Social Welfare (MSPBS), the National Agency for Evaluation and Accreditation of Higher Education (ANEAES), the National Anti-Corruption Secretariat (SENAC), the National Council for Higher Education (CONES), the National Council for Science and Technology (CONACYT), the National Development Bank (BNF), the National Scholarship Programme Carlos Antonio López (BECAL), the National Secretariat for Housing (SENAVITAT), the National Secretariat for Tourism (SENATUR), the National Technical College of Asunción, the National University of Asunción (UNA), the Secretariat for Social Action (SAS), the Social Security Institute (IPS), the Superintendence for Health, and the Technical Unit of the Social Cabinet (UTGS).

The following individuals and organisations are also thanked for their inputs and engagement with the review process: Caja ANDE, Edgar Giménez Caballero, Investigación para el Desarrollo, Juntos por la Educación, Marta Lafuente, Sape'a, the Centro de Analisis y Difusión de la Economía Paraguaya (CADEP), the Development Information Resource Center (CIRD), the Federation of Educators of Paraguay (FEP), the Federation of Production, Industry and Commerce (FEPRINCO), the Inter-american Development Bank, the Micro and Small Enterprise Chamber (*Cámara de Mipymes*), the National Union of Educators (UNE), the National Team for Country Strategy (ENEP) and its members, the National Worker's Central (CNT), Paraguay Educa, the Paraguayan Association of Private Health Clinics, Paz Peña, Promed, the Workers Central Union of Paraguay (CESITP) and the World Health Organisation (WHO).

The team is grateful to Andrew Brenner for editing the manuscript and to the OECD Development Centre Communication and Publications Unit, especially Delphine Grandrieux, Aida Buendía and Elizabeth Nash for their support in editing, laying out and producing the report.

This publication has been produced with the assistance of the European Union. The contents of this publication are the sole responsibility of the OECD and can in no way be taken to reflect the views of the European Union.

Table of contents

Tables

Figures

Boxes

Abbreviations and acronyms

AFD	Agencia Financiera de Desarrollo (*Financial Development Agency*)
AIDS	Acquired immune deficiency syndrome
ANEAES	Agencia Nacional de Evaluación y Acreditación de la Educación Superior (*National Agency for Evaluation and Accreditation of Higher Education*)
APS	Aporte Previsional Solidario (*Solidarity Pension Contribution*)
AUGE	Acceso Universal con Garantías Explícitas (*Universal Access with Explicit Guarantees*)
BCP	Banco Central del Paraguay (*Central Bank of Paraguay*)
BECAL	National Scholarship Programme *Carlos Antonio López*
BEPS	Beneficios Económicos Periódicos (*Periodic Economic Benefits*)
BTI	Bertelsmann Stiftung's Transformation Index
CADEP	Centro de Análisis y Difusión de la Economía Paraguaya (*Centre for Analysis and Dissemination of the Paraguayan Economy*)
CAIS	Centros de Atención Integral en Salud (*Centres of Integral Health Care*)
CCT	Conditional Cash Transfer
CEDLAS	Centro de Estudios Distributivos, Laborales y Sociales (*Centre for Distributive, Labor and Social Studies*)
CELADE	Centro Latinoamericano y Caribeño de Demografía (*Latin American and Caribbean Demographic Centre*)
CEQ	Commitment to Equity
CESITP	Central Sindical de Trabajadores del Paraguay (*Workers Central Union of Paraguay*)
CHE	Catastrophic health expenditure
CIAT	Centro Interamericano de Administraciones Tributarias (*Inter-American Center of Tax Administrations*)
CMNN	Communicable, maternal, neonatal and nutritional diseases
CNET	Consejo Nacional de Educación y Trabajo (*National Council of Education and Labor*)
CONES	Consejo Nacional de Educación Superior (*National Council for Higher Education*)
CR	Contributory regime

CRVS	Civil registration and vital statistics system
DB	Defined-benefit
DC	Defined-contribution
DGEEC	Dirección General de Estadística, Encuestas y Censos (Directorate-General for Surveys, Censuses and Statistics)
EBAIS	Equipos Básicos de Atención Integral de Salud (*Basic Equipment of Comprehensive Healthcare*)
ECLAC	Economic Commission for Latin America and the Caribbean
EEB	Educación Escolar Básica (*Basic School Education*)
ELPS	Encuesta Longitudinal de Protección Social (*Longitudinal Survey of Social Protection*)
ENEP	Equipo Nacional de Estrategia País (*National Team for Country Strategy*)
EPH	Encuesta Permanente de Hogares de Paraguay (*Permanent Household Survey*)
EUR	Euro
FAO	Food and Agriculture Organization of the United Nations
FEEI	Fondo para la Excelencia de la Educación y la Investigación (*Fund for Excellence in Education and Research*)
FONACIDE	Fondo Nacional de Inversión Pública y Desarrollo (*National Fund for Public Investment and Development*)
FONARESS	Fondo Nacional de Recursos Solidarios para la Salud (*National Fund of Solidarity Resources for Health*)
FOSYGA	Fondo de Seguridad y Garantía (*Security and Guarantee Fund*)
GBD	Global Burden of Disease
GDP	Gross Domestic Product
GIZ	Deutsche Gesellschaft für Internationale Zusammenarbeit GmbH
HAQ	Healthcare access and quality
HIV	Human immunodeficiency virus
ICROP	Integrated Community Registration Outreach Programme
IDB	Inter-American Development Bank
IFAD	International Fund for Agricultural Development
IFD	Institutos de Formación Docente (*Teacher training institutes*)
ILO	International Labour Organization
IMF	International Monetary Fund
INAN	Instituto Nacional de Alimentacion y Nutricion (*National Institute of Food and Nutrition*)

IOPS	International Organisation of Pension Supervisors
IPS	Instituto de Previsión Social (*Social Security Institute*)
IRACIS	Impuesto a la renta comercial, industrial o de servicios (*Tax on commercial, industrial or service income*)
IRAGRO	Impuesto a la renta agropecuaria (*Agricultural income tax*)
IRP	Impuesto a la renta personal (*Personal income tax*)
IRPC	Impuesto a la Renta del Pequeño Contribuyente (*Small Taxpayer's Income Tax*)
ISCED	International Standard Classification of Education
IT	Information technology
ITS	Institutos Técnicos Superiores (*Higher Technical Institutes*)
IUD	Intrauterine device
LAC	Latin America and the Caribbean
MAG	Ministerio de Agricultura y Ganadería del Paraguay (*Ministry of Agriculture and Animal Husbandry*)
MDCR	Multi-dimensional Country Review
MEC	Ministerio de Educación y Ciencias (*Ministry of Education and Science*)
MH	Ministerio de Hacienda (*Ministry of Finance*)
MSPBS	Ministerio de Salud Pública y Bienestar Social (*Ministry of Public Health and Social Welfare*)
MTEESS	Ministerio de Trabajo, Empleo y Seguridad Social (*Ministry of Employment, Labour and Social Security*)
NCD	Non-communicable diseases
NEET	Not employed, nor in the education system or training
OOP	Out-of-pocket
PAHO	Pan-American Health Organization
PAI	Expanded Immunization Programme
PANI	Programa Alimentario Nutricional Integral (*Comprehensive Nutritional Food Program*)
PBS	Pensión Básica Solidaria (*Basic Solidarity Pension*)
PISA	Programme for International Student Assessment
PND	Plan Nacional de Desarrollo (*National Development Plan*)
PNTE	Plan Nacional para la Transformación Educativa 2030 (*National Plan for Educational Transformation 2030*)
PPP	Purchasing power parity

PREAL	Programa de Promoción de la Reforma Educativa en América Latina y el Caribe (*Program for the Promotion of Educational Reform in Latin America and the Caribbean*)
PYG	Paraguayan Guarani
REIFOCAL	Registro de Instituciones de Formación y Capacitación Laboral (*Registry of institutions of professional training*)
SAS	Secretaría de Acción Social (*Secretariat for Social Action*)
SASSA	South African Social Security Agency
SDG	Sustainable Development Goals
SEME	Sistema de Emergencias Médicas Extrahospitalarias (*Out-of-hospital Medical Emergency System*)
SENAC	Secretaría Nacional Anticorrupción (*National Anti-Corruption Secretariat*)
SENASA	Servicio Nacional de Saneamiento Ambiental (*National Service of Environmental Sanitation*)
SET	Subsecretaría de Estado de Tributación (*Under-Secretary of State for Taxation*)
SGSSS	Sistema General de Seguridad Social en Salud (*General System of Social Security in Health*)
SIAF	Sistema Integrado de Administración Financiera (*Integrated Financial Management System*)
SSIEV	Sub-Sistema Informático de Estadísticas Vitales (*Sub-Computer System of Vital Statistics*)
SIIS	Sistema Integrado de Información Social (*Integrated Social Information System*)
SINAFOCAL	Sistema Nacional de Formación y Capacitación Laboral (*National Training and Labor Training System*)
SISALRIL	Superintendencia de Salud y Riesgos Laborales de la República Dominicana (*Superintendence of Health and Labor Risks of the Dominican Republic*)
SNEPE	Sistema Nacional de Evaluación del Proceso Educativo (*National System for the Evaluation of the Educational Process*)
SNPP	Sistema Nacional de Promoción Profesional (*National System of Professional Promotion*)
SPR	Sistema de planificación por resultados (*Results-based planning system*)
SR	Subsidised regime
STP	Secretaría Técnica de Planeación del Desarrollo Económico y Social (*Technical Secretariat for Economic and Social Development Planning*)
TERCE	Tercer Estudio Regional Comparativo y Explicativo (*Third Regional Comparative and Explanatory Study*)
TVET	Technical and Vocational Education and Training
UCA	Universidad Católica "Nuestra Señora de la Asunción" (*Catholic University of Asunción*)

UHC	Universal Health Coverage
UN DESA	United Nations Department of Economic and Social Affairs
UN	United Nations
UNA	Universidad Nacional de Asunción (*National University of Asunción*)
UNDP	United Nations Development Programme
UNFPA	United Nations Population Fund
UNICEF	United Nations Children's Fund
USD	US Dollar
USF	Unidades de Salud de la Familia (*Family Healthcare Units*)
VAT	Value-added tax
WHO	World Health Organisation
YLL	Years of life lost

Executive summary

Having achieved robust economic growth and a remarkable level of macroeconomic stability over the past 15 years, Paraguay has set a course to become not only more prosperous, but also more inclusive by 2030. To fulfil its development ambition, the country will need to overcome the multiple constraints. Specifically, it will need to foster structural transformation to unlock new sources of growth. Paraguay will also need to enhance its capacity to further social development and inclusivity.

Poverty reduction is progressing notably: absolute poverty fell from 12% to 4% between 2010 and 2017, a pace that puts the country on track to eradicate it by 2030. Access to electricity, improved sanitation and the Internet is spreading. Progress in addressing inequalities has been slower: Paraguay's tax and benefit system contributes to poverty reduction but decreases inequality by less than 2%, a low figure by regional and OECD standards.

Putting Paraguay on a more inclusive development path requires co-ordinated action to increase the capacity of the state to redistribute, to improve the delivery of public services such as health and education, and to sustain efforts to break the intergenerational transmission of poverty and inequality. The ability of the country's social protection system to address vulnerabilities and improve living standards and that of the education and training system to endow citizens with the necessary skills will be critical in delivering this shift in Paraguay's development.

Achieving social protection for all Paraguayans

Despite notable successes, the social protection system in Paraguay is very fragmented and has limited reach. Only 21% of the employed population contributes to social security. Given the high level of informality, Paraguay has expanded social assistance programmes targeting those most in need. It has established a well-targeted cash transfer programme for poor families. A social pension contributes to almost half of Paraguayans over 64 receiving a pension. However, the flagship social assistance programmes cover less than 30% of poor households.

To ensure that all Paraguayans receive adequate social protection, the reach of both social security and social assistance should be expanded. Bringing the self-employed into the social security system is indispensable for the system's sustainability and coherence and requires adjustments to respond to their circumstances. Major social assistance programmes targeting poor families and the elderly need to be significantly scaled up to reach their target populations.

Social protection is provided by a multiplicity of agencies and programmes, which hinders efficiency and limits synergies. To increase the efficiency of public action, Paraguay should establish an integrated social protection system. This will require rethinking the governance of social protection to endow it with strong leadership and effective co-ordination mechanisms. Essential building blocks such as a single registry of beneficiaries, a unified targeting system for social assistance and a dashboard to support planning and monitoring, are already in place and should be strengthened and integrated. The contributory and non-contributory pension systems should be integrated into a single multi-pillar system, and be put under reinforced oversight. In the short term, parametric reforms to certain regimes in the pension system will be necessary to ensure its financial sustainability, enhance its effectiveness and strengthen its progressivity.

Delivering quality healthcare to all requires systemic reform

In the midst of a marked demographic and epidemiological transition, Paraguay faces a double burden in health. Non-communicable diseases are on the rise, while challenges derived from communicable, maternal, neonatal and nutritional conditions persist. Through the development of primary care delivery units and the elimination of user fees, Paraguay has greatly increased access to healthcare. The population with access to skilled healthcare increased from just over half of the population in 2003 to over three quarters in 2016. Conversely, coverage by health insurance has progressed little and remains low, at 26%. Consequently, out-of-pocket expenditures are large and many Paraguayans are confronted with the prospect of impoverishment in the face of health expenses. Further efforts to generalise preventive care, to increase the quality and to ensure continuity of care are needed to effectively increase the health of the majority of Paraguayan citizens.

To deliver quality healthcare to all Paraguayans, the health system needs to overcome its high level of fragmentation and weak stewardship. Social security covers around 20% of the population, and a collection of scattered public and private schemes a further 8%. The rest of the population has access to the national health service of the Ministry of Health. Fragmentation leads to large inequalities in the availability of resources and limits the pooling of funds and risk. A national dialogue is necessary to set the course for a vision of the future of the health system. Building on existing efforts to develop health networks around primary care, Paraguay should establish the conditions for a more integrated health system to emerge, by generalising inter-institutional agreements, moving towards the separation of purchasing and service provision functions, and developing the necessary governance institutions in the heath sector. On the funding side, Paraguay should consider ways of channelling out-of-pocket expenditure to mandatory pre-paid regimes. To deliver on its commitment to Universal Health Coverage, the country needs to expand health service and insurance coverage and increase financial protection. The establishment of a well-defined guaranteed health package would contribute to this goal.

Reforming the education and skills system to foster inclusiveness and improve school-to-work transitions

Access to education in Paraguay has expanded markedly and primary education is almost universal. However, challenges remain, in particular in supplying pre-primary education and in increasing completion rates: 10% of 14-year-olds are out of school, rising to 28% for 17-year-olds. Socio-economic status and geographical area remain strong determinants of completing secondary education, perpetuating inequalities. The quality of the education system remains a core challenge, with over a third of students performing at the lowest level of proficiency in national evaluations. Poor learning outcomes and the low relevance of skills taught sustain lacklustre transitions to the labour market, especially for those from disadvantaged backgrounds. Indeed, 80% of those with less than upper secondary schooling are in informal employment and 6 out of 10 young people from extremely poor households are not employed, in education or training by age 29.

Transforming the education and skills system in Paraguay is vital to foster inclusiveness and access to good quality jobs and to achieve Paraguay's development objectives. The current quest to develop a National Plan for the Transformation of the Education Sector for 2030 reflects both the size of the challenge and the determination to transform the education system into a driver of inclusion. Five key elements should be included in this renewed drive for reform. First, efforts must continue to expand education coverage and foster completion, supporting access in remote areas and among the disadvantaged and implementing policies to favour school retention and completion, avoiding repetition and dropouts. Second, policies to improve learning outcomes must focus on teachers, reshaping their training and career pathways, educational resources and the management of schools. Improving evidence on learning outcomes is critical to inform policy making in this respect. Third, to make education more relevant, the reform of the secondary education curriculum is critical to favour insertion in the labour market and provide a basis for access to higher education. Fourth, moving towards an integrated Technical and Vocational Education and Training system will favour good quality school-to-work transitions, where stakeholder engagement, including educators, private sector and unions, will be critical. Five, policies to improve the match between the demand and supply should strengthen information, training, intermediation and skills anticipation mechanisms.

Chapter 1. Overview and recommendations to meet Paraguay's development ambition

Paraguay has experienced strong growth since the early 2000s and has committed itself to a development path to become more inclusive, efficient and transparent. To achieve sustainable and inclusive development and deliver on its vision to 2030, Paraguay will have to overcome two key challenges: buttressing the sources of economic prosperity by fostering structural transformation, and making development more inclusive. The objective of the Multi-dimensional Country Review of Paraguay is to assist the country in achieving its development objectives. The second volume provides in-depth analysis and policy recommendations in three key areas to better share the benefits of development: education, social protection and health. This chapter provides an overview of the analysis contained in the report, the main conclusions and their implications for development policy in Paraguay. The chapter also discusses possible scenarios for the future and their implications for development prospects and priorities in the country.

Having achieved a remarkable level of macroeconomic stability and overcome the economic and institutional turmoil that plagued the country during the 1990s, Paraguay has set a course to become not only more prosperous, but also more inclusive by 2030. Economic growth has been robust, outpacing the region even in the face of the difficulties of some of its neighbours and major trading partners. Along with the development of flagship social programmes, economic growth has contributed to lifting many Paraguayans out of poverty since the turn of the century. Well-being outcomes have improved in a range of domains, including access to health services or educational attainment.

The country's development path in the past has capitalised on Paraguay's vast natural wealth. Growth has relied on highly productive mechanised agriculture and extensive animal farming. The production of clean electricity from the two binational dams and the revenues that they produce have not only generated income but also provided room for manoeuvre.

A model of development relying on the exploitation of natural wealth presents limitations in terms of inclusivity and sustainability. In Paraguay, where the ownership of factors of production – especially land – is concentrated, reliance on agriculture generates an unequal primary distribution of income. It also leads to inequalities in the spatial distribution of opportunities and strong pressure on environmental resources (OECD, 2018).

Paraguay has set its sights on a brighter future. The country's ambitions for its future are set out in the National Development Plan (*Plan Nacional de Desarrollo* – PND) to 2030 entitled "Building the Paraguay of 2030". The PND sets a course that involves two key transformations: shifting from an economy based on natural resources towards a knowledge-based economy and from an unequal society towards a society free of extreme poverty that offers equal opportunities to all (National Government of Paraguay, 2014).

The Multi-dimensional Country Review (MDCR) of Paraguay is developed to support Paraguay in achieving its development goals. Volume I of this review (OECD, 2018) provides an assessment of the development process in the country, based on a comparative review across development outcomes. It identifies two key constraints that the country's development faces. On the one hand, there is a need to foster structural transformation to unlock new sources of growth by closing the infrastructure gap, strengthening education and skills, and continuing efforts to strengthen governance. On the other hand, the country needs to increase the capacity of the state to further social development and inclusivity. This requires the country to address informality and the fragmentation of social protection, unlock sources of finance for development and territorialise development policy.

This second volume of the MDCR of Paraguay focuses on three key areas where reforms are needed to increase the inclusivity of the country's development path. It provides an in-depth analysis of the country's performance in social protection, health and education and offers policy recommendations to help the country achieve its ambitious objectives in these areas. The chapter begins by a review of progress achieved in Paraguay towards the Sustainable Development Goals (SDG), to which the PND is largely aligned. It then provides a summary of the conclusions and policy recommendations from each of the remaining chapters in the volume.

Progress and challenges in Paraguay's development path

Paraguay has made progress towards the SDGs albeit in some cases at a pace slower than needed to meet the targets

Paraguay has made great progress along certain key dimensions of development but progress has been slower in others. Figure 1.1 depicts progress achieved since 2005 in each of the 17 SDGs with the exception of maritime life. The indicators are chosen to match those of the SDG indicator framework where available, and the targets are set at the national targets where they exist and the international targets when national targets are not set explicitly.

In terms of poverty reduction, both growth in labour incomes and an expansion of poverty reduction programmes have contributed to poverty reduction at a pace that has the country on track to eradicate extreme poverty by 2030. Progress has also been remarkable in closing the remaining gap in access to certain key public services. Access to electricity, which was already high, is nearly universal, and substantial progress has been made in closing the gap in access to improved sanitation. Internet access has also expanded rapidly, increasing opportunities for better public service delivery.

Despite progress in social infrastructure, transport infrastructure remains a significant hurdle as identified by Volume 1 of this review (OECD, 2018). Paraguay has made significant efforts to increase public investment in transport infrastructure, but has not yet succeeded in leveraging private investment. The establishment of a national system for public investment has set the conditions for better project assessment and evaluation and new frameworks for public-private projects have been established in 2013. However, further efforts are necessary for infrastructure projects to fully reflect the development priorities of the country.

Increasing the inclusivity of the development path remains a major challenge that requires decisive policy action

Across domains, while there has been progress in reducing exclusion, decreasing inequality has been more challenging. Although income inequality has fallen, it remains high relative to the region and OECD countries. Moreover, major drivers of inequality have evolved slowly. This is the case for indicators measuring the quality of employment, including the prevalence of salaried work and informality.

Enabling a more inclusive development path requires addressing inequalities today. Paraguay's tax and benefit system contributes to poverty reduction but only decreases inequality by less than 2 % as measured by the Gini coefficient (OECD, 2018). This places the country among those with the lowest degree of redistribution in the region. In Paraguay, the capacity of the state to redistribute income is well below that of OECD countries. Given its low level of public expenditure, Paraguay could consider reforming both the revenue and the expenditure sides of its redistribution capacity. Among OECD countries, most redistribution happens through the spending side. In Paraguay, the reach of key social protection programmes that can have a major effect on income inequality is still far from their objective.

Figure 1.1. Progress across SDG dimensions in Paraguay

Progress towards the 2030 target (relative to 2005 baseline)

Panel A. People

	Target	2005	2010	2015	Target 2030
1: No poverty	Extreme poverty headcount ratio (%)	9.1	11.8	5.4	3
2: Zero hunger	Prevalence of undernourishment (%)	10.7	12.4	10.4	0
3: Good health and well-being	Life expectancy at birth (years)	71.2	72.4	73.6	79
4: Quality education	Adult literacy rate, population over 15 years of age (%)	92.1	93.9	95.1	100
5: Gender equality	Seats held by women in national parliaments (%)	10	12.5	15	50

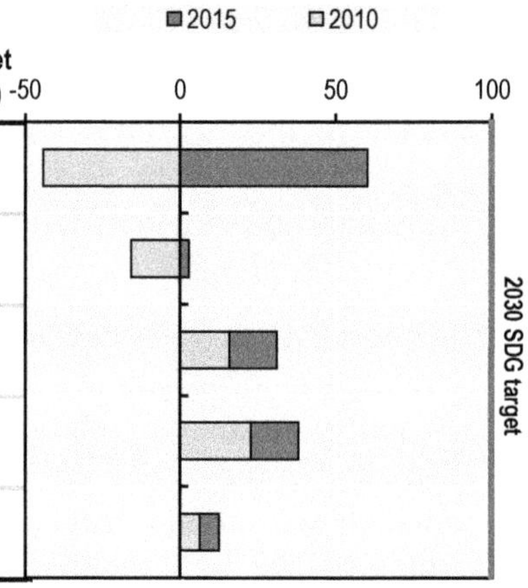

Panel B. Prosperity

	Target	2005	2010	2015	Target 2030
7: Access to electricity	Access to electricity (% of the population)	94.7	97.4	99.3	100
8: Decent work	Wage and salaried workers (%)	38.5	44.1	48.8	100
	Informal workers in non-agricultural employment (%)	-	69.2	64.4	0
8: Access to finance	Account at a financial institution (% aged 15 +)	-	21.7	-	100
9: Industry and innovation	Individuals using the Internet (% of population)	7.9	19.8	48.4	80
9. Infrastructure	Population satisfied with roads and highways (%)	55	49	45	100
10: : Reduced inequalities	Gini Index	0.52	0.51	0.48	0
11: Sustainable cities	Housing deficit, quant. and qual. (thousands of dwellings)	804.017	-	780	360

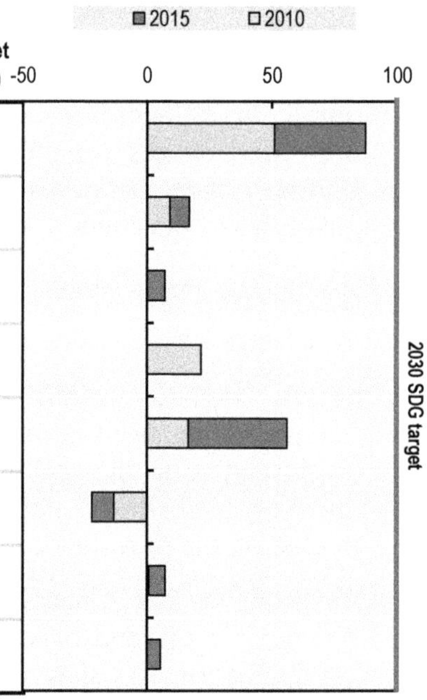

Panel C. Planet

	Target	2005	2010	2015	Target 2030
6. Clean water and sanitation	Access to improved sanitation (%)	62.2	81.4	87.6	100
7. Clean energy	Share of renewable sources in TPES	0.71	0.67	0.65	1
12.Responsible cons. and prod.	Average mean levels of PM2.5 exposure in cities	23.3	17.5	14.9	0
13. Climate action	Greenhouse gas emissions (thousands of CO^2 eq. Gg)	107	-	167	333
15. Life on land	Sites for biodiversity covered by protected areas (%)	23.3	23.3	23.3	45.2

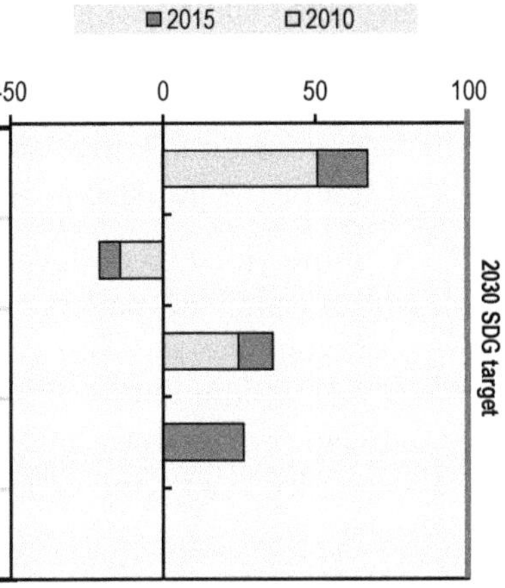

Panel D. Peace and institutions

	Target	2005	2010	2015	Target 2030
16: Peace and justice	Intentional homicides (per 100,000 people)	18.6	11.9	9.3	2.3
16. Empowerment	BTI democracy index (0-10 scale; 10=best)	6.6	7	6.8	10

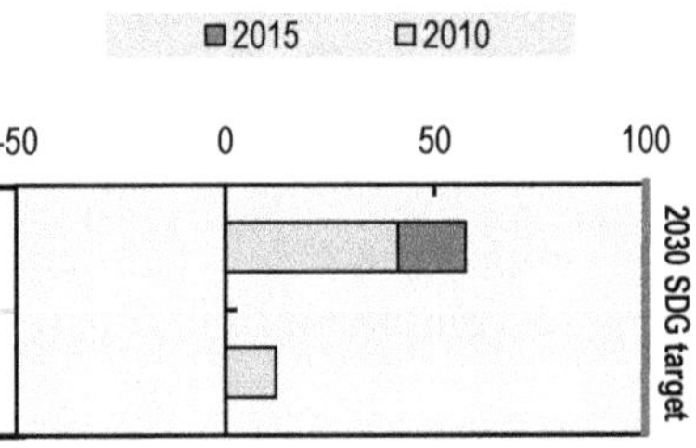

Panel E. Partnerships and financing

	Target	2005	2010	2015	Target 2030
17: Partnerships and Financing for Development	Overall level of statistical capacity (scale 0 - 100)	62.2	70	72.2	85
	Debt service (% of exports of goods and services)	5.8	2.7	2.6	15

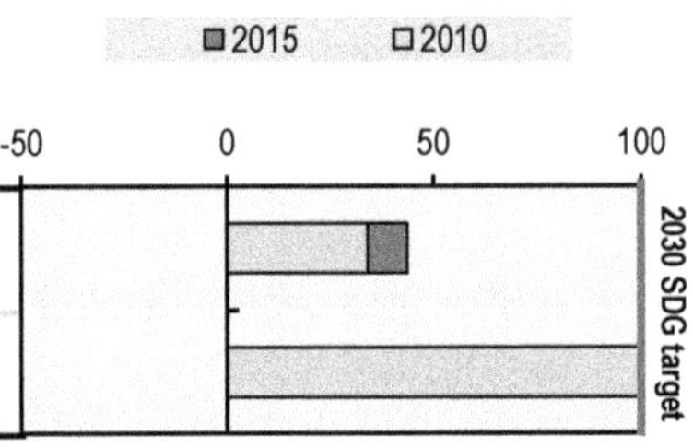

Note: Baseline for informal workers in non-agricultural employment indicator is 2010 instead of 2005. Baseline for access to finance indicator is 0 due to lack of data. Sustainable Cities and communities indicator uses 2002 instead of 2005 and 2012 instead of 2015. Greenhouse gas emissions indicator uses 2012 instead of 2015. Population satisfied with roads and highways indicator uses 2006 instead of 2005. BTI democracy index uses 2006 instead of 2005 and 2016 instead of 2015.

Source: Authors on the basis of official national data when available, and alternatively, international data: *Permanent Household Survey* (DGEEC, 2017); *SDG Indicator system* (United Nations, 2018), https://unstats.un.org/sdgs/indicators/database; *Sustainable Energy for all SE4All database* (World Bank, 2018), http://databank.worldbank.org/data/reports.aspx?source=Sustainable-Energy-for-All; Gallup World Poll (2018); International Energy Agency (2018) database; *Global Burden of Disease Study* (Global Burden of Disease Collaborative Network, 2016); *World Development Indicators* (database) (World Bank, 2018), http://databank.worldbank.org/data/reports.aspx?source=world-development-indicators; *Bertelsmann Transformation Index 2008* (Stiftung, B., 2008); *Reporte Nacional de Inclusión Financiera 2017* (Ministerio de Hacienda, 2017).

StatLink https://doi.org/10.1787/888933822463

The provision of public services, and in particular education and health, can make sizeable contributions to reducing inequalities. Educational attainment determines earnings opportunities and in Paraguay is a strong determinant of the quality of jobs that workers have access to. Paraguay is some way away from achieving quality universal basic education, which could not only provide the skills to the knowledge-based economy of tomorrow but also provide opportunities to all Paraguayans.

A more inclusive development path also requires addressing the intergenerational transmission of poverty and inequality. Several of Paraguay's social policies, and in particular the flagship conditional cash transfer programmes, aim to encourage human capital accumulation among disadvantaged populations, by improving their health and education outcomes and thereby expanding their earning possibilities. Improving access to quality health and education on the supply side is a critical component of this strategy.

Achieving social protection for all Paraguayans requires larger investments and a systemic approach.

In recent years, living standards in Paraguay have improved and investing in social policies will allow the country to continue on this path. Income poverty nearly halved after a hike at the turn of the century; yet many Paraguayans remain vulnerable. Indeed, the burgeoning middle class needs support in order to stabilise. Paraguay recognises the important role of social protection for a sustainable growth path in its National Development Plan *Paraguay 2030* and its Social Protection Sector Strategy Note.

Despite notable progress, social protection coverage remains insufficient

Paraguay's social protection is still evolving. Social protection reduces poverty and inequality in Paraguay, but less than in other Latin American countries. Not all contingencies are covered and many groups of people are unprotected. Only 24.5% of Paraguayans are covered by social protection – measured by the share of the population that is contributing to social security or receiving a contributory or non-contributory benefit – less than half of the Latin American average. High levels of informality and self-employment limit the reach of social security: in 2016, only 21% of the employed population contributed to social security. In this light, Paraguay expanded its social assistance, targeting the population most in need; yet, less than 30% of poor households receive one of the flagship social assistance programmes targeting children and the elderly.

The contributory pension system needs to reform and to expand. The country's young population allowed Paraguay to maintain a generous pension system for the relatively small older population. However, its fragmentation and demographic changes render the system unsustainable. Only 16% of the population above age 64 receive a contributory pension. Contribution rates and periods are not in line with the generosity of the various pension systems and contributors can obtain a more generous pension than in OECD countries at an early age. The net replacement rate of the contributory pension is 40 percentage points higher than the OECD average (103.8% vs. 62.9%). In its current state, the pension schemes are unequal and unsustainable. Contributions to the main pension fund for private sector workers will not suffice to cover pension expenditure as of 2032, and the running deficit of the schemes for non-civilians already accounts for 0.44% of Gross Domestic Product (GDP).

Bringing the self-employed into the social security system is indispensable to create a sustainable and coherent social protection system. Although independent workers can voluntarily contribute to the social security pension system since 2013, in its current state Paraguay's social security system excludes independent workers de facto. Low and irregular income are important impediments for the self-employed to fulfil the contribution requirements. Pension funds do not accept contributions that are based on an income below the minimum wage, and thus exclude 65.7% of own-account workers who earn below the minimum wage in Latin America. The legal minimum social security contributions represent more than 21.5% of income generated every month by a self-employed Paraguayan. For poor workers at the bottom of the income distribution, contributions would even represent 88% of their income, which is higher than the theoretical cost for poor workers in Latin American countries.

The fragmentation of social protection challenges its coverage and governance

Social assistance and social security in Paraguay would benefit from a coherent, co-ordinated and integrated strategy. Currently there is very little interaction or co-ordination between the two pillars of social protection. Social security providers operate without any major oversight and an incomplete information management system complicates the providers' work. And while social assistance plays an important role in the National Development Plan, it lacks clear leadership. Ever since ministerial co-ordination (via the Social Cabinet) came to a halt the only major mechanism for co-ordination between institutions has been based around the national poverty reduction programme *Sembrando Oportunidades*. While this mechanism has succeeded in linking action across programmes and agencies, its limited scope is not conducive to achieving co-ordination for the social protection system as a whole. The secretariat of the Social Cabinet has continued building tools for co-ordination, such as the unified registry of beneficiaries and a social protection matrix which includes budget estimates for social protection programmes until 2023, but has not provided leadership in high-level policy co-ordination.

Paraguay's ambition to expand social protection coverage needs to be financed. Expanding social protection requires mobilising resources, especially for social assistance. Covering the whole target population of Paraguay's flagship social assistance programmes with current benefit levels and inclusion error would demand at least doubling current expenditure levels to 0.7% of GDP for the conditional cash transfer *Tekoporã* and 1.4% of GDP for the social pension programme *Adulto Mayor*. Therefore, it is crucial to mobilise domestic resources so social protection can be sustainably extended to more Paraguayans. Taxes on income, profits and capital gains are among the lowest in Latin America. As a result, Paraguay's tax-to-GDP ratio is one of the lowest in Latin America and is half the OECD average.

Main recommendations

Expand social security coverage

Developing an integrated strategy to enforce social security contributions is indispensable. Informality amongst wage employees is high and so is the evasion of taxes and social security contributions. If the government is to expand social security coverage these impediments need to be tackled. The state needs to strengthen the financial and human resources allocated to inspection and oversight systems that contribute to combatting evasion. In addition to resources, counselling for employers and assistance in registering employees needs to be provided. As part of a broad strategy, the relevant authorities should also follow up on affiliates who cease to contribute and should support, when possible, their re-integration and draw the necessary conclusions when they stop contributing.

Reducing unintended side effects resulting from the legal requirement on minimum contributions could allow more independent workers to contribute to social security. Low and irregular income, paired with the legal requirement that declared incomes be no lower than the minimum wage, are key constraints for independent workers. Lowering the minimum contribution base to the minimum pension could eliminate the legal barrier many independent workers face. It is equally important to regularly review the level of the minimum wage and whether it represents an impediment to contributing to social security.

The social security system should adjust its contribution collection to independent workers' realities. Independent workers rarely have a stable income, which makes it all but impossible to make a set contribution on a regular basis. Allowing flexible contributions for independent workers, including irregular amounts and frequency, can be a way of adjusting the system to independent workers' realities. To effectively allow flexible contributions, the calculation of pension benefits needs to be based on lifelong earnings. An alternative to flexible contributions is a monotax. A handful of countries expanded the coverage to independent workers by charging a fixed fee determined by presumptive income categories as combined tax and social security contribution. Carefully designed and time-limited subsidies to independent workers' contributions can also increase affiliation of independent workers with low income.

Establish an integrated social protection system

Paraguay's social protection system needs to safeguard against all contingencies. Currently not all contingencies are addressed because of the lack of co-ordination between social security and social assistance, as well as the lack of provisions to cover certain risks. An integrated social protection system could provide child benefits also for non-poor formal sector workers. And formal employees should be insured against unemployment.

Contributory and non-contributory pensions need to interact and be integrated into a multi-pillar pension system. This integration can be achieved by creating a three pillar system. First, the social assistance programme for the elderly, *Adulto Mayor*, should be transformed into a basic pension within an integrated system. This requires improving the targeting of *Adulto Mayor*, setting a ceiling for the benefit and – most importantly – allowing a combination of contributory and non-contributory pensions to be paid to an individual. To combine contributory and non-contributory pensions, *Adulto Mayor* would have to be reformed in such a way that its benefits decrease for those with higher contributory pension benefits. Second, the state needs to create an integrated mandatory defined benefit pension system. This can be achieved by integrating pension providers into a single statutory social security provider for private and, ideally, public sector workers. Third, workers should have the possibility to top up their mandatory pensions through voluntary savings plans. Closed pension providers could be transformed into occupational savings plans that complement the mandatory defined-benefit pension system.

Paraguay needs to invest more in social protection. If Paraguay's flagship social assistance programmes are to meet the needs of their entire target populations, their budgets will have to be doubled. A careful budget review should help to finance this expansion, and increasing the efficiency of expenditure could lower the necessary extra funds. Substantial resources should be freed up by decreasing the current fragmentation of social assistance programmes that share similar objectives. If social assistance expenditure were to be defined and recorded in compliance with international standards, then comparisons across countries and time could be made.

Improving domestic resource mobilisation is key to financing social protection. Tax revenues need to increase to finance the expansion of social protection. Current tax burdens do not reflect the growing demand for state services. Thus, tax rates and exemptions could be reviewed to secure the financing of the growing demand for social protection and other state services. The fight against tax evasion and improving tax collection should be of equal importance and intensified. These efforts can increase tax revenues without having to substantially increase tax rates and investment incentives. Finance for social assistance would also benefit from earmarked taxes, which is a way to secure financial resources beyond budgetary cycles.

Improve the governance of social protection

Better co-ordination of agencies would improve the delivery and impact of social assistance programmes. Paraguay needs to effectively align targeting mechanisms and facilitate exchange of information between agencies. Key co-ordination instruments such as the unified targeting instrument, the unified database of beneficiaries and the dashboard for monitoring anti-poverty programmes should be further strengthened and integrated. The delivery of programmes and the relationship between citizens and the state would benefit from joint staff on the ground. A joint presence on the ground would make it easier to engage with beneficiaries, make referrals and reduce costs. This horizontal co-ordination requires re-establishing the co-ordination at ministerial level through the Social Cabinet or assigning to another agency the role of system co-ordinator for social protection or more broadly, social policy.

The pension system needs to be regulated and supervised to increase the system's stability and trustworthiness. A supervisory body for pension providers needs to be created to make up for the oversight and regulation gap. This supervisory body should be endowed with the necessary financial and human resources and its impartiality needs to be ensured. Part of the regulation needs to focus on providing clear guidelines for investments, including ceilings for levels of investment by category, and enforcing diversification of investments. In this process, the supervisory body should enforce a standardisation of financial reports submitted to the Ministry of Finance (and other institutions).

The internal governance of pension providers needs to be improved. Many pension providers need to improve and digitalise their registry of contributions. Better registries can reduce administrative costs, speed up the process of determining pension entitlements and serve as the basis for reliable statistics on future obligations. The biggest social security provider for private sector workers should clearly separate the management of its pension and health branches. And the pension provider for public sector workers should become an independent institution.

Establish a more coherent, fair and inclusive pension system

Paraguay should standardise its pension system to increase the system's equity. At present, the various pension schemes' parameters (e.g. contribution rates, pensionable age and replacement rates) vary widely, which leads to inequities. Paraguay should reform its pension system to overcome these inequities. Key measures for an equitable system are unifying retirement ages, the basis for benefit calculation and replacement and accrual rates. All pension benefits should be indexed using the same method.

Strengthening the link between benefits and contributions is essential to ensure the system's sustainability. This link can be strengthened by increasing the number of years used to calculate the pension benefit, regularly revising the benefit level and contribution rates. Benefit levels should have a ceiling and reflect the decreasing contributor-per-pensioner ratio. The regular revision of contribution rates should be based on actuarial studies, demographic developments, the economic situation, the ratio between pensioners and contributors and the financial soundness of each scheme.

Overcoming fragmentation and accelerating reform can improve the health of Paraguayan citizens

Paraguay faces a double health burden of unresolved and new health challenges

Paraguay has been going through a marked demographic and epidemiological transition. Non-communicable diseases have risen sharply, whereas communicable, maternal, neonatal, nutritional diseases have not decreased as expected. In particular, death rates due to the former have increased by 62.8% between 2000 and 2016, while death rates due to the latter decreased by only 49.4% over the same period. The course of Paraguay's epidemiological transition places a challenging double burden on its health system. In addition to dealing with the simultaneous presence of communicable, maternal, neonatal and nutritional diseases, the system has to deal with the fast-growing burden of non-communicable diseases. Disability and death rates associated to external injuries have been rising in recent decades, mostly due to traffic accidents and interpersonal violence. Between 2000 and 2016, death rates due to external injuries increased by 50.5% (Global Burden of Disease Collaborative Network, 2016).

The epidemiological transition has been accompanied by changes towards sedentary lifestyles and unhealthy dietary habits among the population, deteriorating risk factors and the social determinants of health. In Paraguay, metabolic and behavioural risks are the main contributors to prevalence of non-communicable diseases in Paraguay. Among metabolic risks, the main contributors are high fasting plasma glucose, high blood pressure and high mass index. Among behavioural risks, the main contributors are dietary risks, malnutrition, alcohol and drug use and tobacco.

The health system is fragmented, which limits its capacity and efficiency

Health service delivery is segmented and uncoordinated. The health system in Paraguay consists of the public subsystem, the mixed social security subsystem and the private subsystem. The three subsystems are, for the most part, vertically integrated: they raise revenue, manage funds and deliver service independently. Each of them covers different population groups, mainly based on their employment status and ability to pay. The set of services they provide is not the same and each population segment receives different benefits and quality standards.

A series of reforms failed to transform the health system in a meaningful way. Law 1032, adopted in 1996 was a key milestone in the reform of the health sector in Paraguay.

Although there has been progress in its implementation, a number of key governance provisions in the 1996 reform and subsequent reforms face strong opposition. On primary healthcare, the country has introduced reforms to shift from a pyramidal structure to a network model, though these reforms have not yet fully materialized. The fact that the Paraguayan health system is a mixture of models, with different values and with significant vested interests, makes reform difficult without a national consensus on the way forward.

The weak stewardship of the health authority has limited the country's potential in terms of healthcare access and quality. The fragmentation of the health system (with different modalities for financing, regulation, enrolment, and service delivery) makes stewardship particularly challenging. The regulatory framework and oversight bodies are weak. Information management is inefficient and limits the available evidence base for the formulation of policy and makes continuity of care difficult.

Health financing mechanisms are highly fragmented and insufficient. Health is financed from various funding sources, including public expenditure, contributions to the social security scheme, voluntary advance payments and out-of-pocket expenditure. Revenues for the care of different population groups are held in separate pools, with no potential for cross-subsidy between them. Although past governments have made great efforts to increase public spending on health, funding remains insufficient and inequitable. The health system relies heavily on households' out-of-pocket expenditure.

Despite recent advances, Paraguay faces major challenges to achieve Universal Health Coverage (UHC). Universal Health Coverage strives to ensure that all individuals and communities in a country receive the health services they need without suffering financial hardship. Healthcare access and insurance coverage is still limited, especially among the most vulnerable people. Within the poorest deciles, only a minority is covered by any health insurance. Due to the high reliance of the system on out-of-pocket expenditure, many Paraguayans incur catastrophic health expenditures and are exposed to other financial risks. The entitlement to a specific set of health benefits is very restricted and strongly linked with people's ability to pay. In this regard, almost 80% of the population is uninsured and therefore not entitled to a specific and guaranteed set of benefits.

Main recommendations

Reshaping the system to improve healthcare delivery

Better integration and co-ordination is essential for delivering healthcare services and addressing health policy targets. A national dialogue is necessary to reach a broad consensus on the vision for the future of the health system. The government has a duty to establish the required framework conditions to favour the integration of health service delivery across the public and potentially the private system. Such a framework should aim at generalising inter-institutional agreements for the provision of service across public sector entities. Similarly, public procurement of health services and supplies could be made more agile if the right reforms are introduced. In the long run, the country should consider separating purchasing and service provision functions across the health system. This will entail a reform of how health service providers are paid by funding institutions, be they public or private.

The shift of Paraguay's national health system towards integrated networks based on primary healthcare should be strengthened. A fully-implemented networks model could tackle the major challenges posed by health services fragmentation. Furthermore, primary healthcare is essential for ensuring the continuity of care throughout the system. To progress in this area, the system should (i) ensure that Family Health Units have adequate human and financial resources and (ii) increase the pace of expansion of Family Healthcare Units (USFs).

The governance of the national health system needs to be improved. Paraguay could strengthen the stewardship role of the Ministry of Health and Social Welfare by providing oversight institutions with the necessary autonomy, financial and human resources. The country should also pursue the implementation of the legal framework for the governance of the national health system. In order to increase the quality of health services, the system needs to consolidate and streamline the legal and regulatory bodies pertaining to the health sector. To do so, the system should ensure that regulation applies to all relevant actors, inconsistencies are removed and outdated legislation is either updated or abolished.

Greater investment in the development of information systems in health could improve the delivery of better statistical information and support continuity of care. Paraguay needs to continue past efforts to improve the accuracy of vital statistics and unify systems within institutions and where relevant across the public, private and mixed subsystems. Increasing capacity among stewardship bodies could generate health statistics for the entire health system with the support of the National Statistical Office. In order to ensure continuity of care, the country needs to further develop its medical records system both for recording and access purposes.

Ensuring sustainable funding

Diversifying the sources of funding for health would help ensure the sustainability of health financing. The expansion of social insurance can contribute to securing funds, but will need to be complemented by funding through general taxation. Possibilities to be considered in the case of Paraguay include increasing taxes on goods that generate risks or costs for public health, including tobacco and alcohol, and earmarking part of revenues from these taxes for health financing.

Paraguay should consider ways of channelling out-of-pocket expenditure to mandatory pre-payment regimes. This step is critical in sustaining health financing and in moving towards UHC in a way that is fairer and more efficient. Voluntary enrolment leads to self-selection and is ineffective. Making enrolment mandatory is a critical step, but must be accompanied by the design of a contribution system that ensures contributions are paid from the public purse for those unable to pay and appropriate means are available for those with the ability to pay to contribute. A reform is also needed in the contributory systems to better adapt to circumstances of independent workers. Furthermore, the system could also consider offering partly- or fully-subsidised health insurance for those unable to pay (through a means-tested subsidy).

Paraguay could establish financing mechanisms to cover key contingencies. Certain contingencies are not sufficiently covered by the existing insurance pools and could benefit from a system that channels funds to ensure service provision. The implementation of the National Fund of Solidarity Resources for Health (FONARESS, *Fondo Nacional de Recursos Solidarios para la Salud*), as a pooled fund for highly complex treatment can go some way to achieve this. In this regard, private insurers and IPS could act as revenue collectors and contribute to the fund, while adjusting their financial provisions for the specific set of conditions to be financed through FONARESS.

In the long run, Paraguay could consider options to merge risk pools or create a system that allows for transfers across risk pools.

Ultimately, adequate financing for health will require Paraguay to establish mechanisms to support broader service coverage and pool risk. These mechanisms should ensure that risk and financial flows are pooled, to allow for more efficient allocation of resources across the system. They should also be aligned with the reform of provider payment to generate appropriate incentives for quality care provision, adequate cost management and efficient referral.

Advancing towards Universal Health Coverage

A fundamental way of achieving sustainable UHC is investing more in health promotion and disease prevention. Tackling strategic risk factors is a challenging but worthwhile investment, as it is often more cost-effective than waiting to treat poor health associated with these behaviours.

Paraguay needs to expand health service and insurance coverage, increase financial protection and ensure the delivery of a well-defined benefit package. In particular, the current coverage of the Family Healthcare Units should be expanded to meet the health needs of the entire population. Adequate financial protection could be ensured by providing universal coverage for costly conditions and treatments and by improving the availability and affordability of medicines. Lastly, in order to advance towards UHC, the country needs to define a set of guaranteed services and/or pathologies that can be provided effectively to the population and deliver on that guarantee.

Reforms in the education and skills system are necessary to foster inclusiveness and access to better jobs

Transforming the education and skills system in Paraguay is vital to foster inclusiveness and better access to good quality jobs. Education and development go hand in hand, and Paraguay's success in achieving its main development objectives, as set out in the National Development Plan 2030, will depend in large part on its capacity to improve the education and skills system. Substantial progress has been made, but reforms are unfinished, as presented in Volume I of the MDCR of Paraguay.

Access to education has improved but challenges remain to increase equity and ensure better progression within the education system

Access to the education system has expanded markedly, particularly at the primary level, but hurdles persist in pre-primary and secondary education. There are severe limitations in the availability of administrative data but estimations from survey data show that gaps in school attendance are still relevant both in lower secondary (third grade of *educación escolar básica*) and upper secondary (*educación media*). In particular, net attendance ratios for lower secondary education were at 78% in 2015, and at only 57% for upper secondary. Access to pre-primary education (*educación inicial*) is also a pending challenge. Although coverage is relatively large for pre-school (age 5), with a net enrolment rate of 77% in 2012, access to pre-primary education for children ages 0-4 is insufficient. Figures from 2012 present gross enrolment rates in pre-primary education of around 38% in Paraguay, well below the Latin America and Caribbean (LAC) average of 71% for that same year.

Major inequalities persist in access to the education system, particularly at the secondary level; important factors include gender, socioeconomic status, and geographical location. While access to primary education is widespread, income is still a relevant predictor of access to secondary education: 96% of those in the richest quintile were enrolled in this education level in 2015, but only 67.7% of those belonging to the poorest quintile attended secondary education. Likewise, net enrolment rates in urban areas are significantly higher (87% in 2015) than in rural areas (70%), where 91% of the indigenous population lives (DGEEC, 2014). Unequal access to education is likely to perpetuate socioeconomic inequities in the country.

While more students enter the education system in Paraguay today, keeping kids in school and ensuring they graduate is an ongoing challenge. Attendance has improved, but many students start to leave the education system after the age of 11. Indeed, almost 99% of the population was attending school at age 11 in 2016, but 10% of those aged 14 were out of school in 2016. And as many as 14%, 23% and 28% of those aged 15, 16 and 17, respectively, were not attending school in 2016. Dropouts tend to start during the transition from the second to the third cycle of *educación escolar básica* (i.e. the transition from primary to lower secondary, at the age of around 12). From there, the dropout rate worsens, particularly during the transition from *educación escolar básica* to *educación media* (i.e. the transition from lower secondary to upper secondary, at age 15 approximately) and as students get older. On average, two out of three Paraguayans aged 5-18 who were not attending school in 2016 cited economic issues as the main reason for why they had dropped out of school.

The barriers faced by students with regard to access to the education system and to progress once in it translate into relatively unsatisfactory completion rates, despite progress in recent years. Completion rates reached levels of almost 90% for primary education, but fall to levels of around 68% and 65% in lower-secondary and upper-secondary education respectively, in 2016. Inequalities in completion rates are also significant: only 84.4% of children from the poorest quintile complete primary education, compared to 99.2% of children from the richest quintile.

Learning outcomes remain insufficient, driven by weaknesses in teacher training

Learning outcomes remain insufficient, highlighting the fact that - while schooling has significantly improved - the quality of the education system remains a core challenge. Results from the 2015 evaluation of the *Sistema Nacional de Evaluación del Proceso Educativo* (SNEPE) show that almost a third of students in all the grades where the test is conducted perform at the most basic level of competencies. Relative to the previous SNEPE, which was conducted in 2010, there has been little improvement, and not for all levels. Learning outcomes are lowest in disadvantaged groups or among students in remote areas.

The quality of teaching, probably the single most important factor determining the quality of education, faces various challenges in Paraguay. The number of teachers is relatively high, as shown by the comparatively low ratio of students per teacher, but many of those teachers lack the adequate level of qualification. In fact, in 2012 only 59% of teachers in pre-primary education (*educación inicial*) were qualified to teach at that level. For primary education (first and second cycle of *Educación Escolar Básica* [EEB]), the picture is significantly brighter: 92% had the required qualifications in 2012 (up from

85% in 2004). Most of the more qualified educators teach at the secondary education level.

The quality of teacher-training systems (*Instituciones Formadoras de Docentes*) is inadequate yet they are an important factor in providing quality teachers. Poor quality teaching is directly linked to the weaknesses of evaluation mechanisms and the lack of incentives to improve performance. Teachers' evaluations have been traditionally weak in Paraguay. Evaluations should come with incentives in order to spur an improvement in teacher performance. These incentives have been generally weak, as increases in teachers' salaries are mostly linked to the accumulation of years of experience, accreditations and training. For teachers seeking quality, ongoing training, the options are limited. This represents an additional barrier to effective teaching and the improvement of performance throughout teachers' careers. Also, there is little incentive to participate in this type of training, given the way in which the increases in the remuneration scales (*escalafón docente*) are designed. All in all, deficiencies in the design of the teachers' careers provide little incentive for teachers to improve their performance.

Education and skills can play a major role in enhancing employability prospects and access to good quality jobs in Paraguay. Yet, the transition from the classroom to the workplace still has many hurdles that stand in the way of a successful inclusion in labour markets. In addition to the abovementioned challenges, another fundamental barrier to better employability is the fact that the skills that a candidate has acquired in the classroom often do not match up with what employers are looking for.

School-to-work transitions are hampered by low levels of skills

Transitions from the classroom to the workplace are difficult, with a large share of young people that leave the education system entering bad quality jobs. More than half of students leave the education system to join inactivity, unemployment or informality. This transition is particularly problematic for the most disadvantaged socioeconomic groups. A significant withdrawal from the education system takes place after age 15, with particularly adverse consequences for low-income households. At age 29, and among youth living in extremely poor households, around 6 out of 10 workers are not employed, nor in the education system or training (NEET); 3 out of 10 are informal workers, and only 1 out of 10 workers has a formal job. In vulnerable households, half of workers at age 29 are either NEET or informal. The picture is somewhat brighter for youth living in middle-class households, where only around 2 out of 10 workers are either NEET or informal at age 29.

Low levels of education and skills are a direct cause of poor school-to-work transitions in Paraguay. In particular, a low-skilled labour force is one of the complex and diverse causes of informality in the country. Informality decreases with the level of education among Paraguayans. While informal work remains above 80% for those with no education or who have completed lower secondary school, it affects around 70% of those who have completed upper secondary school, and only 30% of those who have graduated from an institution of higher education.

Low relevance of skills limits the opportunities to access formal jobs, as illustrated by the major difficulties faced by formal firms to find workers with the skills they need. Around 80% of formal firms in the country claim that they face difficulties to fill their vacancies. This is significantly above the LAC average of 65%, which is already high. The skills that are most difficult to find are mainly related to emotional intelligence, communication skills and critical thinking, all part of a group of generic, soft skills that are scarce among

Paraguayan workers. Also, other more specific, technical skills related to budget, financial or computing skills are particularly in demand.

Main recommendations

These challenges suggest the agenda is ambitious and education and skills challenges must be faced with strong political commitment and ambition. The determination to transform Paraguay's education system into a driver of inclusion, economic progress and greater well-being, is reflected in the current quest to develop a National Plan for the Transformation of the Education Sector for 2030. This volume aims to contribute to the definition of this plan, and presents a series of key policy recommendations.

Policies must continue to expand education coverage and foster completion, particularly among most disadvantaged groups. The production of better education statistics is critical to favour policy design, implementation, monitoring and evaluation. Policies to support access in remote areas and across the most disadvantaged socioeconomic groups, particularly in pre-primary and secondary, must be pursued to complete the universalisation of compulsory education. And policies to favour school retention and completion, avoiding repetition and drop-out, must be at the centre of this strategy given the high dropout rates in Paraguay.

Policies to improve learning outcomes must focus on teachers, educational resources, and the management of schools. In this respect, it is critical to improve evidence on learning outcomes to inform policy-making. One of the core policy challenges to transform education and improve teaching in Paraguay is re-shaping teachers' career pathways. The goal is to attract talent, strengthen incentives to continuously develop and improve teachers' pedagogical skills, and establish a stronger, more systematic system for the evaluation of teachers' performance. This must be complemented by improving the quality of the *Instituciones de Formación Docente*, which entails better evaluation and accreditation mechanisms.

Policies to make education more relevant must focus on reforming the curriculum of upper secondary school (*educación media*), so that it favours labour market insertion and provides a more solid basis for accessing higher education. The curriculum of *educación media* must be oriented towards training students with skills for the 21st century. This should include a mix of occupation-specific skills. Workers in the 21st century must also have a stock of information-processing skills and various "generic" skills, including interpersonal communication skills, self-management skills, and the ability to learn.

Policies to favour good quality school-to-work transitions in Paraguay must move towards a national, integrated Technical and Vocational Education and Training (TVET) system. This should be oriented at improving the quality and relevance of skills provided by the different modalities of TVET training that exist in the country, including both formal and non-formal options. An integrated system must favour the transparency of learning outcomes and the transferability of qualifications, as well as providing clear career pathways. Stakeholder engagement, including educators, private sector and unions, will be critical.

Policies to improve the match between the supply and demand of skills in Paraguay should go beyond the improvement of the relevance of skills. The reach of active labour market policies (ALMPs) must be extended in order to support training and intermediation programmes that favour access to job vacancies. Improving labour market information can be an effective tool to support better education and career choices. And setting up institutional mechanisms such as skills councils to foster dialogue between educators, private sector and workers can be critical to anticipate and identify skills needs.

Anticipating trends and preparing for future challenges: scenarios for the future of Paraguay

As part of the OECD MDCR methodology, a series of workshops are organised throughout the Review. These workshops seek to connect with a diversity of perspectives of Paraguayan society and identify challenges and solutions to inclusive, sustainable development together with local stakeholders and experts.

To ensure that the recommendations in this report not only address current challenges but can withstand shifts in the global economy and in domestic trends, future state scenarios were developed to test the recommendations. These scenarios were used to anticipate how future trends might shape recommendations and, more specifically, how different contexts could affect the incentives and the prioritisation of policy reform or even create new policy trade-offs.

This section details four scenarios for Paraguay developed with a time horizon of 2030 and their implications for policy in the country. The scenarios were developed on the basis of trends in the global economy and in Paraguay that have particular bearing on the areas of focus of this report and were developed through the participatory workshops organised in the context of the MDCR.

Box 1.1. Scenarios for the future of Paraguay

Four alternative scenarios with a 2030 horizon were developed as part of the MDCR of Paraguay. They highlight the implications of external and domestic shocks on the context in which Paraguay will pursue its development strategy. The scenarios were developed as part of a series of participatory strategic foresight workshops held in March and December 2017 in Asunción.

The March workshop focused on the identification of priority areas, while the workshop entitled "Scenarios for the future of Paraguay" discussed several alternative future scenarios and their implications for Paraguay. During this workshop, 40 participants including government officials and representatives of the private sector, civil society, and the academia modified the draft scenarios prepared by the OECD team on the basis of the work carried out in the first phase of the MDCR. Participants discussed the implications of the various scenarios for policy, with specific reference to the three main focus areas in the report, namely education and skills, social protection, and health. Four scenarios emerged from this exercise:

Scenario 1. The new super-cycle

The world economy recovers thanks to sustained growth in India, which raises global demand for goods and services. China continues to grow, although at lower rates. The expansion of the global middle class with new consumption and dietary habits generates new demand for certain products, buttressing the global price of meat and livestock inputs, such as soybeans and their derivatives. By 2030, the Paraguayan economy has diversified: exports of automotive components and pharmaceutical products have become significant. Paraguayan essential oils are popular in the large global cities of the United States, Europe and Asia. Paraguay has managed to strengthen its commercial ties with China. People associate Paraguay with quality and traditional knowledge. A new automobile assembly plant is installed in Presidente Franco, near Ciudad Del Este, to serve the Brazilian market. Despite this growing dynamism, the economy suffers from a growing skills gap. The wage gap increases, especially between those who obtained employment in the new sectors and other workers. This growing gap raises concerns about the persistence of inequality

Scenario 2. Villages without youths

The fertility rate falls rapidly, accelerating the demographic transition and the depopulation of rural areas. In rural areas the population ages rapidly as young people migrate to the cities. The budget for transfers to older adults is doubled as they become increasingly isolated. Without access to appropriate skills and opportunities, the young migrate to cities in search of new livelihoods. However, there are multiple barriers to settling in Asunción, which is already saturated, and young people go to secondary cities or further away in the Central department. In these regions, informal settlements grow due to the limitations of zoning regulations. Public services in these new cities are overloaded. Private schools and clinics multiply to serve a wealthy population that escapes the saturation of public services. The state struggles to regulate these new actors.

Scenario 3. The rise of the middle class

In 2030, around half of the population of Paraguay is middle class, even though many still work informally. Extreme poverty has been eradicated, but more than 3 million Paraguayans still live in precarious conditions. The middle class mobilizes to demand better health and education services from the government through protests and increased participation in electoral processes. Citizens also demand better leisure infrastructure and the improvement of other public services. The population also becomes more demanding in the honesty of political leaders and demands more transparent and equitable management of public resources. The government responds by implementing new regulatory measures so that the private sector improves the provision of health and education services. However, private sector prices are not affordable for many Paraguayans. Increased incomes also lead to changes in consumption patterns. Increased consumption generates demand for the services sectors in which the vulnerable classes work. However, certain changes in consumption behaviour create conditions that worsen health outcomes: overweight and obesity continue gaining ground, as do risky leisure activities and traffic accidents.

Scenario 4. The acceleration of climate change

Rains are increasingly unpredictable in the country as a consequence of climate change. The fertility of deforested areas is reduced, which increases the demand for fertilizers to maintain their productivity. Floods increase in winter, while droughts become more frequent and harsher, especially in the Chaco. The harsh conditions in the countryside increase the rural exodus, increasing the population of informal settlements in the cities. In urban areas, more frequent floods expose the failings of urban design, making transport more unpredictable and forcing populations to move to less vulnerable areas. In particular, new settlements have to move away from wetlands that are more vulnerable to the effects of flooding. The greater volatility of exports of agricultural commodities impacts the macroeconomic balance, due to the fact that the entry of foreign currency becomes increasingly uncertain.

Scenario 1 "The new super-cycle" presents a favourable external environment and highlights the importance of capitalizing in Paraguay's advantages, including its natural endowment, its capacity to generate clean electricity and chiefly, its capacity to develop skills for the workforce. This scenario highlights important avenues to ensure that economic prosperity benefits all, in particular through the extension of social protection and health coverage. In this context, developing practical and technical skills that are relevant to the new opportunities is particularly important to ensure fair distribution of the proceeds of economic growth. In a positive environment as described in the scenario, economic prosperity offers avenues for financing the extension of public services. However, this will require efforts to increase the formalisation of the economy and greater control of tax evasion. The scenario also highlights the importance of continued efforts on the part of Paraguay towards the integration of the country in global networks, through the creation of a global image as well as the development of trade relationships with key new global actors.

Scenario 2 "Villages without youths" highlights two issues in Paraguay's development path. First, territorial inequalities in economic opportunities and public services remain large today. This calls attention to the need to territorialise policies to support the emergence of local growth poles beyond the large cities of Asunción and Ciudad del Este. This implies an attention to territories' comparative advantages in terms of their economic development, as well as greater attention to the development of public service provision at the local level. Among other things, the provision of technical and vocational training in areas that are relevant at the local level is an important factor to encourage the development of economic activity where populations reside. Second, internal migration is often perceived as a threat, in particular if it converges in informal and precarious settlements, leading to growing security concerns. In contrast, appropriate urban planning and skills formation policies can transform internal migration into a motor for the economy, by capitalising on agglomeration economies and the young and vibrant workforce.

Scenario 3 "The rise of the middle class" would have implications for policy and politics. A growing and vocal middle class is likely to call for fairer and more transparent governance, through electoral channels but also through other channels, including demonstrations and the use of social media. In this scenario, the challenge of quality in public service provision is posed acutely. Better-off Paraguayans tend to turn to the private sector for health and education provision. The expansion of the middle class would put pressure on health and education systems to deliver greater quality. In this scenario, the capacity of the Paraguayan economy to generate formal employment would be critical not only to sustain the middle class but also to ensure that the public sector can provide appropriate social protection, including health coverage to this segment of the population.

Scenario 4 "The acceleration of climate change" puts emphasis on the need for Paraguay to ensure it is robust to climate change. Improving urban planning and zoning is a key area to ensure that urban areas are prepared. Better quality streets will be able to withstand increased flooding. Climate change is likely to disrupt livelihoods and accelerate internal migration. In turn, without appropriate urban planning policies, internal migration will result in urban sprawl, multiplying health and other risks for the population. Better roads will also be critical to ensure that public services can reach populations if floods become more frequent. The management of feeder roads is already a major issue in some parts of the country, where certain population centres are very difficult to reach when rains are heavy. This problem could become more acute should floods become more frequent. This scenario also highlights the importance of economic diversification, both to reduce the impact of rainfall variability on the economy and to generate employment opportunities for internal migrants.

References

DGEEC (2018), *Principales Resultados de Pobreza y Distribución del Ingreso*, Dirección General de Estadísticas, Encuestas y Censos de Paraguay, Fernando de la Mora, www.dgeec.gov.py/Publicaciones/Biblioteca/pobreza/Boletin%20de%20pobreza%202017.pdf (accessed on May 2018).

DGEEC (2017), *Encuesta Permanente de Hogares* [Permanent Household Survey] (database), Dirección General de Estadísticas, Encuestas y Censos de Paraguay, Fernando de la Mora, www.dgeec.gov.py/datos/encuestas/eph.

DGEEC (2014), "III Censo Nacional de Población y Viviendas para Pueblos Indígenas" in Censo 2012, Dirección General de Estadísticas, Encuestas y Censos de Paraguay, Fernando de la Mora, www.dgeec.gov.py/Publicaciones/Biblioteca/indigena2012/Pueblos%20indigenas%20en%20el%20Paraguay%20Resultados%20Finales%20de%20Poblacion%20y%20Viviendas%202012.pdf.

Global Burden of Disease Collaborative Network (2016), Global Burden of Disease Study 2016 (database), Institute for Health Metrics and Evaluation, Seattle.

National Government of Paraguay (2014), *Plan Nacional de Desarrollo: Paraguay 2030* [National Development Plan: Paraguay 2030], Asunción, www.stp.gov.py/pnd/wp-content/uploads/2014/12/pnd2030.pdf.

OECD (2018), *Multi-dimensional Review of Paraguay. Vol I: Initial Assessment*, OECD Publishing, Paris, https://doi.org/10.1787/9789264301900-en.

Chapter 2. Towards social protection for all in Paraguay

To sustain and further improvements in living standards and well-being, Paraguay will need to review its social protection policies and transform them into a coherent system for all. This chapter analyses social protection in Paraguay and provides policy recommendations to foster coherence, equity and an integrated system. Social protection is split along the line of informality, leaving parts of society unprotected. Formal dependent workers are covered by social security, whose fragmentation results in unequitable provisions. The high degree of self-employment limits the reach of social security, while informality and evasion further reduce its coverage. Means-tested social assistance needs to be better targeted and scaled up to fully address the needs of the population not covered by social security. Key bottlenecks to expand social protection to the whole population are its governance, insufficient financial resources for social assistance and the inclusion of independent workers into social security. Independent workers' low and unstable incomes, as well as the system's design itself are barriers to the inclusion of independent workers.

The statistical data for Israel are supplied by and under the responsibility of the relevant Israeli authorities. The use of such data by the OECD is without prejudice to the status of the Golan Heights, East Jerusalem and Israeli settlements in the West Bank under the terms of international law.

In recent years, living standards in Paraguay have improved, but the state has to review its social policies to continue along this path. Since increasing in the early 21st century, income poverty has nearly halved; yet poverty and inequalities remain high (OECD, 2018). Many Paraguayans remain vulnerable and the expanding middle class needs support to stabilise (UNDP, 2016). Volume 1 of the MDCR of Paraguay lays out that steering the economy in a sustainable growth path and furthering improvements in living standards require addressing the coverage and fragmentation of the social protection system.

Paraguay puts social protection at the core of its national development. Countries are increasingly recognising the value of social protection to achieve and sustain well-being (OECD, 2015). Paraguay is no exception; social protection plays a key role in achieving the objectives of the National Development Plan *Paraguay 2030*: reducing poverty, fostering social development and inclusive growth. The strategy even sets the ambitious goals of eradicating extreme poverty and reducing inequality. The state recognises that social protection is a key instrument to achieve these goals, as it sets the goal of universalising access to social security.

However, high informality and self-employment limit social security's impact and force Paraguay to have a parallel social assistance system. Traditionally, social security safeguards the population against various risks. Yet, low levels of formality (35% in 2015) and salaried work (55% in 2015) limit the reach and expansion of social security (OECD, 2018). The National Development Plan recognises that large swaths of society are left unprotected. In response to this Paraguay expanded social assistance to provide minimum living standards. While social assistance is an important element of social protection, Paraguay's high informality and self-employment risk creating parallel systems for formal and informal workers, which is the case for the pension system.

Demographic changes require preparing the social protection system for population aging if deficits for the treasury are to be averted. Complying with *Paraguay 2030*'s definition of vulnerable groups, the country's principal social protection provisions target the elderly and children. However, the demographic profile is changing: the share of children will have halved by 2050, while the elderly population will have nearly tripled (Figure 2.1 Panel A). Expectedly, the dependency ratios will revert with the old-age dependency ratio surpassing the child dependency ratio (Figure 2.1 Panel B). In addition, life expectancy at age 60 is expected to continue to increase, to reach 84 by 2050 (Figure 2.1 Panel C). Until now, Paraguay's youthful population allowed the country to maintain a generous pension system. These favourable conditions are slowly reversing, which could jeopardize the sustainability of the contributory and non-contributory pension system. The treasury is already covering the running deficit of the pension funds for non-civilians (police and military personnel). And the contributions to the major pension fund for private sector workers will not suffice to cover pension expenditure as of 2032 (IPS, 2014).

This chapter assesses Paraguay's social protection system and provides recommendations to reach the objective of providing for the population in need. Paraguay's health and education system are assessed in Chapter 3 and Chapter 4. First, the chapter analyses social protection's coverage and adequacy. Second, given the demographic transition and future liabilities the chapter assesses the pension system equity and sustainability. Third, it sets out three principal challenges Paraguay needs to overcome to universalise social protection: the system's governance, including independent workers into social security and the financing for non-contributory social assistance. It concludes with a set of policy recommendations to establish a social protection system for all.

Figure 2.1. Paraguay's aging society poses challenges for the provision of social protection

Projections of selected demographic indicators for Paraguay

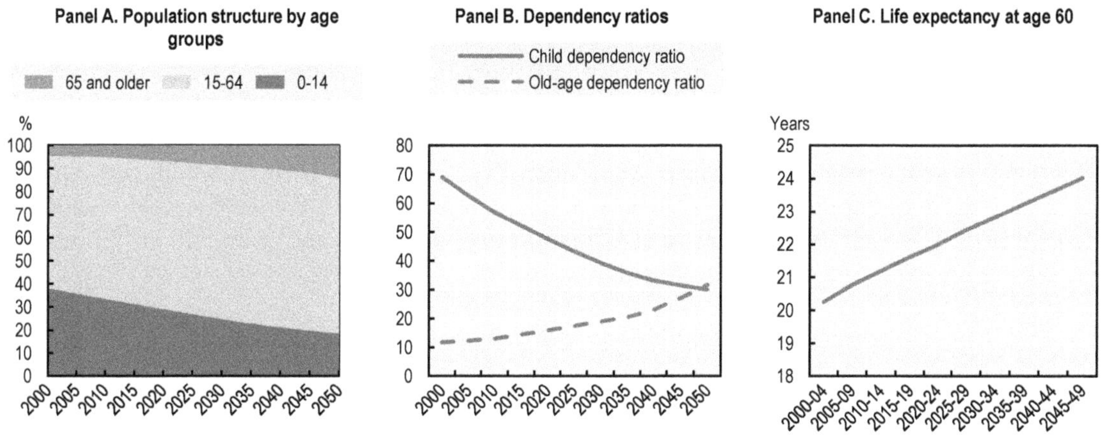

Note: The child dependency ratio is the ratio between the population aged 0-14 and 15-59. The old-age dependency ratio is the ratio between the population above age 60 versus individuals aged 15-59. Panel C presents life expectancy at age 60 projections for a five years average.
Source: CELADE - Population Division of ECLAC (2013).

StatLink https://doi.org/10.1787/888933822482

Paraguay's social protection system provides too little for too few

Despite social protection's key role in national development, Paraguay only has a working definition of social protection. In absence of a universally accepted definition, Paraguay guides its social protection system by the objective of mitigating social risks, guaranteeing a minimum living standard and promoting decent work and access to opportunities. A range of education, health and labour policies contribute to achieving these objectives, focusing on vulnerable groups, such as children, adolescents, indigenous people, people with disabilities, as well as the elderly, who are considered especially vulnerable (National Government of Paraguay, 2014; Gabinete Social, 2017).

Paraguay's social assistance and social security systems capture most aspects of the International Labour Organization's (ILO) holistic definition of social protection. Paraguay's social assistance aims at protecting children, enabling household's income generation and securing a minimum income in old-age; social security mitigates the loss of income due to sickness, occupational injuries, invalidity, death of the income earner and old-age; this is complemented by (basic) medical care. While covering fewer contingencies, these policies reflect the ILO's view on social protection. The ILO defines social protection as "the set of public measures that a society provides for its members to protect them against economic and social distress that would be caused by the absence or a substantial reduction of income from work as a result of various contingencies (sickness, maternity, employment injury, unemployment, invalidity, old age, and death of the breadwinner); the provision of healthcare; and the provision of benefits for families with children" (ILO, 2000).

Key provisions currently focus on children and the elderly, but social protection needs to address vulnerabilities at all ages. Since the first poverty reduction strategy in 2003 (*Estrategia Nacional de Reducción de la Pobreza, Desigualdad y Exclusión Social*), poverty and inequality reduction have been at the heart of country's social assistance programmes. Indeed, poverty and inequality have fallen since the 2002 crisis, and eradicating extreme poverty is within reach; but the reduction has been less impressive than in Latin America as a whole (OECD, 2018). While poverty remains a concern across ages (especially among minors), non-monetary vulnerabilities should be of equal concern (Figure 2.2). Many of these vulnerabilities are insufficiently addressed by the country's social protection system. Key vulnerabilities of the working age population, such as unemployment or – more frequently – underemployment, are insufficiently addressed by Paraguay's social protection system. Many, across all ages, live without health insurance. Literacy is a prerequisite for inclusion in a modern society. While literacy is not a concern for younger Paraguayans, a sizeable minority of adults above age 40 are illiterate and rates are even higher among the elderly.

Figure 2.2. Vulnerabilities are distributed across the life cycle

Vulnerabilities by age in Paraguay (2016)

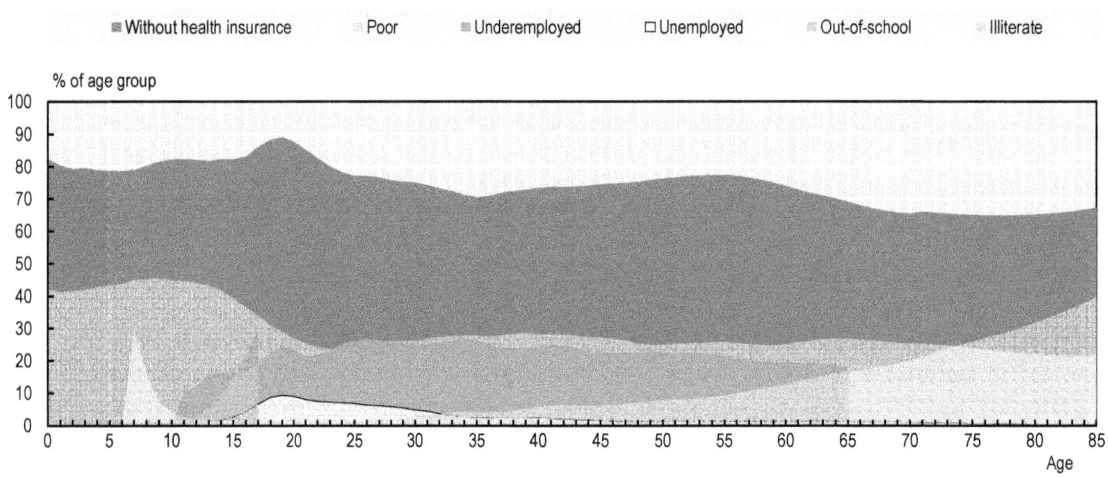

Source: Own calculations based on the Permanent Household Survey of Paraguay (DGEEC, 2017).

StatLink https://doi.org/10.1787/888933822501

Paraguay does not protect all its population against all contingencies. A comprehensive social protection system needs to cover at least the aforementioned contingencies; this, however, is not the case in Paraguay. Social security for formal workers does not protect against unemployment, and formal workers do not receive child or family allowances, unless they qualify for the means-tested conditional cash transfer programme *Tekoporã* (Table 2.1). The inactive population and informal workers – until recently excluded from social security – are only partially protected against contingencies: contingencies such as income loss due to unemployment or sickness are not covered, other contingencies (except health) only in case of poverty or voluntary contribution to social security.

Table 2.1. Paraguay's social protection system does not cover all contingencies

Paraguay's social protection responses to contingencies

Contingencies	Social protection responses		
	Dependent workers	Independent workers	Inactive
Sickness (medical expenses, loss of income)	Contributory health insurance (IPS) Private insurance (civil servants and employees of the state)	Public medical care	Public medical care
Child and family benefits	means-tested CCT (*Tekoporã, Abrazo*)	means-tested CCT (*Tekoporã, Abrazo*)	means-tested CCT (*Tekoporã, Abrazo*)
Maternity	Contributory social security (IPS, Caja Fiscal), employer financed in case the mother is not affiliated with the IPS	means-tested CCT (*Tekoporã*)	means-tested CCT (*Tekoporã*)
Unemployment	no	no	n.a.
Occupational injury and illness	Contributory occupational injury insurance (IPS, Caja Fiscal, closed pension funds)	Voluntary social security (IPS)	n.a.
Disability	Contributory disability insurance (IPS, Caja Fiscal, closed pension funds)	Voluntary social security (IPS)	means-tested CCT (*Tekoporã*)
Death	Contributory survivors pension (IPS, Caja Fiscal, closed pension funds)	Voluntary social security (IPS)	no
Old-age	Contributory old-age pension (IPS, Caja Fiscal, closed pension funds)	Voluntary social security (IPS)	means-tested (*Adulto Mayor*)

Note: n.a. = not applicable. See Annex 2.A for details.
1. CCT stands for conditional cash transfer.
2. Civil servants' sickness benefits are covered by private pre-paid insurances or the health agencies of the Armed Forces and Police.
3. Dependent workers whose contract was terminated without a due cause are entitled to a compensation corresponding to 15 daily wages for each year of service.
Source: Own elaboration.

Paraguay's commitment to protect children targets the poor. Flagship programmes, such as the conditional cash transfers *Tekoporã* and *Abrazo*, provide for families with children in need; the conditionalities and the guidance of social workers have improved health indicators and school attendance of children (MH, 2016; Casalí and Velásquez, 2016) but exclude by design non-poor children and families, for whom social protection lacks an alternative offer.

Social assistance for the working age population concentrates on small-scale programmes providing support for income generation. While mandatory social security has a provision for most of the contingencies of the working age population, the country's economic structure excludes large groups of society from the system. Informal and independent workers' contingencies are de facto unaddressed. In absence of these provisions, informal and independent workers benefit from small-scale programmes providing financial and technical support to small, family run businesses and farms (see Annex Table 2.A.1). These measures include provisions that reach beyond traditional social protection, such as the land accreditation programme in the peri-urban areas from the SAS (*Tekoha*).

In addition to traditional social assistance programmes, Paraguay is increasingly investing in improving families' productive capacities and resilience. Programmes like *Tenonderã* and *Familia por Familia* aim at reducing poverty sustainably by helping families to become self-sufficient. *Tenonderã* is a graduation programme for families in the final years of their eligibility for *Tekoporã*. *Familia por Familia* was designed by the *Secretaría Técnica de Planificación* (STP) to target extreme poor families. Both programmes aim at sustainably reducing poverty by promoting social and economic inclusion of families through enhancing families' business ideas, providing skills training and (seed) capital to invest in assets, as well as coaching and technical support. In contrast to *Tenonderã*, *Familia por Familia* includes intensive individual coaching and a strong social work component to assist the needs of extreme poor families, it also helps to connect them to local markets.

Paraguay's progress in providing for its elderly is split in parallel systems. With the flagship programme for the elderly (i.e. *Pensión Alimentaria para los Adultos Mayores*, henceforth *Adulto Mayor*), Paraguay grants a non-contributory pension to poor residing citizens above age 65. Poor elderly without labour income, contributory pensions and other cash transfers from the state are entitled to receive a benefit representing 25% of the minimum wage.[1] This is an important complement to contributory old-age pensions and its expansion is in line with the ILO's and Paraguay's working definition of social protection. However, the strong reliance on non-contributory pensions risks cementing the costly split between formal and informal workers.

The social protection system's coverage is low

Paraguay's social protection system covers considerably fewer people than in comparator countries. A quarter of Paraguayans are covered by at least one social protection programme (24.5%). One in ten Paraguayans (of all ages) either contributes to social security or receives a contributory benefit (11%); an additional 13.5% of the population receives exclusively social assistance. This places Paraguay at the bottom of an international comparison and considerably below the Latin American average (Figure 2.3 Panel A).

Figure 2.3. Paraguay's middle class is left unprotected

Effective social protection coverage

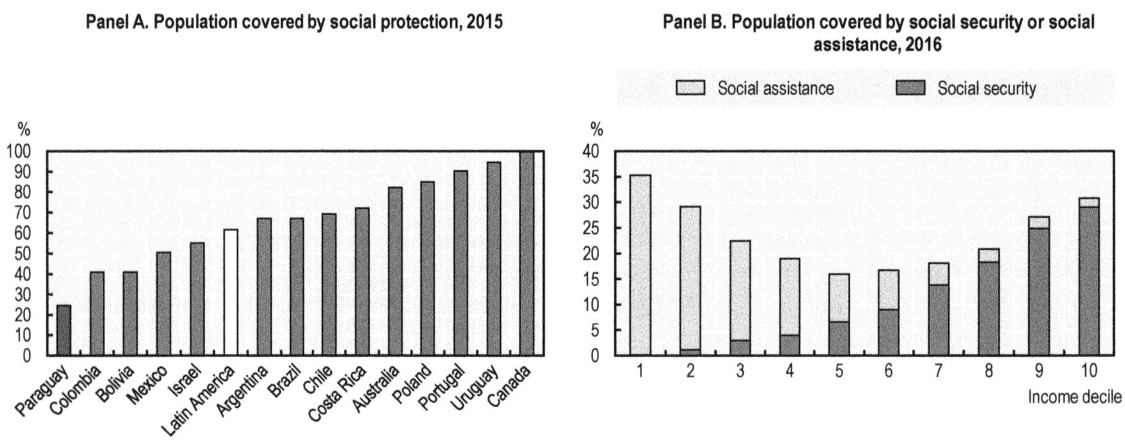

Note: Effective coverage of social protection is measured as the percentage of people actively contributing to a social insurance scheme or receiving at least one benefit (contributory or non-contributory, excluding health). Panel A: 2016 for Paraguay, 2015 or latest available for other countries. Panel B: Social assistance includes conditional cash transfers (*Tekoporã*); in-kind transfers (food) and non-contributory pensions (merit, veterans, survivors of veterans and military or police personnel, *Adulto Mayor*). Social security includes contributions to a social security scheme and receipt of contributory pensions.

Source: Panel A: Paraguay based on the Permanent Household Survey of Paraguay (DGEEC, 2017), others based on ILO (2017). Panel B: Own elaboration based on the Permanent Household Survey of Paraguay (DGEEC, 2017).

StatLink https://doi.org/10.1787/888933822520

Paraguay's social security and social assistance systems leave the middle class and certain contingencies unprotected. Social assistance plays an important role in increasing social protection's coverage rates, but large gaps remain. As a consequence of social assistance targeting the poor and social security being skewed towards high income individuals, the centre of the income distribution is insufficiently covered by the system (Figure 2.3 Panel B). Moreover, the system does not provide adequate protection against key contingencies set out in national strategies: the effective coverage of maternity benefits is low, insurance against unemployment does not exist and the effective coverage against other contingencies is low (Table 2.2). Since 2015, Law No. 5508/2015 extends paid maternity leave to informal workers. In that case employers have to cover the full salary during 18 weeks of maternity leave (the *Instituto de Previsión Social* [IPS] covers the salary during the maternity leave of formal workers).

Table 2.2. Coverage of contingencies, 2015

Contingency	Sickness (loss of income)[a]	Child and family benefits	Maternity	Unemployment	Occupational injury and illness	Disability	Old-age
Indicator	Insured (% of employed)	Cash transfer recipients, children (age 0-14)	Cash transfer recipient, Women giving birth	Cash transfer recipient, unemployed	Legal coverage[d]	Cash transfer recipient, persons with severe disabilities	Cash transfer recipients, above statutory pension age
Paraguay	19.6[b]	32.8	3.0[c]	n.a.	52.8	21.6	22.2
Argentina	..	84.6	34.0	7.2	69.7	..	89.3
Australia	..	100.0	..	52.7	77.9	100.0	74.3
Brazil	42.4	96.8	45.0	7.8	62.9	100.0	78.3
Canada	..	39.7	100.0	40.0	78.8	67.2	100.0
Chile	18.1	93.1	44.0	45.6	93.8	100.0	78.6
Colombia	..	27.3	..	4.6	44.6	6.0	51.7
Costa Rica	72.1	17.7	..		68.6		68.8
Israel	2.2		..	29.4	90.0	90.4	99.1
Mexico	..	25.0	..	..	49.3		64.1
Peru	..	..	..	..	48.4	3.9	19.3
Poland	..	100.0	100.0	..	100.0	100.0	100.0
Portugal	86.1	93.1	100.0	15.5	87.6	89.2	100.0
Thailand	25.4	18.9	..	43.2	41.0	35.7	83.0
Uruguay	88.0	66.2	100.0	45.6	68.3		76.5

Note: n.a. = not applicable.
.. = missing data.
a. 2015 or latest available year.
b. The percentage of the working population having an IPS insurance.
c. The percentage of women giving birth who benefit from paid maternity leave. The figure represents the situation before enacting Law No. 5.508/2015 which extends paid maternity leave to informal workers.
d. The legal coverage is the percentage of the labour force theoretically captured by the scheme. For Paraguay this is the population formally obliged to contribute to social security, thus dependent workers.
Source: ILO (2017), a. ILO (2018). b. own elaboration based on ELPS (STP, 2016).

Social security coverage

Paraguay's low provision against key contingencies is a result of social security's focus on dependent employees. The Paraguayan social security system uses wage employment as the standard even though barely half the working population is in dependent wage employment (Figure 2.4 Panel A). The consequence of this focus is a low legal coverage:

only half of the working population are legally covered. Since November 2015, domestic workers and their employers are mandated to pay social security contributions. Given the country's high informality, the actual coverage of dependent employees is even lower (37.7%) (Figure 2.4 Panel B) and few domestic workers, self-employed and employers contribute voluntarily to the system. The high level of informality and self-employment in the private sector manifests in a lower share of private sector workers contributing to a social security scheme compared to public sector employees.

Figure 2.4. Paraguay's social security system reaches few of its target group

Employment distribution and affiliation to a social security scheme, in percent, 2016

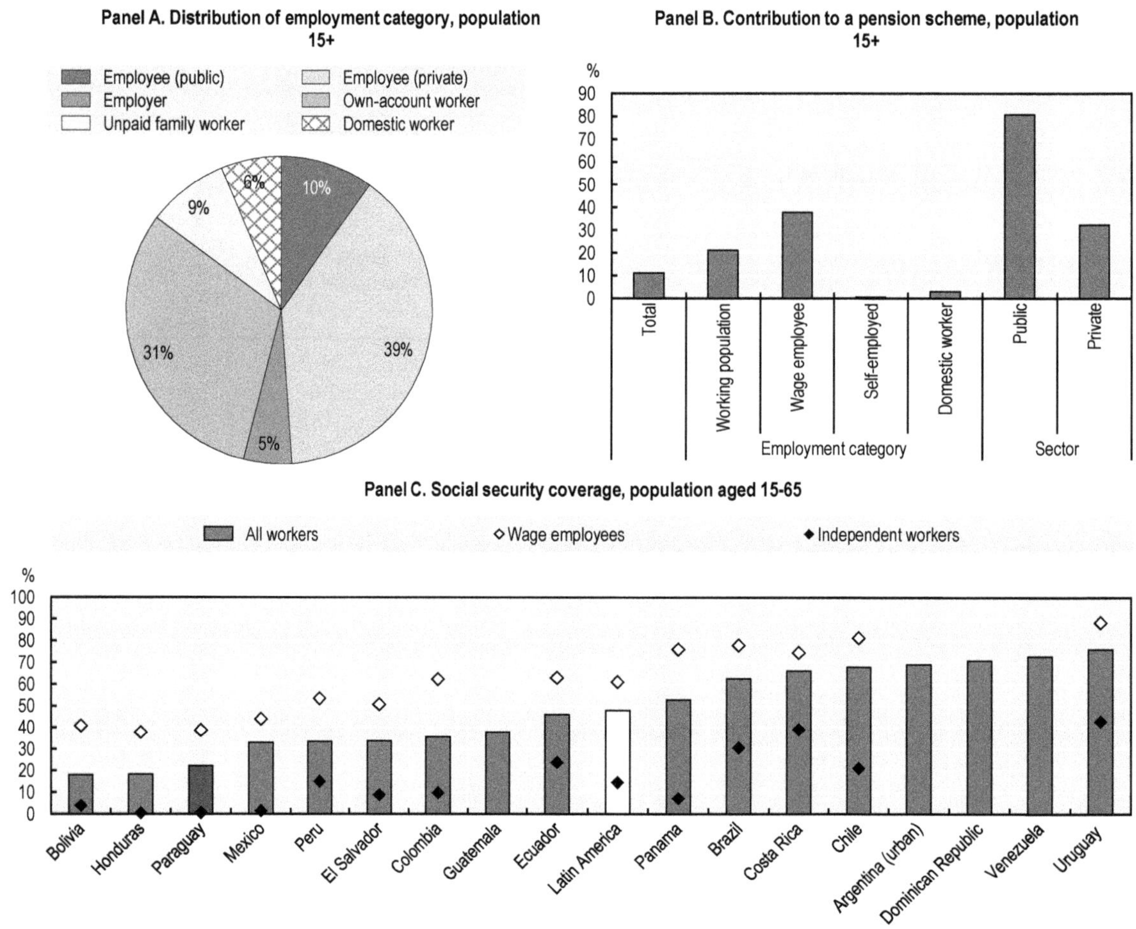

Note: Panel B: Public and private sector workers refer to wage employees. Self-employed refer to employers and own-account workers. Panel C: Social security coverage is defined by active contributions to the pension system. In Paraguay, these contributions include all provisions of the social security system. Data from 2015; 2014 for Argentina, Guatemala, Mexico and Venezuela.

Source: Panel A and B: Own calculations based on the Permanent Household Survey of Paraguay (DGEEC, 2017). Panel C: ECLAC (2017).

StatLink https://doi.org/10.1787/888933822539

A regional comparison confirms Paraguay's challenge in providing social security to its citizens. The share of Paraguayan workers actively contributing to social security is half the Latin American average, placing the country at the lower end of a regional comparison (Figure 2.4 Panel C). Only Bolivia and Honduras have a lower coverage rate. Social security coverage among independent workers is low across Latin America (14.6%), but Paraguay's social security system leaves independent workers virtually uncovered.

The social security system is skewed towards people with higher incomes. While social security coverage is generally low, it is especially low among Paraguayans from low and middle-income households (Figure 2.3 Panel B). Like in most countries, coverage rates increase with company size, income and years of schooling (Navarro and Ortiz, 2014; 2014; Casalí and Velásquez, 2016; ECLAC, 2017). Coverage is also comparatively high among urban and unionised workers, as well as workers in high income and productivity sectors. Lower labour market participation, higher incidence of underemployment and less stable employment history due to household responsibilities hamper women's possibilities to contribute sufficiently to social security. Consequently, coverage among women is lower than among men, leading to fewer women receiving contributory old-age pensions (MTESS, 2017).

Social assistance coverage

Paraguay's social assistance correctly identified its target group, but few of the target group receive cash benefits. The flagship social assistance programmes (*Tekoporã*, *Abrazo* and *Adulto Mayor*) target poor families with children and elderly. Focusing on these target groups is indeed adequate to achieve the National Development Plan's (*Plan Nacional de Desarollo* – PND) goal of reducing poverty: only 3.2% of poor households do not have a child or old person among their members (Figure 2.5). However, less than 30% of poor households receive one of the flagship social assistance programmes targeting children and elderly.

Figure 2.5. Social assistance has the right target group, but covers few

Poor households' generational structure and share of poor households receiving social assistance, in 2016

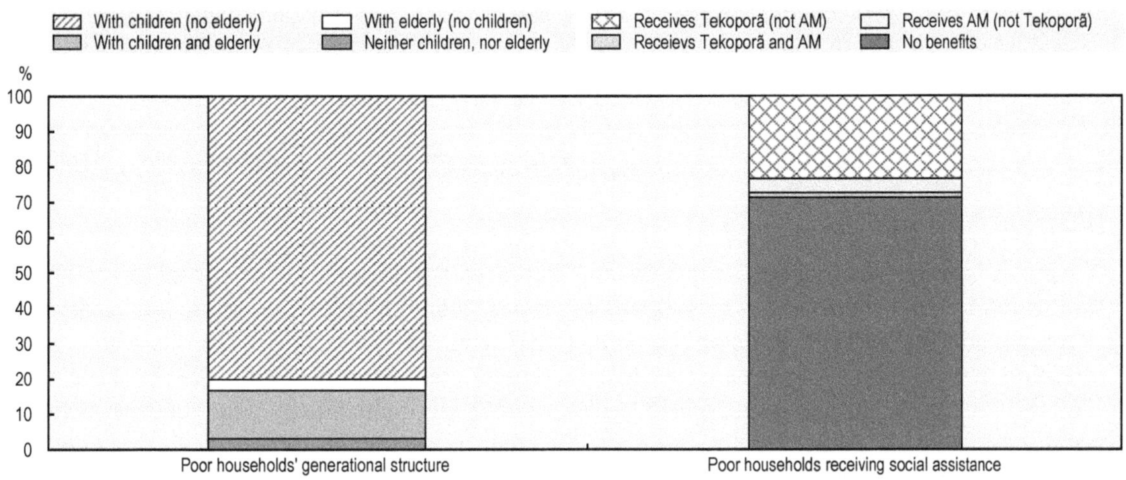

Note: AM = *Adulto Mayor*. A household member below age 18 is considered a child. A household member of age 65 or above is considered elderly.
Source: Own elaboration based on the Permanent Household Survey of Paraguay (DGEEC, 2017).

StatLink https://doi.org/10.1787/888933822558

Tekoporã is well targeted, but provides for few. As discussed earlier, Paraguay's social assistance targets lower income individuals and households. Yet, only 25% of poor children below age 15 benefit from *Tekoporã*, among the extreme poor children the rate is higher but still far from complete (Figure 2.6 Panel A). For the extreme poor recipients, the benefit is an important income source; it represents 18.6% of household income for the first decile, but the ratio reduces to 10.6% among recipients in the second decile (Figure 2.6 Panel B). While *Tekoporã* still needs to expand to fully cover its target group (currently only 23.7% of poor households are covered), it is a considerably well-targeted benefit: coverage is higher among poorer households and four-fifths of total spending goes to the four bottom deciles. Still, approximately a third of benefiting households with children are not poor (own elaboration based on EPH, 2016).

Figure 2.6. *Tekoporã* benefits the most in need

Coverage and incidence of *Tekoporã*, 2016

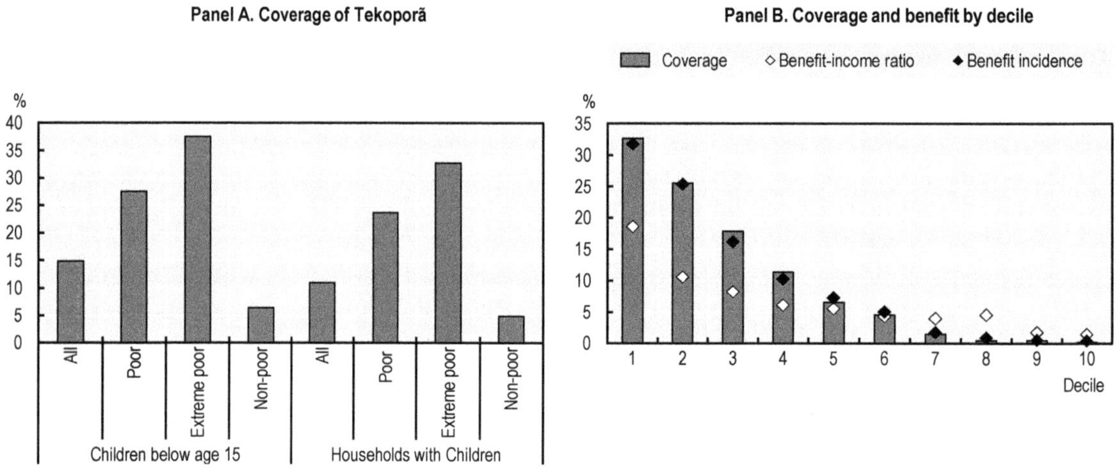

Note: The benefit-income ratio presents the *Tekoporã* benefits as a share of the household's income. The benefit incidence is the percentage of benefits going to each decile of the income distribution relative to the total benefits going to the population.
Source: Own elaboration based on the Permanent Household Survey of Paraguay (DGEEC, 2017).

StatLink https://doi.org/10.1787/888933822577

Pension coverage

Paraguay's main non-contributory pension increases the provision for the elderly. The introduction of *Adulto Mayor* helped to more than double the share of elderly Paraguayans receiving a pension between 2008 and 2015 (ECLAC, 2017). Since its creation the number of beneficiaries has increased considerably, from 909 in 2010 to 162 000 in 2016. In the same period, the number of contributory pension recipients increased as well. Whereas the number of other non-contributory pension receivers decreased from 15 000 to 10 000 (mostly due to a reduction in pensions for veterans and their surviving dependents (Figure 2.7). Without non-contributory pensions, pension coverage and the well-being of the elderly would be drastically lower in Paraguay.

Figure 2.7. The number of non-contributory pension recipients increased sharply

Number of pension recipients, 2010-16

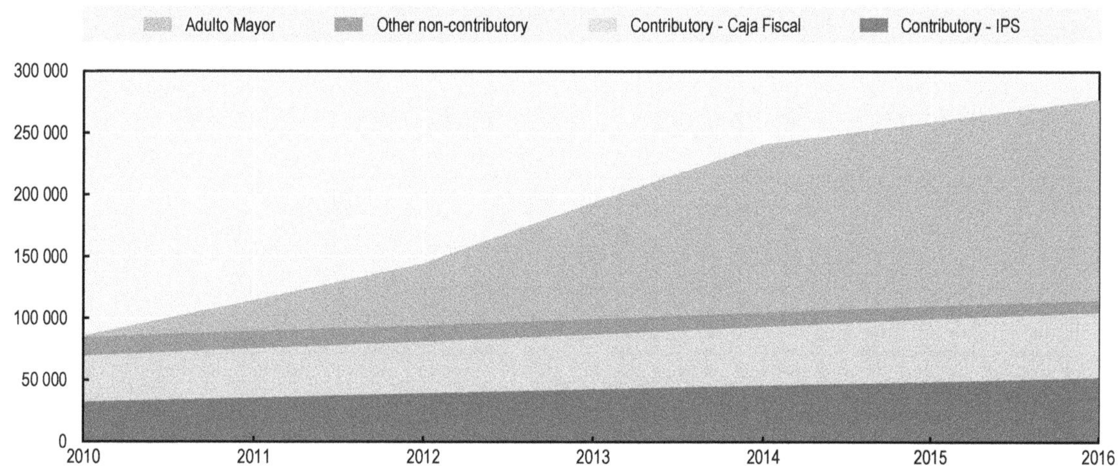

Note: Recipients of a contributory pension depicted are IPS and Caja Fiscal beneficiaries. Other non-contributory pensions include merit pensions, and pensions for veterans and survivors of veterans as well as military and police personnel.
Source: Data for 2010-15 are from MTESS (2016); Data for 2016 are from MH (2017).

StatLink https://doi.org/10.1787/888933822596

While closing the coverage gap, the non-contributory pension *Adulto Mayor* created a parallel system. Since the introduction of *Adulto Mayor*, the non-contributory pension system surpassed the number of contributory pension recipients. In 2015, more elderly Paraguayans received a non-contributory pension (30.3%) than a contributory pension (16%); in turn, more than half of the elderly are without a pension (53.7%). In fact, the share of contributory pension recipients is one of the lowest in Latin America; and, in general, the share of elderly pension recipients is below the regional average (Figure 2.8 Panel A).

Non-contributory pensions help to counter the contributory pension system's focus on the top income deciles. The coverage of contributory pensions among elderly in the first quintile is very low and lower than the Latin American average (0.9% vs. 6.2%) (ECLAC, 2017). Only thanks to non-contributory pensions this low coverage increases, and the percentage of pension recipients among the lower and middle deciles increases to numbers comparable to the top deciles (Figure 2.8 Panel B). In fact, Paraguay's non-contributory pensions contribute more to closing the coverage gap between the rich and poor than the Latin American average (ibid.). Compared to *Tekoporã*, *Adulto Mayor* is less well targeted, many recipients can be found in the centre of the income distribution. And at 43% the *Adulto Mayor*'s inclusion error is superior to *Tekoporã*'s inclusion error (own elaboration based on EPH 2016).

Figure 2.8. Few elderly Paraguayans receive a pension, but social assistance reduces inequities

Coverage of social security by decile, 2016

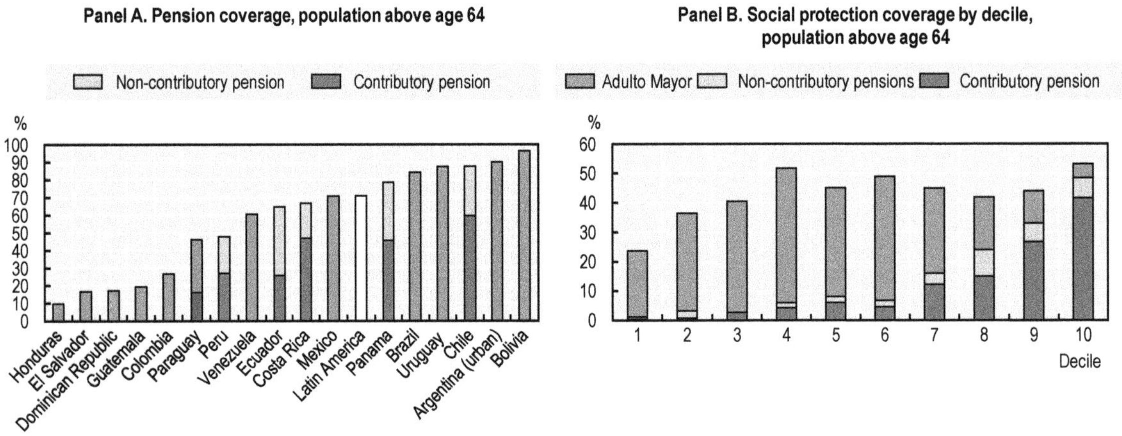

Note: Panel A: Data from 2015; 2014 for Argentina, Guatemala, Mexico and Venezuela. Non-contributory pensions include merit pensions, pensions for veterans and survivors of veterans, military and police personnel.
Source: Panel A: ECLAC (2017). Panel B: Own elaboration based on EPH (2016).

StatLink https://doi.org/10.1787/888933822615

Social assistance reduces poverty and inequality less than in other countries

Paraguay's fiscal system reduces poverty. The fiscal system, measured via direct taxes and social assistance (*Tekoporã*, *Adulto Mayor*, scholarships and school lunch programmes), plays an important role in achieving the National Development Plan's goal of reducing poverty.[2] Thanks to direct taxes and benefits, the poverty headcount (measured with the $4 PPP a day poverty line) reduces by 1.8 percentage points (Figure 2.9 Panel A). This is a decent achievement compared to other countries in the region, but considerably below top performers such as Argentina, Chile, Ecuador and Uruguay. In absence of *Adulto Mayor*, the extreme poverty rate would be 0.9 percentage points higher; and without *Tekoporã*, extreme poverty would increase by 0.7 percentage points (Giménez et al., 2017). The higher benefit value of *Adulto Mayor* explains its bigger impact on poverty reduction.

The effects of social assistance and direct taxes on inequality are less marked. Income inequality decreases (but a reduction of only 0.9 Gini points), which places Paraguay at the bottom of a regional comparison (Figure 2.9 Panel B). The comparatively low redistributive effect is explained by Paraguay's low tax collection and especially low tax rates. Just as with poverty, *Adulto Mayor* reduces inequality. Without the non-contributory pension, income inequality would be 0.4 Gini points higher (ibid.).

Figure 2.9. Paraguay's fiscal system reduces poverty and inequality

Reduction of poverty and inequality rates due to direct taxes and social assistance

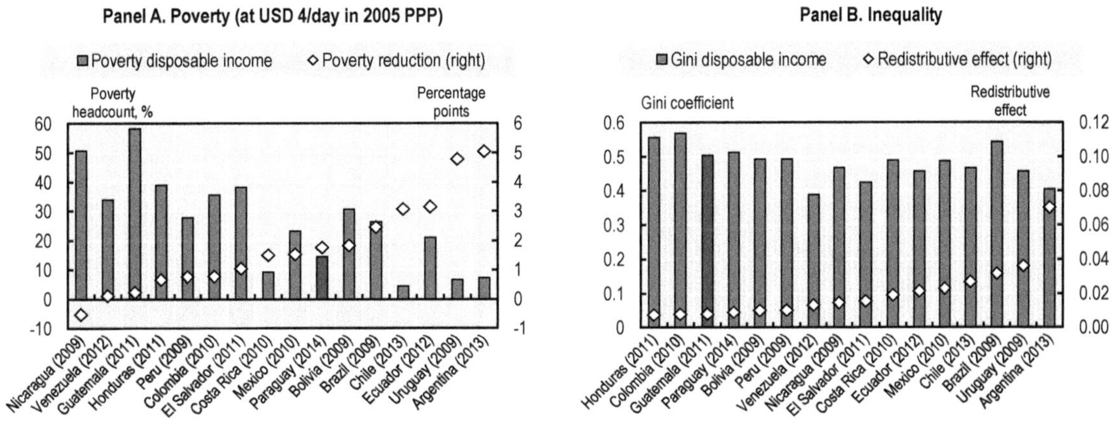

Notes: 1. Poverty and inequality reduction is measured as the difference between the market income including contributory pensions and the disposable income, which is the market income without direct taxes but with direct transfers.

2. Bolivia does not have personal income taxes.

3. In Bolivia, Costa Rica, Ecuador and Honduras market income does not include consumption of own production because the data was either not available or not reliable.

4. For Brazil, the results for the analysis presented here differ from the results published in Higgins and Pereira (2014) because the latter include taxes on services (ISS), on goods and services to finance pensions (CONFINS) and to finance Social Workers (PIS), while the results presented here do not include them. The authors concluded, after the publication of this paper, that the source for these taxes was not reliable.

5. Gini coefficients for Chile are estimated here using total income and, thus, differ from official figures of inequality, which are estimated using monetary income (i.e. official figures exclude the owner's occupied imputed rent).

6. For the Dominican Republic, the study analyses the effects of fiscal policy in 2013, but the household income and expenditure survey dates back to 2006-07.

Source: Commitment to Equity Institute Data Center on Fiscal Redistribution (CEQ, 2017). Based on information from: Argentina (Rossignolo, 2018); Bolivia (Paz Arauco et al., 2014); Brazil (Higgins and Pereira, 2014); Chile (Martinez-Aguilar et al., 2018); Colombia (Melendez and Martinez, 2015); Costa Rica (Sauma and Trejos, 2014); Dominican Republic (Aristy-Escuder et al., 2018); Ecuador (Llerena et al., 2015); El Salvador (Beneke, Lustig, and Oliva, 2018); Guatemala (Icefi, 2017a); Honduras (Icefi, 2017b); Mexico (Scott, 2014); Nicaragua (Icefi, 2017c); Paraguay (Giménez et al., 2017); Peru (Jaramillo, 2014); Uruguay (Bucheli et al., 2014) and Venezuela (Molina, 2016).

StatLink https://doi.org/10.1787/888933822634

Despite the decent performance in reducing poverty headcount, the depth of poverty falls than in other countries. A closer look into *Tekoporã* and *Adulto Mayor* reveals that they lead to smaller reductions in the extreme poverty gap than in other countries in the region (Figure 2.10). *Tekoporã* and *Adulto Mayor* reduce the depth of extreme poverty by 20.1% and 12.2% respectively.

Figure 2.10. Social assistance reduces the poverty gap less than in other countries

Extreme poverty gap reduction in Latin America

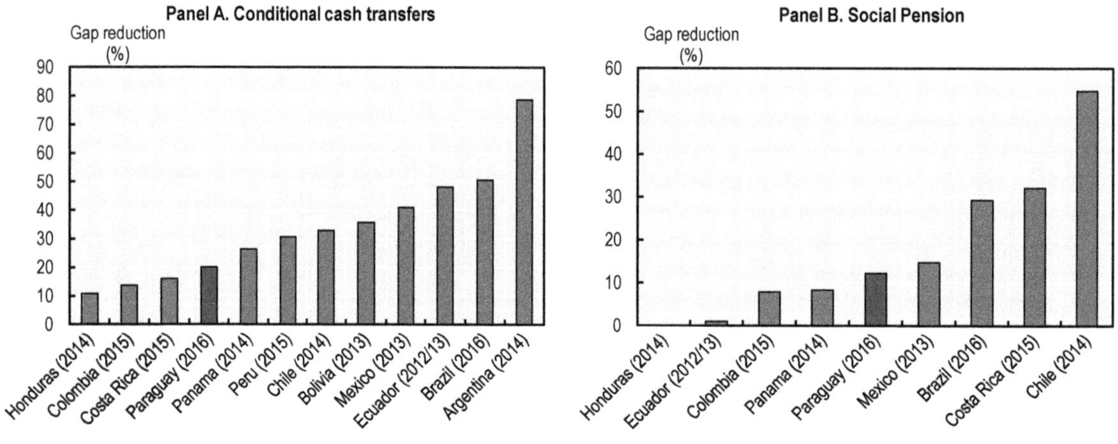

Notes: 1. In Paraguay extreme poverty is measured based on the national 2016 definition, in the remaining countries extreme poverty is based on the international USD 1.9 PPP line.

2. Extreme poverty gap reduction is the difference between the extreme poverty gap pre-transfer and post-transfer divided by the extreme poverty gap pre-transfer.

Source: World Bank (2018a). Except extreme poverty gap reduction for Paraguay: own elaboration based on the Permanent Household Survey of Paraguay (DGEEC, 2017).

StatLink http://dx.doi.org/10.1787/888933822653

Paraguay's contributory pension system needs to become more equitable and to expand

Paraguay's pension system is characterised by a multitude of providers with few affiliates. The number of affiliates in each pension scheme is symptomatic of the fragmentation of Paraguay's pension system. The approximately 750 000 active contributors and 110 000 contributory pension recipients are scattered among eight different pension funds offering 11 different pension schemes (see Annex Table 2.A.1 for more details). The two major funds, the IPS and the *Caja Fiscal*, cover more than 90% of the affiliates. The remaining affiliates are scattered among six closed pension funds. In recent years, private providers started offering voluntary pension schemes, such as the *Caja Mutual de Cooperativistas, Caja Médica, Caja de Profesores de la UCA*; these loosely-regulated voluntary private schemes cover approximately 30 000 people (Casalí and Velásquez, 2016). The contributory schemes are complemented by non-contributory pensions for veterans, survivors of killed police officers and military, poor elderly (*Adulto Mayor*) and merit pensions. *Adulto Mayor* is not officially a pension, but functions de facto as one and, with 162 000 benefit recipients, is larger than the contributory pension system. The present analysis focuses on the largest public contributory programmes, as most affiliates contribute to them and their future funding gaps constitute a potential risk for the treasury.

Retirement age, contribution periods and contribution rate are unequal

Paraguay does not have a harmonised standard retirement age. Each pension scheme has a different retirement age for its affiliates and most are below the Latin American average

(Figure 2.11). Affiliates of the IPS, the *Caja Bancaria*, the *Caja de la ANDE* and the *Caja de Itaipú Binacional* can access a full standard pension at age 60 if a minimum contributory period is reached (discussed below). Affiliates of the *Caja Municipal and Caja Parlamentaria* can retire with a standard pension at age 55, affiliates of the *Caja Ferroviaria* even at age 50. Civil servants of the central administration have the strictest scheme within the *Caja Fiscal*: they receive a standard pension only at age 62. All other *Caja Fiscal* schemes (military, police, teachers and university professors) have no official retirement age; their retirement is only subject to a minimum contributory period. Retirement becomes obligatory at age 65 for all *Caja Fiscal* affiliates, irrespective of the number of years contributed.

The minimum contributory periods for a standard pension differ for each scheme. The minimum contributory periods range from as little as 10 years (scheme for police) to 30 years (*Caja Bancaria*). The contributory periods are unrelated to the retirement age: schemes with low contributory periods (such as the schemes for police or military, *Caja Municipal and Caja Parlamentaria*) also have low retirement ages (Figure 2.11). The *Caja de Itaipu Binacional* has a high retirement age (age 60), but a low contributory period. The Caja Ferroviaria has one of the highest contributory periods (25 years), but also one of the lowest retirement ages (age 50).

Figure 2.11. Contributory periods and retirement age do not stand in relation

Retirement age and minimum contributory periods for a standard pension, in years

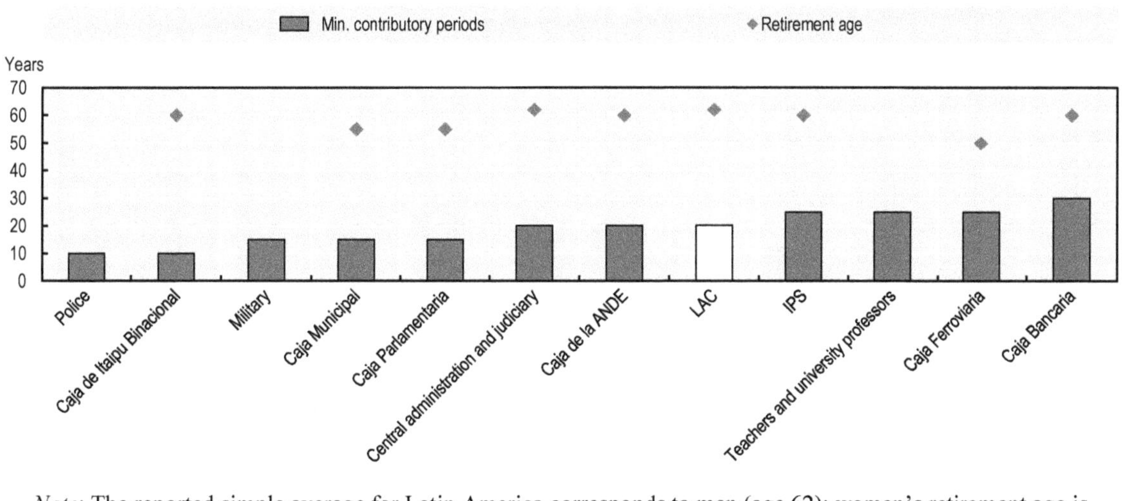

Note: The reported simple average for Latin America corresponds to men (age 62); women's retirement age is age 60.5. The schemes for teachers, military and police personnel have no official retirement age.
Source: Based on Navarro and Ortiz (2014). LAC average from OECD/IDB/World Bank (2014).

StatLink https://doi.org/10.1787/888933822672

Some providers offer early retirement schemes. Typically, the early retirement schemes are conditioned on longer contributory periods or grant lower replacement rates. IPS affiliates can already retire at age 55 with 30 years of contributions. *Caja Municipal* affiliates can retire at age 50 with 20 years of contributions. Civil servants of the central administration can retire at age 50 with a lower replacement rate. Police officers, military, teachers and university professors can retire at any age, as long as they have reached the minimum contributory period. Teachers and university professors who have been certified to be physically or mentally unfit for work can request an early retirement (different from a disability pension) with a minimum contribution period of 15 years and a lower replacement rate (40%).

The IPS offers a proportional pension for affiliates not qualifying for a standard pension. As of 2011 these affiliates can claim a proportional pension at age 65 with 15 years of contributions (Law 4.290/11). An alternative to the proportional pension is settling the missing years of contribution by contributing 12.5% of the average wage of the last three years until requirements are met (Law 3.404/07).[3]

Since 2013, the IPS includes independent workers and employers to its pension scheme on a voluntary basis. However, in 2016, only 518 affiliates belonged to this voluntary scheme (IPS, 2018). Independent workers can voluntarily contribute 13% of their income (which cannot be below the minimum wage) and obtain an early, standard or proportional pension. Independent workers are only entitled to the IPS's health benefits once retired, not during working life.

Contribution rates are low. Like retirement age and minimum contributory period, the contribution rates differ for every scheme (see Annex 2.A). While the closed pension funds demand relatively high contribution rates, the main pension providers (IPS and *Caja Fiscal*) demand low rates compared to OECD countries (Figure 2.12). The low contribution rates are paired with a low retirement age and high replacement rate, making it a costly system (see next section).

Figure 2.12. Contribution rates are low

Mandatory pension contribution rates for employees and employers, 2016

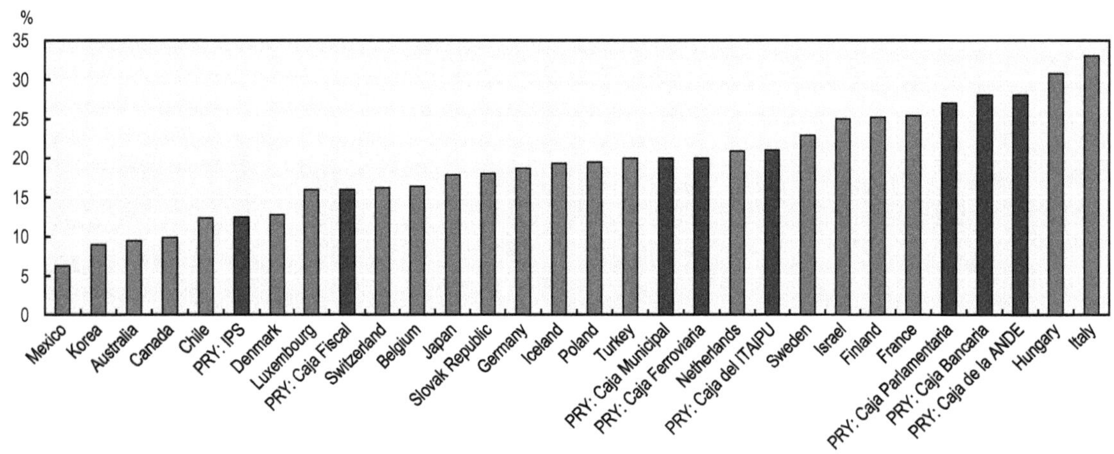

Note: The IPS contributions depicted are the contributions to the IPS pension fund (excluding contributions to the health benefits). The Caja de la ANDE is a complementary system. Employers and employees contribute 5% each to the Caja de la ANDE and 12% and 6%, respectively, to the IPS.
Source: OECD (2017) and Navarro Ortiz (2014) for Paraguay.

StatLink https://doi.org/10.1787/888933822691

The IPS contributions differ from other schemes. The IPS provides health and pension benefits to its affiliates, which are financed by employers' and employees' contributions. The contribution to the pension and health benefits are mandatory for all IPS affiliates, except voluntary contributions of independent workers who are excluded from the health benefits. The contributions from employers (14% of the salary) and employees (9% of the salary) finance both benefits. These contributions are divided into the IPS pension, health and administrative funds. The actual contribution rate corresponding to the pension scheme would be 4.9% for the employee and 7.6% for the employer.[4]

Paraguay's pension funds have high replacement rates

The pension benefit calculation induces the underreporting of earnings. In Paraguay, the calculation of the pension benefits (earnings measure) is based on fewer years than in other countries. The earnings measure ranges from the last month (*Caja Parlamentaria*) to five years (*Caja Fiscal*). This is considerably below OECD countries, who typically take the lifelong earnings or at least the best 24 years to calculate the benefit value (OECD, 2017). Basing the pension calculation only on a few years disconnects pension benefits and contributions made; it also encourages contributors to underreport their early earnings in order to decrease contributions, as the benefit would not be affected.

The pension benefit calculation disadvantages independent workers. The IPS bases its pension calculation on the last three years before retirement, except for independent workers who make voluntary contributions. The earnings measure for the benefit calculation of independent workers is extended to ten years instead of three (Law 4.933/13). This difference with dependent workers creates inequity within the system, both groups have the same contribution rates, retirement age and replacement rate, but a different earnings measure.

Figure 2.13. Replacement rates are high

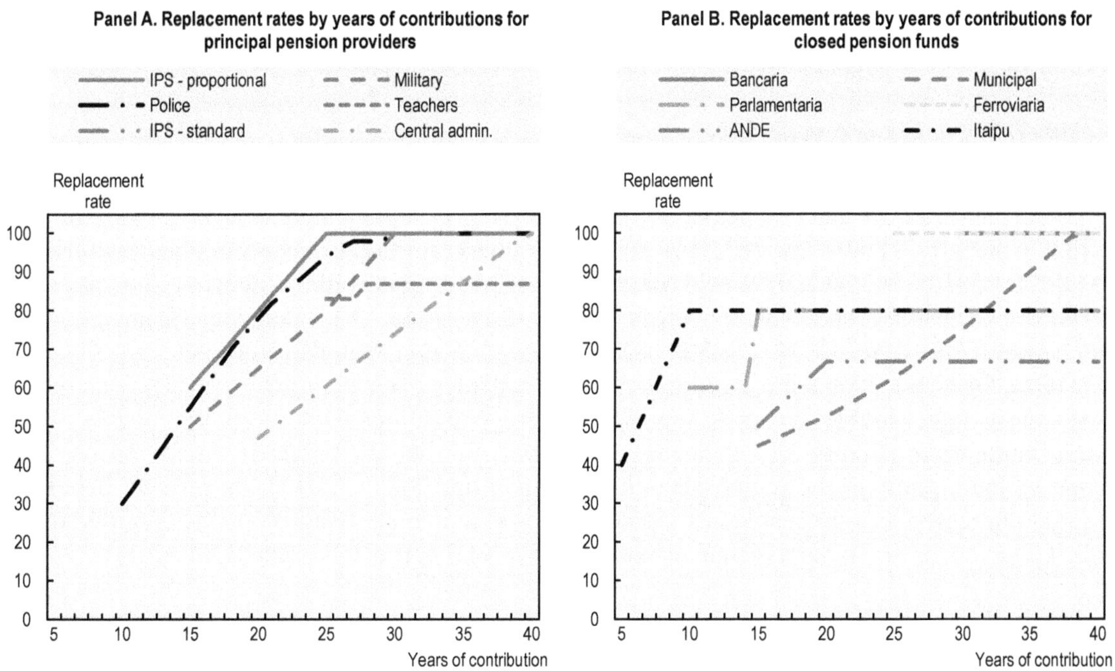

Note: The IPS proportional pension is granted at age 65 and available for affiliates not meeting the requirement for a standard pension.
Source: Own elaboration.

StatLink https://doi.org/10.1787/888933822710

Most pension benefits increase progressively with years of contributions. Except the IPS standard pension, all pensions increase with years of contributions. Initial replacement rates are high in most schemes and increase quickly with additional years (Figure 2.13). After 25 years of contributions the IPS's proportional pension grants a pension equal to IPS's standard pension.

The differentiated replacement rate of the *Caja Fiscal* highlights the inequity within that provider. *Caja Fiscal* offers different schemes to the military, police, teachers, university professors, central administration and judicial personnel. These schemes differ in their retirement age, replacement rate and minimum years of contribution required. However, the employee contribution rates are the same for all schemes (16%). This makes the *Caja Fiscal* an inequitable system, especially within the civilian segment, as funds can be transferred between the different civilian schemes to cover deficits.

Generous retirement benefits provide little incentive to contribute more than necessary. Benefit levels differ for each of Paraguay's schemes. The standard pension of the main social security provider, the IPS, is set at 100% with 25 years of contribution. Most other schemes also grant a pension benefit equal to 100% of the salary. The high replacement rates do not provide incentives to contribute more than the required minimum. Data from the IPS (2014) confirm that most affiliates retire as soon as they meet the requirements and only a negligible number of individuals contribute more than needed.

Under Paraguayan pension schemes, benefit entitlements can accumulate rather quickly. The accrual rate measures this speed; it indicates the percentage of the earnings that are covered with each year of contribution. In the standard pension of the IPS each year of contribution covers 4% of the earnings. This accrual rate is superior to those of OECD countries, which range between 0.55% and 2.81% (OECD, 2017).

Pension benefits are generous

Contributory and non-contributory pension benefits are comparatively high. The net replacement rate of the IPS pension was 103.8%. This replacement rate is considerably above the OECD average (62.9%) and the highest among Latin American countries (OECD, 2017; OECD/IDB/World Bank, 2014). Most contributory pensions are above 100% of current contributors' wages (Figure 2.14 Panel A).[5] Pensions from closed schemes (*Caja de la ANDE*, *Caja Bancaria*, *Caja de Itaipu*) but also from the *Caja Fiscal* scheme for non-civilians are even higher: these schemes offer their affiliates pensions that are more than double the economy-wide average earnings and more than triple the minimum wage (Figure 2.14 Panel B). Moreover, the benefit value of *Adulto Mayor* is one of the highest in the region (Bosch, Melguizo and Pagés, 2013). Its relative benefit value expressed as a percentage of the economy-wide average wage (20.1%) is above the OECD average for social assistance benefits (18.1%) (Figure 2.14 Panel C).[6]

Figure 2.14. Pension benefits are generous

Value of pensions in relation to the average wage

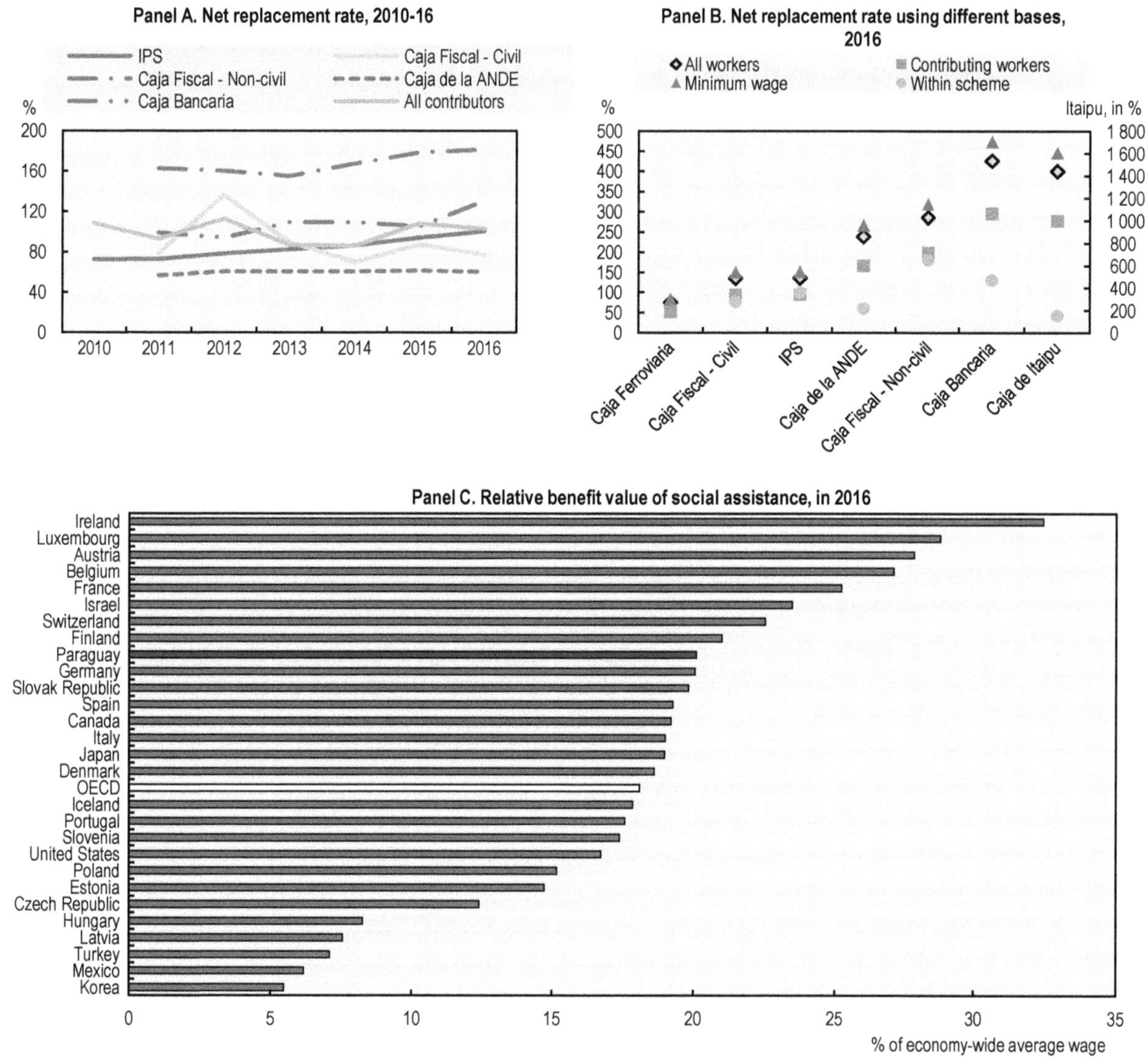

Note: The replacement rate presents the average net pension value as a ratio of the average net income of current workers. Panel A depicts the ratio between the average pension and the net income of contributors to the scheme. Panel B depicts the ratio between the average pension and a range of net incomes. The replacement rate for the Caja de la ANDE reports only the benefit stemming from Caja de la ANDE, not the complementary IPS benefit.

Source: Panels A and B: Own calculations based on MTESS (2017). Panel C: For OECD countries OECD (2017), for Paraguay own calculations based on the Permanent Household Survey of Paraguay (DGEEC, 2017).

StatLink https://doi.org/10.1787/888933822729

Contributory and non-contributory pensions are an important part of households' income. Most contributory pension recipients are situated in the top income deciles. Among contributory pension recipients the benefit represents an important part of household income: the pension represents more than a third of total consumable household income

(Figure 2.15 Panel A). *Adulto Mayor* is of great importance for low-income households; the benefit represents more than 30% of the consumable household income for the first to third decile (Figure 2.15 Panel B).

Figure 2.15. Pensions are a major income source

Pension recipients and benefit-income ratio by decile, population aged 65 or above in 2016

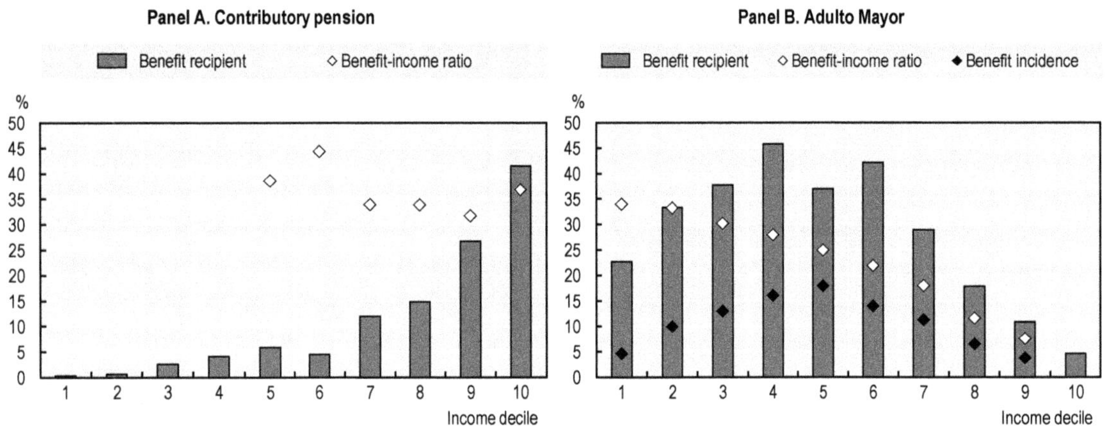

Note: The benefit-income ratio presents the *Adulto Mayor* benefits as a share of the household's income. The benefit incidence is the percentage of benefits going to each decile of the income distribution relative to the total benefits going to the population. Decile based on per capita consumable household income. The consumable income is the market income plus pensions, direct and indirect transfers minus direct taxes.
Source: Own elaboration based on the Permanent Household Survey of Paraguay (DGEEC, 2017).

StatLink https://doi.org/10.1787/888933822748

Figure 2.16. Poverty is lower among pension recipients

Poverty rates among pension recipients, 2016

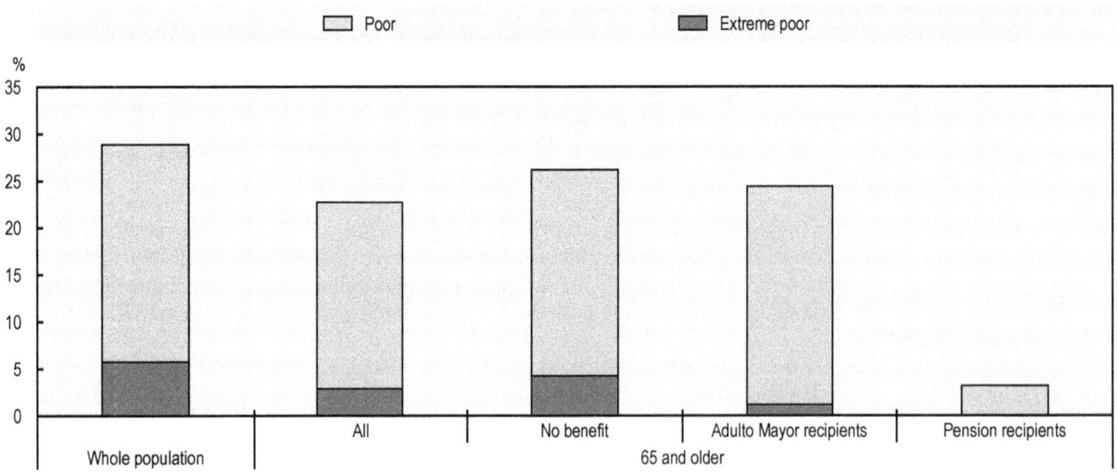

Source: Own calculations based on the Permanent Household Survey of Paraguay (DGEEC, 2017).

StatLink https://doi.org/10.1787/888933822767

Pensions are an important instrument to reduce old-age poverty. Elderly without any pension benefits have a much higher poverty rate than contributory pension recipients, but also higher than *Adulto Mayor* recipients (Figure 2.16). Indeed, analyses confirm *Adulto Mayor*'s impact on reducing poverty and inequality among the elderly (Bruno, 2017; Rodríguez and Benítez, 2018).

Certain segments of the current system are not financially sustainable

Demographic trends threaten the sustainability of the pension schemes. An expanding elderly population with higher life expectancies leads to low and decreasing contributors-per-pensioner rates; in other words, expenditure outstrips revenues. Most pension schemes, especially the closed schemes, have a low contributors-per-pensioner ratio (Table 2.3). This ratio has been decreasing over the years and will continue to fall with the demographic transition. For example, the *Caja de la ANDE*'s contributors-per-pensioner rate decreased from 3.7 in 2005 to 2.4 in 2016 (*Caja ANDE*, 2017). The IPS still has 10.1 contributors per pensioner, but this ratio is projected to halve to 5.0 by 2050 (IPS, 2014). Given the current replacement and contribution rates, the IPS requires at least eight contributors per pensioner to fully finance (with affiliates' contributions) an ordinary old-age pension equal to 100% of the current average wage.

The fragmentation of Paraguay's pension system increases administrative costs. The small closed pension funds are not very efficient in offering and running pension plans, judged by total operating costs in relation to assets managed. The operating costs are equal to 1.1% to 7% of the total assets managed (Table 2.3),[7] which surpass those in OECD countries, which typically range between 0.1% and 1.5% (OECD, 2017). The low efficiency in managing the assets is explained in large part by the size of the closed pension funds. Indeed, hardly any economies of scale are generated given the low number of affiliates. A consolidation between the small funds could reduce administrative costs.

Few contributing affiliates and actuarial deficits endanger public finances and cement inequalities. The low number of contributing affiliates constitutes a latent liability for the treasury: poor elderly without a contributory pension might qualify for a non-contributory pension. This would increase both the target population and programme costs, which already accounted for 0.7% of GDP in 2016 (MH, 2018). On the other hand, due to the public character of the pension funds, the state will need to bail out the funds that turn unprofitable. These future liabilities are a serious concern for public finances. Eventual bailouts are also problematic from an equity perspective: the non-affiliated population has lower income than affiliates to social security; a bailout for any pension fund would thus have regressive distribution effects.

The IPS's positive financial situation will turn negative by mid-century. Currently, IPS revenues exceed its expenses and, thus, the IPS holds reserves worth USD 1 140.3 million (Box 2.1). Yet, this situation is not expected to last. By 2032, the IPS's expenses for pension and administration are projected to be higher than revenues from employers' and employees' contributions (IPS, 2014). The turning point could be postponed by seven years, if the state were to actually contribute the 1.5% of affiliates' payroll stipulated in the Law No. 375/56, which it currently does not. The turning point could be postponed by an additional five years if the IPS were to stop paying a year-end bonus to its beneficiaries. Indeed, end-of-year bonuses are not part of the base for social security contributions. Moreover, actuarial predictions indicate that the accumulated reserves will be depleted ten years after the running expenses surpass the contributions collected.

Table 2.3. Indicators of the funds' financial situation, 2015 or latest available

		Caja Fiscal								
	IPS	Military and Police	Teachers and university professors	Central Administration and judicial personnel	Caja Bancaria	Caja Municipal	Parlamentaria	Ferroviaria	ANDE	ITAIPU
Contributors per pensioner [a]	10.1	2.3	3.8	7.1	4.7	5.1	0.6	0.0	2.4	0.8
Contributions (% of GDP) [b]	3.2		1.4		0.3	0.0	n.a.	n.a.	0.0	0.2
Benefits (% of GDP) [b]	1.1		1.5		0.2	0.0	n.a.	n.a.	0.1	0.2
Management costs (%) [c]	n.a.	n.a.	n.a.	n.a.	4.0	7	n.a.	n.a.	1.1	5.7
Reserves (in million USD) [c]	2 067.7[d]	0	n.a.	604.9	213.8	41.3	n.a.	0	148.7[e]	283.0

Note: n.a. = not available. 0 = smaller than 0.0%. Management costs are the ratio between operation costs and the value of the assets managed.

a. Data from 2016. b. 2015 for IPS, Caja Bancaria, Caja de la ANDE, Caja del Itaipu, 2014 for Caja Fiscal and Caja Municipal.

Source: Own elaboration based on MTESS (2017); b. IMF (2017); c. Navarro and Ortiz (2014); d. IPS (2017). e. Caja ANDE (2017).

Box 2.1. IPS affiliates without entitlements make the generous system possible

Only one in two Paraguayans of age 65 or above, who contributed to the IPS, receives a pension: 46.3% receive an old-age pension, 3.1% receive an invalidity or survivors pension. More than half of the elderly above age 65 who contributed to the IPS at one point in their working life do not receive a contributory pension: 22.8% continue to work, 16.9% finished their working life (inactive) but do not receive a pension and 9.1% of former contributors receive a non-contributory pension (*Adulto Mayor*) (Figure 2.17). These affiliates typically did not contribute sufficiently to be entitled to a pension. According to the former affiliates' own accounts, the median number of months they have contributed is 120 months (ten years).

The IPS partially owes its current good financial situation to the large number of former affiliates who do not receive a pension. IPS affiliates who did not contribute sufficiently to obtain a standard, proportional or early pension are not entitled to a refund of their contributions. In a pay-as-you-go system, without a refund possibility, not receiving a pension benefit means that the contributions of these affiliates finances the pensions of actual recipients. Thus, having a considerable number of affiliates not entitled to pension benefits increases the IPS's revenues, without obligations on the other side of the balance sheet.

Affiliates with more than 25 years of contributions also generate additional revenues for the system. Standard pension benefits are capped at 100% with 25 years of contributions. Thus, excess contributions would also help the IPS to maintain its generous benefits, but in practice few contribute longer than the required minimum contributory period.

Figure 2.17. IPS affiliates without entitlements subsidise pension recipients

Situation of population of age 65 and above who contributed to the IPS (as a percentage)

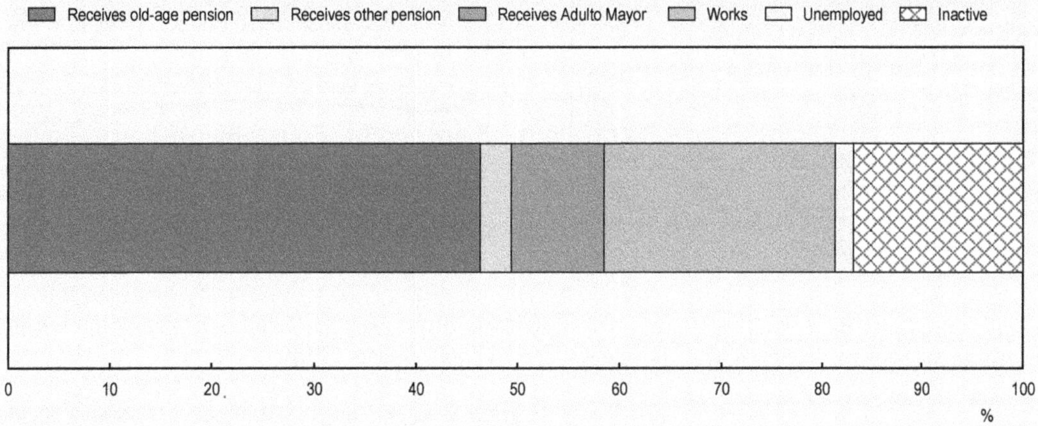

Note: The population considered are the elderly (age 65 or older) who report having contributed to the IPS at one point in their life; they are not necessarily active affiliates currently.
Source: Own calculations on ELPS (STP, 2016).

StatLink https://doi.org/10.1787/888933822786

The financial situation of the *Caja Fiscal* is especially alarming. The *Caja Fiscal* is already unable to cover its liabilities: in 2016 the running deficit of the non-civilian schemes represented 0.44% of GDP (Figure 2.18 Panel B). The treasury covers this deficit with general tax revenues, which is especially regressive as Value-added tax (VAT) (paid also by the poor and non-affiliates) is the largest tax revenue in Paraguay. Without reforms, the situation will only get worse: the IMF (2017) forecasts that the discounted value of the *Caja Fiscal*'s deficits to 2065 accounts for 28% of current GDP.

The imbalance of the *Caja Fiscal* originates from the generosity of certain pension schemes. Retirement age and the required years of contributions are low, paired with a high replacement rate. This is especially true for military and police personnel: the average old-age pension for non-civilians is 181.6% of the current average income for non-civilians, for the civilians within the *Caja Fiscal* this ratio is only 77.2% (MTESS, 2017). The system is not only inequitable, but has been running a deficit for several years (Figure 2.18). While the law No. 4.252/2010 allows cross-financing between the civilian schemes (teachers and university professors, central administration and judicial personnel), a surplus of the civilian scheme cannot be used to cover deficits in the non-civilian schemes (police and military) and vice-versa. Actuarial studies predict that the turning point for the civilian schemes will be between 2021 and 2023; as of then, the overall surplus of the civilian schemes will turn into a deficit (Larrain, Viteri and Zucal, 2013 as cited in Alaimo and Tapia, 2014).

Figure 2.18. Only one of the *Caja Fiscal*'s schemes is in good shape

Financial situation of the Caja Fiscal, percent of GDP

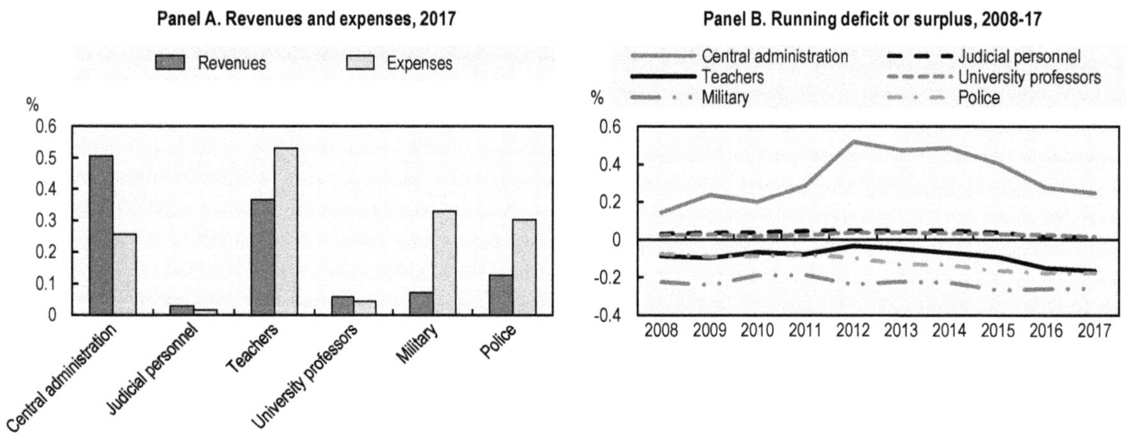

Source: Own elaboration based on Ministry of Finance (MH, 2018) data, *Revenues and Expenses by Schemes*, www.hacienda.gov.py/web-hacienda/jubilaciones (accessed on February 2018).

StatLink https://doi.org/10.1787/888933822805

Most pension funds run actuarial deficits. The complementary pension schemes of the *Caja de la ANDE* and *Caja Itaipu* will be in deficit by the middle of this century. Given their smaller scale, the actuarial deficits are low compared to the IPS and the *Caja Fiscal* (Navarro and Ortiz, 2014; IMF, 2017). While the financial position of the *Caja Bancaria* will also deteriorate over time, it has no actuarial deficit (IMF, 2017).

The way forward

In its efforts to build a social protection system for all, Paraguay must tackle three key challenges: enhancing the governance of the system, encouraging independent workers to contribute to social security and securing financial resources for non-contributory social assistance. The Social Cabinet (2018) recognises these challenges and calls to tackle them.

The governance of the social protection system needs to be enhanced

Paraguay's social assistance and social security systems act in isolation. The two mainstays of the social protection system do not interact; the only provisions in common are old-age benefits. Non-contributory and contributory pensions are administrated separately and are incompatible. A coherent social protection system needs to bring these two important schemes together.

An uncoordinated pension system could have deterring effects on social security contributions. Social assistance benefits for elderly reduce poverty; however, they risk segmenting the pension system into an informal (non-contributory) and formal (contributory) pillar. This can happen if non-contributory pension benefits reduce incentives to contribute to social security. A non-contributory pension can represent a sort of tax on contributions, when the non-contributory pension reduces with the receipt of a contributory pension; it, thus, discourages contributions to social security (Bosch, Melguizo and Pagés, 2013).

Box 2.2. Chileans can receive both a non-contributory and contributory pension

Chile's pension system has three components: a redistributive first tier, a second tier of mandatory individual accounts (defined contributions) and voluntary savings plans as a third tier. The redistributive first tier was introduced in March 2008 following sustained criticism about low contributory pensions (Santoro, 2017). The special feature of this first tier is that it is gradually phased out to decrease eventual deterring effects on pension contributions. Thanks to this reform, pension coverage increased by 10 percentage points and extreme poverty among elderly reduced to 1.5% in 2015 from an initial 7.5% in 2006 (ECLAC, 2017).

The first tier is organised in a non-contributory pension (*Pensión Básica Solidaria [PBS]*) and a supplementary welfare pension (*Aporte Previsional Solidario [APS]*). The PBS is a basic non-contributory pension entitlement for individuals without other pensions. The PBS is payable from the age of 65 to the poorest 60% of the population complying with a set of residency criteria. The APS is a state funded supplementary welfare pension for individuals who made contributions to the second tier but receive low pensions (the same wealth and residence criteria apply). Pensioners with a pension below a set threshold receive the APS, which is gradually phased out until reaching said threshold. The maximum level of the APS is equal to the PBS, in case the person's contributory pension is equal to zero.

Figure 2.19. Chile phases its non-contributory pension out

Stylised value of Chilean pension

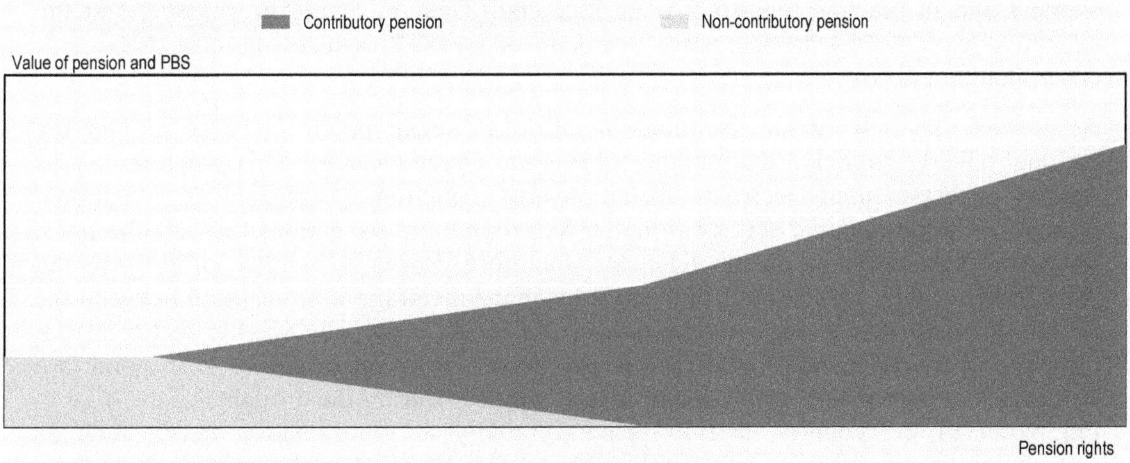

Source: Own elaboration.

StatLink https://doi.org/10.1787/888933822824

Source: ECLAC (2017), Santoro (2017), OECD (2011), OECD (2017).

A holistic pension system must consider the interactions between its main parts. Further research must show whether the difference between the *Adulto Mayor* benefit and the minimum contributory pension benefit (33% of the minimum wage in place) is too small and dampens incentives to contribute to social security. To avoid such negative side effects, the transition between non-contributory and contributory pensions has to be carefully designed. To avoid such negative effects, Chile, for example, phases out its non-contributory pension while the value of the contributory pension increases (Box 2.2).

Social assistance and social security face governance challenges, beyond the challenges involving the interaction of non-contributory and contributory pensions.

Social assistance needs a national champion

While social assistance plays an important role in the National Development Plan, it is a field orphaned of clear leadership and suffering from a lack of political level co-ordination. In the past, the Social Cabinet (*Gabinete Social*), created in 2003 used to act as the ministerial co-ordinating body for all government entities providing any kind of social programme (18 entities). Its function was to promote, co-ordinate and steer the management of social programmes and policies (Decree 751, November 2013). The Social Cabinet is chaired by the President and co-ordinated by the Secretary-General of the Presidency. A more reduced executive team led by the STP and comprising six of the 18 entities was also created by Presidential decree within the Social Cabinet. The Social Cabinet also has a Technical Secretariat to support its work. The Social Cabinet was deemed inefficient and the co-ordination at ministerial level through regular meetings was discontinued in 2013. The Executive Team, led by the STP has maintained regular meetings and driven co-ordination efforts. The Technical Secretariat of the Social Cabinet remains active and has focused on areas beyond day-to-day co-ordination of social policy. It has led the development of an integrated database of beneficiaries of social programmes and the development of a medium-term framework for social protection. The institutional divide between the Technical Secretariat, situated directly at the Social Cabinet and in practice reporting to the Secretary-General of the Presidency, and the executive team, led by the Executive Secretary of the STP, reduces the effectiveness of co-ordination efforts.

At present, the only major co-ordination effort in social policy is based around the national poverty reduction programme *Sembrando Oportunidades*. This programme was created by Presidential Decree to foster poverty reduction, established as a "national priority". The programme acts as an umbrella programme for actions towards the poor, under the co-ordination of the STP and therefore covers a number of pre-existing programmes. Once a week the STP hosts a technical meeting (*mesa técnica*) between the 27 entities that have a stake in *Sembrando Oportunidades*. The weekly technical co-ordination between technical staff and policy makers offer opportunities to respond in a co-ordinated manner to specific needs, as was the case during the droughts of 2014/15 in the North of the country, and to respond rapidly to co-ordination needs such as articulating the intervention of several actors in specific areas in the field. However, its technical nature limits its decision-making and strategic capacity. To improve their effectiveness and reach, meetings could be structured around particular themes or population groups, follow-up could be intensified and stakeholders should attend the meetings more regularly (FAO/STP, 2018). Furthermore, *Sembrando Oportunidades* would benefit from stronger political guidance (ibid).

The lack of leadership and co-ordination leads to overlapping programmes and unexploited synergies. Numerous programmes provide income generation support for family businesses and farms; these programmes are dispersed and reach less than 10% of rural households with agricultural activities (Serafini, 2016). Two major programmes were recently created and have received a lot of attention: *Familia por Familia* (a pilot programme implemented by the STP) and *Tenonderã* (implemented by the SAS). Although target groups and intervention methods differ, both programmes are designed with the aim of integrating social transfers and promotion actions following the graduation methodology and could benefit from a stronger co-ordination and synergies.

Key co-ordination tools have been implemented and need to be consolidated

Paraguay has put in place key instruments to improve policy co-ordination. The country recently designed a single targeting instrument (*Ficha Social*) and is rolling out a single beneficiary register (the Integrated Social Information System [SIIS]) and a reporting matrix (*Tablero de Control*). These instruments reflect the positive experiences in the region, such as Brazil's development of the Single registry of beneficiaries (*Cadastro Único*) (see Box 2.3). To be more effective co-ordination tools, these building blocks need to be enhanced and integrated. Ultimately, beneficiary identification, programme promotion and service delivery can be further integrated through single agents as in the case of South Africa's one stop service vehicles (Box 2.4).

A unified targeting instrument has been set up and data collection efforts are ongoing. A targeting mechanism was developed in the context of the implementation of the national anti-poverty programme *Sembrando Oportunidades.* It consists of a questionnaire (*Ficha Social*) to collect information on households, including their civil status, education, living standards, health, employment and agricultural activities. This questionnaire is complemented by an algorithm to classify the surveyed population as extreme poor, poor, vulnerable and neither poor nor vulnerable. Information was collected from almost 1.1 million people (16% of the population) between 2013 and the end of 2017. The households included were largely from the administration of questionnaires to beneficiaries of social programmes of the SAS and the Ministry of Agriculture. Systematic surveying of areas with high prevalence of poverty complemented the roster. Creating the single targeting instrument was an important step to create synergies and a more co-ordinated and coherent delivery of social assistance. The information is available to public entities and linked to the information in the dashboard of the programme.

Generalising the use of the *Ficha Social* as a targeting instrument is still a challenge. The agencies implementing social assistance programmes lack a common approach to target beneficiaries. Different institutions implement the flagship programmes *Tekoporã, Abrazo* and *Adulto Mayor*, with few possibilities for mutual learning and synergies. All of these programmes use different targeting instruments and none of these is the single targeting instrument (*Ficha Social*) put forward by *Sembrando Oportunidades*. While the SAS, which implements *Tekoporã*, has applied the *Ficha Social* to its beneficiaries, it still relies on a different data collection instrument and a different means test, based on a quality of life index, to identify beneficiaries. To overcome the current institutional resistance and effectively enforce the take-up of the single targeting instrument, it is essential that the *Ficha Social* receives political backing. *Adulto Mayor* currently uses a modified algorithm of the *Ficha Social*, including additional information. This partial deviation of the standard methodology exemplifies how the single targeting instrument can be adjusted to specific programmes' needs.

Box 2.3. A unified registry for Brazilian social policies

The *Cadastro Único* is a single registry of Brazilian households living in poverty and extreme poverty. The *Cadastro* aims to register all low-income families with a household income below 3 monthly minimum wages or individuals earning less than half a minimum wage. The Federal Government, States and municipalities use this information to implement social programmes aimed at improving the lives of these families.

Before introducing the *Cadastro Único*, each government programme had its own mechanisms to collect data about potential beneficiaries, to process that information and to determine the allocation of benefits. Even within the same government agencies, registries were kept separate. Consequently, social protection programmes were segmented and uncoordinated. This frequently led to inclusion and exclusion errors and limited outreach. The lack of unified and more detailed information on poor families hindered policy-making and therefore timeliness and effectiveness of social policies (ILO, 2014).

In 2001, the Brazilian government formally created by law the Single Registry (*Cadastro Único*) and launched the *Bolsa Familia* programme two years later, which unified four similar cash transfer programmes targeting poor and vulnerable families. The goals of the *Cadastro Único* were to identify poor families, develop an understanding about their characteristics, and geo-reference poor households. Following the initial success in registering poor households, the government invested in improving data collection and launched an exhaustive legislative and regulatory review of the registry, resulting in a new online version of the registry launched in 2010. Three years later all municipalities had access to the online database, helping them to target policy interventions more accurately.

In practice, *Cadastro Único* is based on a decentralized data collection and entry scheme and a centralized database consolidation and management. Municipalities are responsible for collecting data and registering families. Municipalities survey households in geographically targeted areas for their inclusion in the *Cadastro*. Citizens can also request their registration directly through dedicated structures in municipalities. Once data are collected, municipal officials enter registry data into a unified software and make some crosschecks to identify potential inconsistencies or gaps in the data. *Caixa Econômica Federal* consolidates data from municipalities, assigns identification numbers and runs some additional crosschecks. The resulting consolidated family registry is the *Cadastro Único* and includes information from all registered families, regardless of whether they are eligible or not for government's social programmes. Finally, the Federal Government, the States and the municipalities use this information to determine families' eligibility for social programmes and subsequent attribution of benefits (Lindert et al, 2007).

Source: ILO (2014) and Lindert et al. (2007).

Plans to enhance the single beneficiary register can contribute to reaching all Paraguayans in need. The SIIS lists all people currently or previously benefiting from one or more social assistance programmes. It is an important management and monitoring tool and helps to identify eventual inclusion errors in programmes. Expanding the SIIS and integrating it with a database of potential beneficiaries registered with the single targeting instrument would be a welcome step towards more co-ordination, efficiency and synergies, bringing the information system closer to the Brazilian *Cadastro Unico*.

The planning and monitoring system of *Sembrando Oportunidades* is a major co-ordination tool for social policy. One of the functions of the *Mesa técnica* is to populate and monitor the on-line dashboard (*Tablero de control*) of the programme. Participating entities set out their targets for implementation actions, including when and where they will carry them out. They also record the delivery of services, so that the same system serves to co-ordinate at the planning stage and to monitor progress. Regular progress reports for all programmes at the regional level are published regularly. The public has access to the online tool, where they can check the degree of advancement of a programme at the district level.

Box 2.4. Reaching South Africa's rural poor with mobile one-stop service vehicles

The Integrated Community Registration Outreach Programme (ICROP) consists of fully equipped mobile one-stop service vehicles bringing the social protection system to rural South Africa. Created by the South African Social Security Agency in 2007 to deliver their child benefits, the ICROP quickly developed to become a whole-of-government initiative bringing all social services to the rural population under the same umbrella. Entities involved in the ICROP include the South African Social Security Agency, the Department of Health, the Department of Education, the Department of Home Affairs, the South African Police Services, municipalities, community leaders and NGOs.

The one-stop service vehicles provide a variety of services. They inform the population about existing benefits and services and help them sign up for social assistance programmes. They also identify potential beneficiaries, update the beneficiary registry, facilitate access to appeals procedures, process identity documents and birth certificates, promote access to health services and ensure involvement of community members in service delivery. Each service vehicle is equipped with a modern IT system and staffed with a driver, two attesting officers, a medical doctor (on-site assessment of medical/disability condition and basic health services), an approval officer (on-site approval and quality control), an IT support technician and a customer care official (managing enquiries and outreach).

Programme beneficiary numbers increased faster in areas served by the ICROP than in areas excluded from the programme. The shared delivery mechanism increased outreach at lower administrative costs and improved institutional co-ordination by using shared processes and tools.

Source: Van Panhuys et al. (2015) and DSD/SASSA/UNICEF (2016).

The *Sembrando Oportunidades* dashboard is integrated into the results-based planning (SPR) system and linked to the budgeting process. The STP has developed and manages a tool to assist in planning, managing and monitoring the achievement of the goals related to the National Development Plan. The service delivery plans of each institution are part of the entity's operational plan, which is linked through the SPR to specific strategies of the PND, and to the annual budget. The link to the budgetary process ensures that co-ordination at the planning stage leads effectively to co-ordinated action plans. There is still scope for improving the functioning of results-based planning, in particular through improvements in the quality of the performance indicators, the establishment of links with the medium-term expenditure plan and the development of the evaluation function (OECD, 2018b; Medina-Giopp and Codas Salinas, 2018).

Social security providers need to be supervised and strengthened

At present, social security providers operate without any major supervision. The only supervision comes from the Supreme Audit Institution (*Contraloría General de la República*), which audits pension providers.[8] However, the Supreme Audit Institution lacks the resources to carry out its vast remit. More importantly, there is a conflict of interest: the auditors contracted by pension providers are paid by the audited institution (Navarro and Ortiz, 2014). The Ministry of Labour, Employment and Social Security (MTESS) – officially in charge of social security – was only created recently and is still working to build up its authority. A bill to create a supervisory body – to be presided by the Minister of Labour Employment and Social Security – is in parliament awaiting approval (Box 2.5).

Box 2.5. The draft legislation of the supervisory authority for pension providers

The draft legislation is well crafted, but certain aspects need to be enhanced

The investments that have been made for Paraguay's pension funds are less diversified than elsewhere in Latin America (IMF, 2017). Little diversification and regulation can pose a threat to affiliates' contributions and pension entitlements. The IPS primarily invests in savings deposits, real estate (principally health facilities), as well as bonds issued by the *Agencia Financiera de Desarollo* (AFD). Due to its internal regulation, the *Caja Fiscal* invests exclusively in bonds issued by the AFD or deposits any eventual surplus with the central bank. The closed pension providers' investments are slightly more diversified; still, they mostly hold loans to their members. The *Caja de la ANDE* invests more than four-fifths of its assets in loans to its members (Caja Ande, 2017). Such practices should be generally limited according to the OECD Core Principles of Private Pension Regulation (OECD, 2016b); the draft legislation promises to remedy this and enforce sound management of providers' assets.

According to the OECD Core Principles of Private Pension Regulation, the supervisory body should promote the stability, security and good governance of pension funds, pension entities and/or pension plans with the aim of protecting the interests of plan members and beneficiaries. Effective supervision of pension funds and plans must be set up and focus on legal compliance, financial control, actuarial examination and supervision of those with the responsibility of operating or managing the plan. Supervisory bodies should be endowed with appropriate regulatory and supervisory powers over private pension plans, pension funds and pension entities, including powers over the functions that are outsourced.

Paraguay's draft law on the creation of a supervisory body, its governing board and pension funds' investment standards complies with most of the OECD Core Principles of Private Pension Regulation and IOPS' (2013) Good Practices for Governance of Pension Supervisory Authorities. However, certain aspects, insufficiently addressed in the draft legislation, deserve special attention, such as:

- establishing a clear and transparent funding mechanism for the supervisory body and its director to ensure independence;

- auditing the supervisory authority regularly and reporting about its activities to allow for the assessment of how well the authority is fulfilling its responsibilities;
- granting indemnity from civil prosecution for the staff of the supervisory authority; and
- requiring internal reviews for important supervisory decisions.

The rules for intervening in pension funds are clearly laid out, but a potential intervention in the *Caja Fiscal* could pose problems, as the *Caja Fiscal* is directly managed by the Ministry of Finance.

The bill provides a clear basis for pension funds to develop sound investment strategies, and even gives pension funds a voice in setting the ceilings for levels of investment by category (no minimum). However, the ceilings for the transitory period stipulated in the legislation might be difficult to meet for many pension providers.

The OECD Core Principles further recommend:

- financing and staffing the supervisory body adequately. The hiring, training and retention of qualified staff is key to the functioning of the body;
- adopting risk-based supervision. This requires a legal framework allowing suitable discretion in terms of interpretation and exercise of supervisory powers; and
- consulting, as appropriate, with pension providers when determining its approach to supervision.

Source: OECD (2016), IOPS (2013) and IMF (2017).

An imperfect separation of the IPS pension and health branches can pose a risk to the institute's governance. As an integrated social security provider the IPS offers health, pension and other cash benefits (maternity, disability, sickness, occupational injury, death) to its affiliates. The health and pension branches are managed separately and the IPS divides employers' and employees' contributions into three separate funds for (i) pensions, (ii) health and (iii) administrative expenses. However, the IPS's charter would allow a joint management of the pension and health services, as evidenced by a common fund for administrative expenses. While the charter does not allow transfers between the pension and health funds, a joint management can still expose the IPS's pension branch to the risk of bad practices (Alaimo and Tapia, 2014; Casalí and Velásquez, 2016). Most of the IPS's real estate investments are in hospitals. These investments yield low returns, can only be sold with parliamentary approval and the market value of the investments is often unknown to the IPS. Furthermore, the IPS does not split the resources destined to finance old-age pensions and other cash benefits (such as invalidity), which complicates the management of the benefits (IPS, 2014).

The lack of independence of the *Caja Fiscal* impedes good governance. The *Caja Fiscal* is not an independent legal entity, but part of the Ministry of Finance, and, thus, lacks a charter and governing board that would set strategic guidelines, supervise the performance and take responsibility for results. The principal risk of this institutional arrangement is that the Ministry of Finance has to directly cover any deficits of the *Caja*

Fiscal (Alaimo and Tapia, 2014; Navarro and Ortiz, 2014), which strips the Ministry of Finance of its tools to demand good governance in return for a bailout. Furthermore, the *Caja Fiscal* – and hence the Ministry of Finance – is subject to political pressure of its clients and other interest groups. For example, the parliament diluted the 2003 reform of the *Caja Fiscal* (Law 2.345/03) bowing to the pressure of civil servants demanding better benefits and disregarding the technical advice of the Ministry of Finance.[9]

An incomplete information management system complicates the work of the IPS and the *Caja Fiscal*. The digital registry of the contribution of IPS affiliates dates back to the year 2000, earlier entries have to be retrieved from the books. This insufficient digitalisation increases administrative costs, slows the process of determining pension entitlements and, thus, makes it difficult to have reliable statistics on future obligations. Registries and data availability are also inadequate in the *Caja Fiscal*, which makes it difficult to assess the *Caja Fiscal*'s management efficiency or carry out periodic actuarial studies. Moreover, annual balance reports submitted by the pension providers to the Ministry of Finance lack a standardised structure, information and language, which handicap the analysis.

Some of the historic reasons for creating closed pension programmes became obsolete. The closed pension funds were created to provide pension schemes for previously uncovered workers (*Ferroviaria* in 1924, *Caja Municipal* in 1978) or to improve the situation of a specific group of workers (*Caja Bancaria* 1951, *Caja de la ANDE* in 1968, *Caja del Itaipú*, 1988). The scheme from ANDE is complementary to the pension provided by the IPS. The complementary scheme for electricity utility employees was created at a time in which the IPS pension represented 42.5% of the salary after 15 years of contribution. Since then the IPS reformed its pension scheme offering more generous pensions. Nevertheless, the ANDE maintained the arrangement of providing its personnel a pension from two schemes: 42.5% from the IPS and 66.7% from the *Caja ANDE*. Another extreme case is the *Caja Ferroviaria*. The Paraguayan railways ceased their activity many years ago and the *Caja Ferroviaria* consequently manages the pensions of retired employees and the sole contributors are the administrators of the *Caja Ferroviaria*.

Including independent workers is the next frontier for Paraguay's social security

Expanding social security coverage requires including independent workers into the system. Yet, in its current state Paraguay's social security system de facto excludes independent workers from contributing. The system's principal challenge is to include this group without creating a parallel system. In response to this challenge, many countries in the region experiment with innovative approaches such as fostering formalisation with simplified tax codes, lowering the contribution base and matching contributions. Furthermore, independent workers should have the possibility to access full social security.

Independent workers want the full social security package, including health. Among the uninsured, half would consider contributing to social security if the health insurance provided were better (Figure 2.20). Having (better) health insurance is more important to the uninsured than having a higher pension or lower contribution rates. The aspects that could motivate the uninsured to contribute to social security do not differ by employment category. Even among actual IPS affiliates, close to half contribute because of the medical care offered (STP, 2016). The high importance people place on health insurance can partially explain the low voluntary affiliation of independent workers, as the current voluntary scheme for independent workers excludes them from contributing to the IPS health insurance until retiring.

Figure 2.20. Independent workers want health insurance

Aspects that would motivate the uninsured to contribute to social security, in 2015

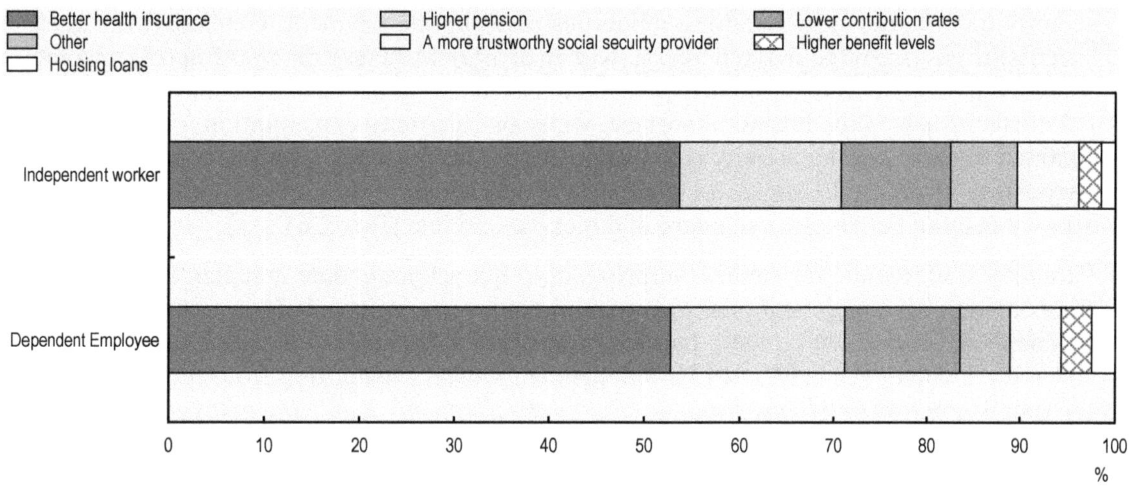

Source: Own calculations on ELPS (STP, 2016).

StatLink https://doi.org/10.1787/888933822843

Simplifying contribution collection for independent workers

Frequent employment changes hinder regular contributions to social security. Paraguay's labour market is very dynamic; large sections of the working age population frequently transit between employment status and category. This high turnover can lead to interrupted contribution payments. Indeed, close to 15% of formal employees in the private sector in Greater Asuncion regularly transits into informality, unemployment or inactivity (Alaimo and Taipa, 2014; Ovando, 2017; Ruppert Bulmer et al. 2017). Job changes are especially common among independent workers: close to 40% of independent workers in Greater Asuncion change their job from one year to the other (Ruppert Bulmer et al. 2017). This instability and the aforementioned low income of independent workers hinder affiliation and regular contributions to social security.

Flexible contribution schedules and innovative collection mechanisms can be a positive response to independent workers' volatile income. Monthly contribution payments can be a challenge for independent workers given their volatile income. In response to such a challenge, Chile, for example, allows irregular contributions corresponding to the income pattern of seasonal industries and workers (Hu and Stewart, 2009). Innovative contribution collection, such as agreed withdrawals with utility bills, can help to substitute the automatic withdrawal independent workers lack compared to their dependent counterparts, whose contributions are automatically deducted by employers (Bosch, Melguizo and Pagés, 2013). And modern communication technology can help to bridge the divide between pension providers and independent workers. In 2014, the Brazilian Ministry of Social Security experimented with reminders by post to independent workers about their obligation to contribute to social security; compliance rates increased by 7 percentage points within the first three months after sending the reminders (Bosch, Fernandes and Villa, 2015).

Many Latin American countries simplified tax and contribution collection to foster formalisation and accommodate independent workers' unstable employment histories. Such a response is the "monotax" levied on micro- and small enterprises with low revenues. This tax regime simplifies registration and collection of taxes (and social security contributions) by bundling numerous taxes in one payment. Generally, the most successful cases charge a fixed fee (lower than normal taxes) on presumptive income categories; income categories are presumed based on gross revenues and a range of parameters, such as the business' surface, water or electricity consumption, or the capital destined to carry out the activity (González, 2006). The regimes with the biggest traction (Argentina, Brazil and Uruguay) include social security contributions in the monotax and allow transiting between the standard and monotax regime (Box 2.6).

Paraguay's tax regime for small enterprises does not accommodate independent workers' frequent job changes and limited administrative capacity. Indeed, only 12% of independent workers have their business registered (*Registro Único de Contribuyente*) and issue invoices (DGEEC, 2017). Independent workers benefiting from the tax regime for small enterprises (*Impuesto a la Renta del Pequeño Contribuyente*) still need to determine their revenues and pay a 10% tax on their real or presumed revenues (equal to 30% of the annual sales), whichever is lower. However, not all independent workers record their transactions, especially microenterprises active in the informal economy.

Box 2.6. Uruguay's simplified tax regime for small independent workers

Uruguay owes its high social security coverage among independent workers (the highest in Latin America; Figure 2.4 Panel C), to a large extent, to the introduction of the monotax (*Monotributo*). Independent workers paying the monotax are entitled to the standard social security benefits, except the unemployment benefit, and can voluntarily contribute to health insurance.

The monotax regime is open to micro and small enterprises with a maximum of one employee (three during harvesting period in case of agricultural businesses), an office surface area smaller than 15m², assets and revenues up to a set amount (changing annually) and providing products and services to the end consumer.

The Uruguayan Social Security Institute collects the monotax and transfers the fraction corresponding to taxes to the tax authority. The monotax is a flat rate contribution for all independent workers replacing all national taxes and social security contributions. Newly contributing micro and small enterprises pay a reduced rate in the first few years, gradually increasing to 100% after the third year. This gradual phasing-in of the contribution rate incentivizes entrepreneurs to start contributing and helps enterprises to ease into the transition.

After a reform in 2007 – making affiliation easier by eliminating previous restrictions, such as place of the activity, type of activity and maximum billing – the number of contributors increased sharply reaching more than 30% of all micro and small enterprises.

Source: Cetrángolo et al. (2014), Duran-Valverde (2014).

A high minimum wage represents a barrier to accessing social security

A high minimum wage limits many Paraguayans' possibilities to contribute to the social security system. Pension funds do not accept contributions that are based on an income below the minimum wage (Law 4.933/13). Yet, 45.4% of the working population earn below the minimum wage, among own-account workers this figure even reaches 65.7% (Figure 2.21 Panel A). This makes it impossible for them to contribute to social security. A regional comparison shows that Paraguay has one of the highest shares of workers earning below the minimum wage (Figure 2.21 Panel B). Paraguay's minimum wages in relation to the median wage places the country at the top end of a regional comparison. This impacts social security affiliation, as social security coverage and the level of the minimum wage are negatively correlated in Latin America: coverage rates decrease with high minimum wages-average wage ratios (Navarro and Ortiz, 2014).

The combination of contribution rules and a high minimum wage drives contribution costs up. According to national legislation, the monthly social security contributions for independent workers cannot be below PYG 255 386 (13% of the 2016 minimum wage). For half of the independent workers this represents more than 21.5% of their income (own calculations based on EPH). For poor workers in the first income decile, contributions would even represent 88% of their income, which is higher than the theoretical cost for poor workers in Latin American countries (72% of the worker's wage) (OECD, 2018). In response to this, countries, like Panama, take the minimum pension as minimum earnings for contribution calculation purposes – the minimum pension is below the minimum wage.

Overall, Paraguayans' median and mean labour income is centred on the minimum wage. However, only workers situated higher than the sixth decile earn comfortably above the minimum wage; workers in the bottom deciles earn well below the minimum wage while workers in the centre of the income distribution earn close to the minimum wage (Figure 2.21 Panel C). Supporting social security contributions of workers situated in the fourth, fifth and sixth decile could help them to access social security (see subsequent section).

For the self-employed, low and unstable income is a major reason for not contributing to social security. According to the accounts of self-employed, 64.4% do not contribute to social security because of low and instable income (Figure 2.22). Indeed, the median and average income of own-account workers is well below the minimum wage (Figure 2.21 Panel B). Few have the financial leeway to contribute to social security. Taking the prevalence of individual savings (savings accounts, long-term deposits, savings funds, stocks, and other) as a proxy for the ability and inclination to defer consumption, few have the financial ability to defer consumption. In fact, among the self-employed only 9.6% currently save (STP, 2015). Only 21.7% of the self-employed report that they do not contribute to social security because there is no obligation to do so. This could be interpreted as being in support of the assertion made by Navarro and Ortiz (2014) whereby 57% of independent workers would like to contribute to social security if they could.

Dependent workers' perception is that low social security affiliation rates are due to evasion rather than low wages. Inspection and supervision are important to wage workers' affiliation with social security. While one in five wage employees report that they avoid contributing to social security because their income is low and unstable, evasion is a bigger concern. Two in five wage employees report that they do not contribute to social security because their employers are unwilling to register them with social security (Figure 2.22). In response to this, Paraguay needs to strengthen systems of inspection and supervision.

Figure 2.21. Many earn below the comparatively high minimum wage

Workers' income in relation to the minimum wage

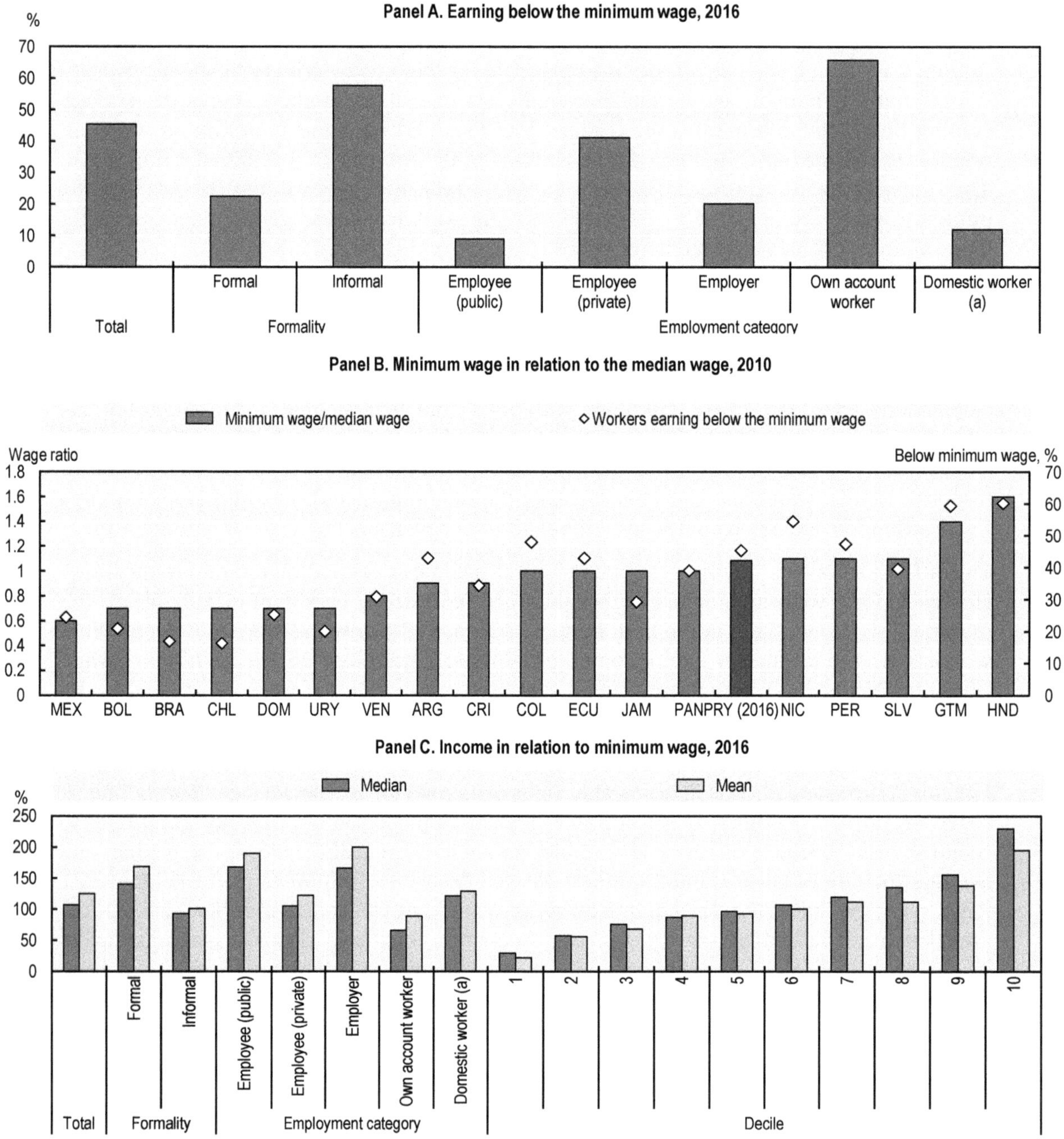

Note: The analysis includes only income from their full-time, main job. (a) The minimum wage for domestic workers is 60% of the standard minimum wage. Compared to the standard minimum wage, 77.4% of domestic workers earn less than this figure.

Source: Panel A and B: Own calculations based on the Permanent Household Survey of Paraguay (DGEEC, 2017). Panel C: Paraguay own calculation based on the Permanent Household Survey of Paraguay (DGEEC, 2017); other countries Bosch, Melguizo and Pagés (2013).

StatLink https://doi.org/10.1787/888933822862

Figure 2.22. Most do not contribute to a social security scheme because of unstable income

Self-reported reasons for not contributing to a social security scheme, as a percentage

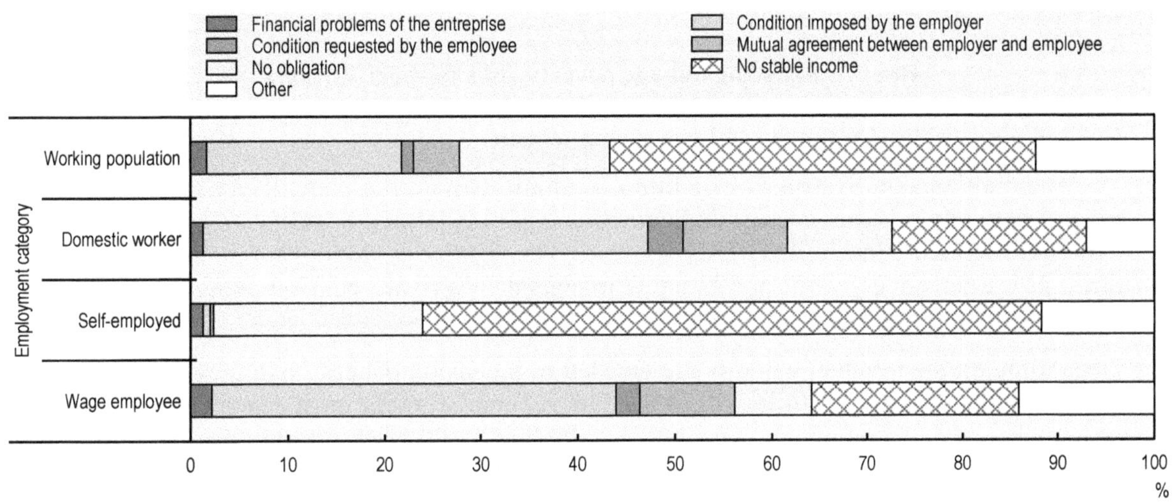

Source: Own calculations on ELPS (STP, 2016).

StatLink https://doi.org/10.1787/888933822881

Subsidising contributions can remedy low affiliation rates of independent workers

Paraguay can learn from other countries' experiences in matching contributions. Several countries with low social security coverage rates, especially among independent workers, are moving towards matching contributions. Most experiences are recent and are principally from countries with defined contribution systems. The Colombian example and Dominican plan are particular good examples. Colombia's subsidised voluntary old-age saving scheme is a good example of a policy respecting independent workers' needs (Box 2.7). However, combining voluntary old-age saving schemes with Paraguay's defined benefit system is difficult; if copied by Paraguay it could create a parallel system for independent workers, which is best avoided (Stuart, Samman and Hunt, 2018). To avoid creating a parallel system such voluntary old-age saving scheme could be introduced in Paraguay as the third tier of an integrated pension system. The Dominican Republic's envisioned subsidised contributory scheme is an example of how to keep independent workers within the standard social security system and could be applied as well in a defined benefit system, such as Paraguay's (Box 2.8).

Matching contributions have to be carefully designed. While matching contributions can be a way to support workers in the centre of the income distributions, who have a stable yet low income above the minimum wage, experience suggests that such policies need to be designed with care (Carranza, Melguizo and Tuesta, 2017). Poorly-designed matching contributions policies could trap independent workers in a subsidised regime and reduce the incentive to bear social security costs autonomously and thus create parallel systems. The period during which independent workers can benefit from matching contributions should be limited and their economic situation regularly monitored.

In response to independent workers' volatile and infrequent income, Colombia introduced in 2015 a subsidised voluntary old-age saving scheme (*Beneficios Económicos Periódicos* [BEPS]). The contributions made by poor and vulnerable independent workers earning below the minimum wage can be irregular and lower than pension contributions within the General Pension System. Both tend to be a barrier for independent workers to contribute to a traditional social security scheme (Navarro, 2016).

Box 2.7. Reducing old-age poverty risks for poor workers

Colombia's subsidised voluntary old-age saving scheme

The General Pension System in Colombia is mainly based on a compulsory contributory pillar where two schemes coexist and compete: a public defined-benefit (DB) scheme and a private defined-contribution (DC) scheme. The former is administered by the State through Colpensiones, while the latter is managed by private pension funds (AFPs for their acronym in Spanish).

Depending on the scheme, workers are entitled to a pension benefit once they meet some minimum requirements. While within the DB scheme workers must reach the statutory retirement age and a minimum contributory period of 1 300 weeks, within the DC scheme workers only need to reach a minimum amount of individual savings enough to ensure a pension higher than 110% of a monthly minimum wage. Contributors within the DC scheme who are not able to reach the minimum amount of savings, but have reached the statutory retirement age and have contributed for at least 1 150 weeks, are entitled to a minimum pension guarantee. By law, the monthly minimum pension is equal to the legal minimum wage. Although this ensures a basic income for those who manage to retire, such a tie creates rigidities that leave out a large part of the population that is not able to satisfy the requirements for receiving a minimum pension. In both schemes, those who are not able to meet the requirements receive a refund. For this reason, the system tends to disadvantage low-income workers, mostly informal, as they typically earn few and irregularly, preventing them to meet the minimum requirements.

In response to independent workers' volatile and infrequent income, and given the restrictions set by Colombian law regarding minimum pensions, the government introduced in 2015 a subsidised voluntary old age saving scheme (*Beneficios Económicos Periódicos* [BEPS]). In this scheme, the state tops up retired workers' accumulated savings and returns with a subsidy of 20%. The contributions made by workers earning below the minimum wage can be irregular, allowing overcoming barriers for independent workers to contribute to a traditional social security scheme (Navarro, 2016). BEPS' subsidised bimonthly benefit is capped at 85% of the minimum wage. Thus, in principle, it allows for a contributory old age scheme without the minimum wage constraint, as these bimonthly benefits are not a pension from a legal point of view.

The Colombian system allows individuals to transit easily between BEPS and General Pension System when needed. In 2018, the third year after launching BEPS, more than 1 million poor workers saved with BEPS and 5 300 receive a pension (Colpensiones, 2018). However, creating the right incentives to raise workers' voluntary saving levels in BEPS remains a challenge.

Source: Bosch, M. et al. (2015), *Diagnóstico del sistema previsional colombiano y opciones de reforma* and OECD (2015), *Pension Policy Notes Colombia.*

The Dominican Republic envisions subsidising independent workers' contribution to make up for the missing employers' contributions. Under this scheme, which has yet to be implemented, the state would contribute to independent workers' social security with a subsidy equal to the contribution of what employers pay for their dependent workers (Lavigne, 2013). National legislation stipulates that the subsidised scheme should function identically to the standard contributory scheme, once it is fully rolled out. Currently, this subsided system offers basic healthcare and childcare facilities to independent workers and could be extended to include benefits for occupational injuries (SISALRIL, 2018). Such a matching scheme can be costly when the number of independent workers is high and it represents de facto a subsidy for independent employment, but it allows to transit between dependent and independent employment while remaining in the social security system.

Box 2.8. Subsidising contributions could be cheaper than granting *Adulto Mayor*

Given the low number of independent workers contributing to social security, the government could consider subsidising independent workers' contributions. The most effective way would be to target those individuals who are capable of setting aside additional savings (Hu and Stewart, 2009), which, in Paraguay, would include independent workers earning close to the minimum wage (Figure 2.21 Panel C).

We assume a hypothetical scenario, in which the government would subsidise independent workers' contributions to the current system. Like in the planned Dominican system, the government would match contributions at the level of the missing employers' contribution (i.e. 7.6% of the minimum wage plus 0.5% for administrative costs with no contributions to the IPS health fund).

Subsidising contributions up to a maximum of 180 months (15 years) would be cheaper for the government than paying the *Adulto Mayor* benefit for more than 60 months (4.9 years). Indeed, the current life expectancy at age 65 is an additional 17 years. The net present value of paying *Adulto Mayor* for 17 years (assuming an average inflation equal to the last 15 years: 6.2%) equals 31 times the annual minimum wage. The present value of matching 180 months of contributions equals 23 times the annual minimum wage. Hence, the government could save PYG 188 million (8 times the annual minimum wage) per beneficiary, or even more if it has to subsidise less than 180 months of contribution. While subsidising contributions can increase the number of contributory pension recipients it can also generate liabilities for the IPS health branch as it may add a higher risk population to the health fund's pool.

Source: Own calculations on ELPS (STP, 2016). The life expectancy at age 65 stems from OECD/IDB/World Bank (2014). The average inflation of 2003-16 is based on World Bank (2018b).

Peru recently introduced a subsidised pension regime for micro-entrepreneurs (*Sistema de Pensiones Sociales* [SPS]): micro-entrepreneurs contributing up to 4% of the minimum wage into personal accounts to the SPS benefit from a matching contribution deposited by the state. At age 65 and 300 months of contributions, micro-entrepreneurs receive a pension benefit calculated on the basis of the personal accounts' development (Navarro, 2016). While granting micro-entrepreneurs the possibility of obtaining a pension benefit, it creates a parallel system which is generally not advisable (OECD, 2016).

Mexico reformed in 2009 its 'Social Contribution' to prevent affiliates of the defined contribution scheme from discontinuing contributions. The 'Social Contribution' consists of a government subsidy of up to 5.5% of the minimum wage in Mexico City for affiliates earning less than 15 times the minimum wage. The value of the state's matching contribution decreases incrementally, i.e. multiples of the minimum wage (Carranza, Melguizo and Tuesta, 2012). To qualify for the 'Social Contribution' the worker had to be contributing to the defined contribution pension system; thus its main object is not to attract new affiliates, but prevent affiliates from ceasing contributions due to low income.

Expanding social protection needs financial commitment

Paraguay's ambition to expand social protection coverage needs to be financed. Expanding social protection requires mobilising resources, especially for social assistance which is not financed by contributions. In the foreseeable future, the bottom deciles will hardly be able to contribute to social security. Their low income and heavy reliance on agriculture make regular social security contributions unrealistic and will thus need to be covered by social assistance. Covering the whole target population of Paraguay's flagship social assistance programmes would demand at least doubling current expenditure levels.

Domestic resource mobilisation is crucial for a sustainable expansion of social protection. More workers need to contribute to social security, and tax revenues need to increase to finance social assistance. Paraguay took important steps to expand the tax base and collection, but further efforts are needed to respond to the growing demand for goods and services provided by the state, such as social protection.

Social expenditure needs to be reviewed

Social expenditure as a whole is high. Paraguay spends more than half of its government budget on the social sector. This share has been steadily increasing from 53.3% in 2007 to 59.4% in 2016 (Figure 2.23 Panel A). This importance given to social expenditure (12% of GDP) places Paraguay among the top spenders in the region and above the Latin American average (Figure 2.23 Panel B). Nonetheless, social protection expenditure is below countries with a more developed safety net such as Argentina, Brazil, Chile and Uruguay.

Social protection expenditure increased slowly but surely. Expenditure on social security increased from 2.7% of GDP in 2007 to 3.6% in 2016, reflecting the aforementioned increasing number of affiliates (Figure 2.24 Panel A). Based on Serafini's (2016) findings this review calculates the social assistance expenditure on non-contributory pensions, conditional and unconditional cash transfers. Following this definition, social assistance expenditure increased from 0.7% of GDP in 2007 to 1.2% in 2016.

Figure 2.23. Paraguay's social expenditure is above the Latin American average

Government and social spending in Paraguay and Latin America

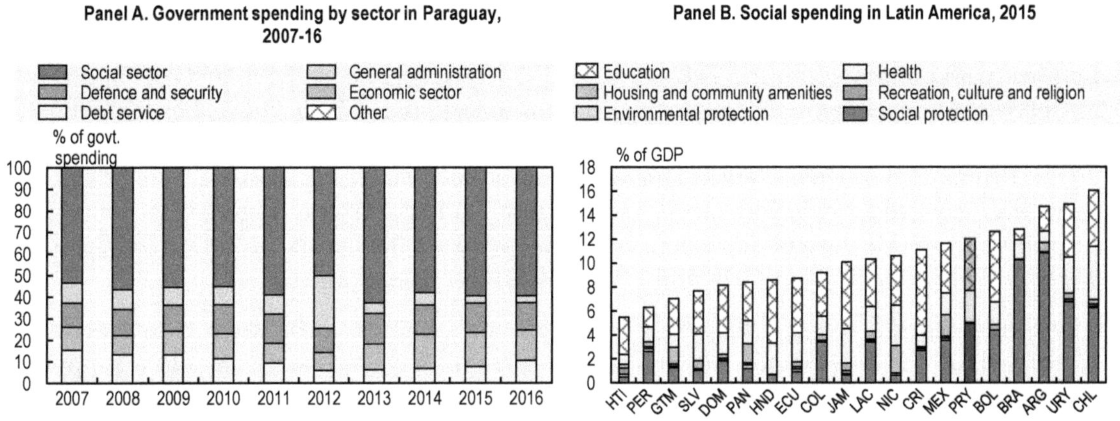

Note: All panels consider only the spending of the central government. Panel A: Paraguay defines the social sector as expenditure on health, social assistance, social security, education and culture, science and technology, labour relations, housing and community services. Panel B: The average for Latin America is the simple average of the 19 countries in the figure. 2014 for Jamaica and Panama.
Source: Own elaboration based on the expenditure database BOOST (MH, 2018). Panel B: CEPALSTAT (2018).

StatLink https://doi.org/10.1787/888933822900

Figure 2.24. Social protection expenditure is on the rise

Social security and social assistance spending, 2007-16

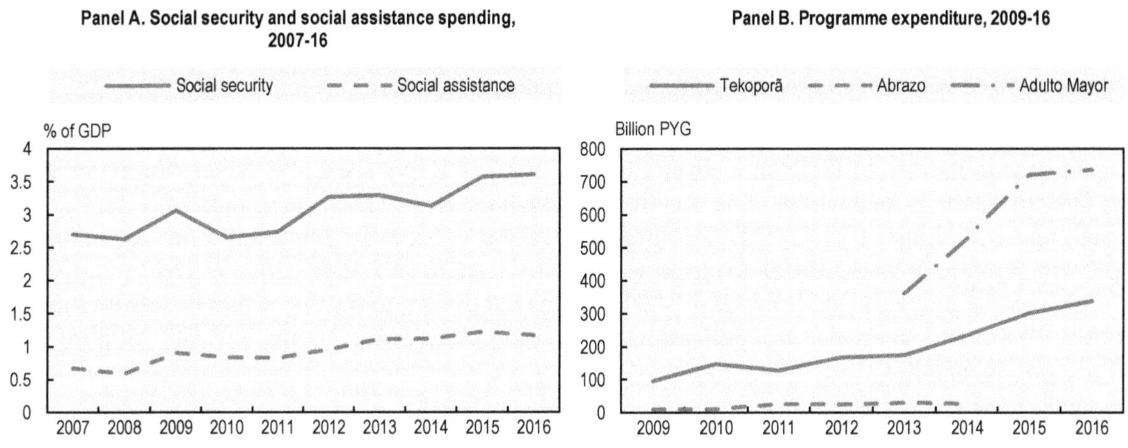

Note: Social security spending is measured as the social expenditure of the IPS, Caja de la ANDE, Caja Bancaria, Caja Municipal and Caja Fiscal. Social assistance expenditure is measured by the spending on non-contributory pensions (Adulto Mayor, pensions for veterans and merit pensions) and other cash transfers proxied by the social expenditure of the Instituto Paraguayo del Indígena, Dirección Beneficencia y Ayuda Social and of the Presidency, the latter includes spending from the Secretaría de Acción Social (*Tekoporã*), Secretaría Nacional de la Niñez y la Adolescencia (*Abrazo*), Secretaría Técnica de Planificación del Desarrollo Económico y Social (*Sembrando Oportunidades*), Secretaría de Emergencia Nacional, Secretaría de Derechos Humanos de las Personas con Discapacidad.
Source: Own elaboration based on the expenditure database BOOST (MH, 2018).

StatLink https://doi.org/10.1787/888933822919

Expenditure for the major flagship programmes is insufficient to cover the whole target population. Expenditure for *Tekoporã* and *Adulto Mayor* increased strongly during the initial phase, but has reached plateaued in recent years (Figure 2.24 Panel B). Expenditure would have to increase substantially versus current levels to cover the whole target population of Paraguay's flagship social assistance programmes. Providing all poor families with children with the *Tekoporã* benefit would have cost 0.5% of GDP in 2016 as opposed to the actual 0.2%. Granting all poor elderly the *Adulto Mayor* benefit would have cost 1% of GDP as opposed to the actual 0.7% (own elaboration based on EPH, 2016; Bruno, 2017; MH, 2018). This assumes perfect targeting; however, in practice there are important inclusion errors (see Figure 2.6 Panel B and Figure 2.15 Panel B respectively). With current inclusion errors factored in, the costs of full coverage of *Tekoporã* would be 0.7% of GDP and 1.4% of GDP for *Adulto Mayor*.

Reviewing expenditures can help to free up resources that could be used to finance the expansion of *Tekoporã* and *Adulto Mayor*. Streamlining income generation support programmes for family business and farms, which reach a paltry 10% of rural households with agricultural activities but cost 0.41% of GDP in 2014, can create additional fiscal space (own calculations based on Serafini, 2016). The continuous reduction in expenditure for pensions for veteran and survivors (0.13% of GDP in 2016) will free up resources that should be used to finance an expansion of *Adulto Mayor* (own elaboration based on MH, 2018).

Tax levels and collection need to reflect the growing demand for state services

Paraguay collects little taxes. Among Latin American countries Paraguay has one of the lowest tax-to-GDP ratio, it is considerably below the regional average and half the OECD average (Figure 2.25 Panel A). While tax evasion is high, low tax rates are also a principal reason for this low ratio. Paraguay has the lowest tax rates in the region: the corporate tax rate does not exceed 10%, taxes on personal income are a flat rate of 10% and VAT is a maximum 10% (Borda and Caballero, 2018). In fact, households pay a mere 1% of what they earn in income tax (Gímenez et al., 2017).

Yet, tax revenues, especially from VAT, have actually increased in recent years. The increase in the tax-to-GDP ratio from 2005 to 2015 is above the Latin American average. This increase is principally due to higher revenues from taxes on goods and services (Figure 2.25 Panel B). VAT is the largest revenue source for Paraguay and above the Latin American and OECD average (OECD/ECLAC/CIAT/IDB, 2017). Tax revenues from goods and services (including VAT) increased thanks to a reform that broadened the VAT base and improved tax collection; VAT rates, however, remain low and loopholes are prevalent (ibid).

Figure 2.25. Tax revenues increased, but remain low

Tax revenues as a percentage of GDP and by tax classification

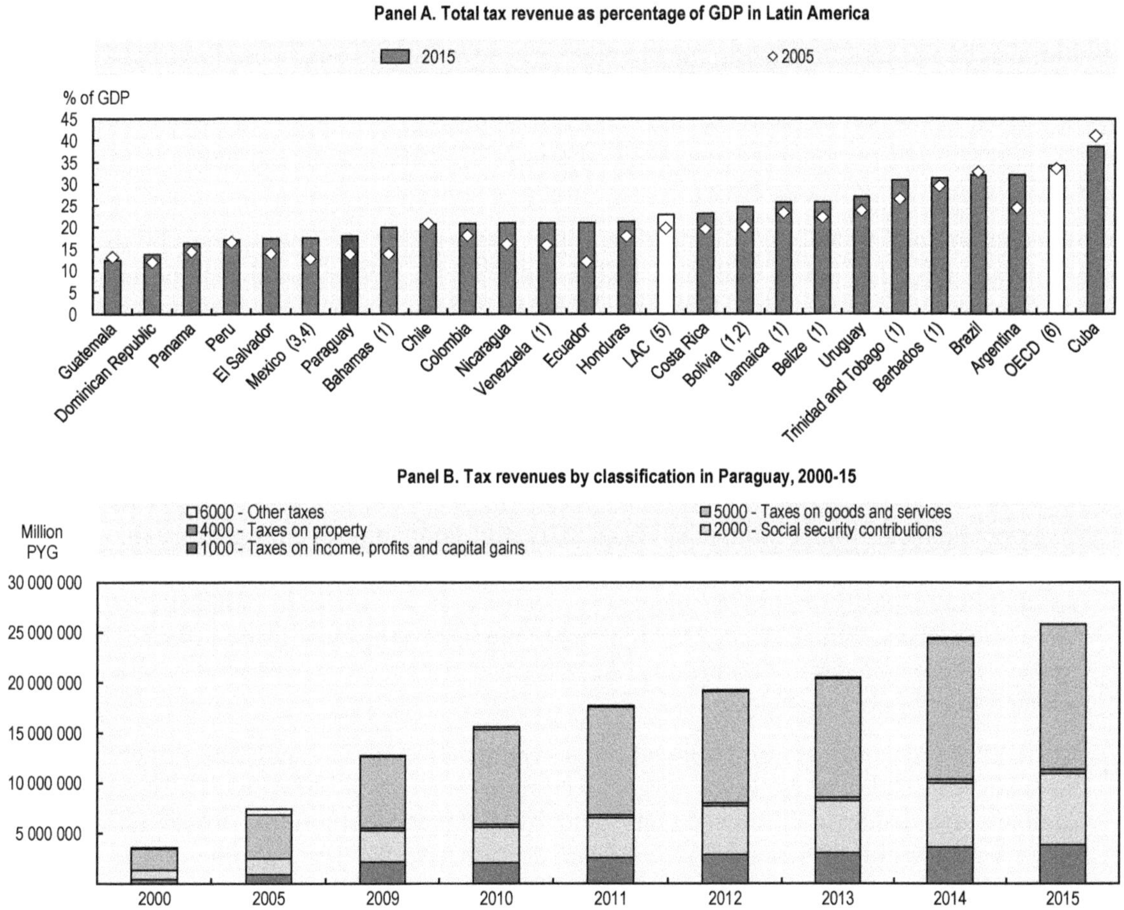

Note: A. Total tax revenues include revenues at the national and subnational level and social security contributions.

1. The data are estimated for the following countries: Bahamas (social security contributions for 2015), Barbados (social security contributions for 2015), Belize (social security contributions from 2013 onward), Bolivia (social security contributions from 2013 onward), Jamaica (environmental levy for years 2014 and 2015), Trinidad and Tobago (local property taxes for 2015) and Venezuela (social security contributions from 2011 onward)..
2. Excludes revenues from hydrocarbon production.
3. Revenue in Latin America and the Caribbean and revenue in OECD countries included fees levied on hydrocarbon production at the federal level. From the data provided for revenue in OECD countries (2016) and for this publication, revenues from hydrocarbon production have been excluded from tax revenues and are instead treated as non-tax revenues.
4. The data are estimated for 2015 including expected revenues for state and local governments.
5. Represents a group of 24 Latin American and Caribbean countries, the average is calculated using calendar year data, except for Bahamas and Trinidad and Tobago where fiscal year data are used. Chile and Mexico are also part of the OECD (35) group.
6. Calculated by applying the unweighted average percentage change for 2015 in the 32 countries providing data for that year to the overall average tax-to-GDP ratio in 2014.

Source: Based on OECD/ECLAC/CIAT/IDB (2017).

StatLink https://doi.org/10.1787/888933822938

Paraguay's tax code has a range of exemptions and deductions, some favouring high-income earners. Interest and returns on capital gains and deposits in national financial institutions, pensions and inheritances are exempt from personal income tax; enterprises' gains from stock trading are exempt from corporate income tax (IRACIS) (Box 2.9). Personal and family expenditures such as education, health, clothing, housing and leisure activities can be reduced, impacting the already high floor for personal income taxes. The intention of these numerous exemptions and deductibles is to encourage formalisation, but they complicate tax declarations and reduce revenues significantly. Tax exemptions for the corporate and personal income, VAT and import tariffs cost an estimated 1.7% of GDP in 2016 (CIAT/SET/GIZ, 2015).

Tax revenues are additionally undermined by high evasion. Only 48.2% of households in the top decile and 23.7% of households in the ninth decile pay personal income taxes. Among the remaining households, less than 20% pay personal income taxes (Gímenez et al., 2017). Despite VAT reforms, evasion remains high (30.9% in 2014) and above the Latin American average (25.9%) (Borda and Caballero, 2018).

Box 2.9. Taxing financial transactions in Brazil for social protection

Taxes on financial transactions can be an easy and equitable revenue source for social protection. Such taxes levied on banking institutions can be implemented and monitored easily thanks to electronic records. It is extremely difficult to evade such taxes. Financial transaction taxes are also collected from informal workers who evade payroll contributions. Moreover, it is a progressive tax as the rich tend to rely more on banks.

Brazil collected such a tax on financial transactions between 1997 and 2007. Each financial transaction was taxed at a maximum rate of 0.38%, which was automatically deducted from accounts held by financial institutions. Revenues from the financial transaction tax (*Contribuição "Provisória" por Movimentação Financeira*) financed public health, social insurance, Bolsa Familia and other social purposes. In 2007, the revenues from the financial transaction tax exceeded the total cost of *Bolsa Família*. After mounting pressure from the financial sector, the financial transaction tax was abolished in 2007. However, the tax returned for a brief period (2009-13) and there is an ongoing debate on whether to reintroduce the tax for social justice reasons.

Source: Ortiz, Cummins and Karunanethy (2017).

Policy recommendations

Box 2.10. Policy recommendations towards social protection for all in Paraguay

1. Expand social security coverage:

1.1. Put in place a strategy to expand coverage of social security.

- Strengthen inspection and supervision systems to fight evasion.

- Assist employers in registering employees. Associate inspection and supervision with an information campaigns and counselling.
- Follow up on affiliates who cease to contribute. When possible support their re-integration into the system. Analyse and learn from the reasons for ceasing to contribute.
- Approve the strategy to inform the general public of the benefits of social security on a regular basis.

1.2. Improve incentives for formalisation and social security contributions.

- Review the minimum wage:
    - Review the level of the minimum wage and introduce a mechanism to determine its future fluctuation, linking it to productivity and prices.
    - Consider taking the minimum pension as minimum earnings for contribution calculation purposes.
- Put a more attractive system for independent workers in place:
    - Allow voluntary contribution to the health system.
    - Allow flexible contributions for independent workers. This may include irregular contributions in terms of amount and frequency.
    - Make contributions payment easier. This could be in form of a monotax or automatic deductions (e.g. with utility bills).
    - Consider matching contributions for independent workers with low income.

2. Reform to establish an integrated social protection system:

2.1. Protect against all contingencies:

- Introduce unemployment insurance.
- Introduce child benefits for non-poor formal sector workers.

2.2. Review social expenditure:

- Define social assistance expenditure according to international standards.
- Increase the budget for flagship social assistance programmes.
- Review expenditure of programmes with little impact and high costs due to programme fragmentation.

2.3. Broaden tax collection:

- Decrease tax exemptions.
- Improve tax collection and fight evasion.
- Increase tax rates to reflect the growing demand for state services.
- Earmark specific revenues for the financing of social protection.

2.4. Integrate the contributory and non-contributory pensions into a multi-pillar pension system:

- Transform *Adulto Mayor* into a basic pension within an integrated system
  - Improve the targeting of *Adulto Mayor*.
  - Revise the *Adulto Mayor* law to set a fixed benefit value or at least include a ceiling.
  - Allow a combination of contributory and non-contributory pensions. Phase *Adulto Mayor* out with the value of the contributory pension benefits favouring recipients with a meagre pension.
- Create an integrated mandatory, defined benefit pension system.
  - Explore the possibility of establishing a single statutory social security provider for private sector workers to reduce administrative costs and increase economies of scale.
  - Explore the possibility of integrating the social security system for public and private sector workers.
- Create a voluntary savings mechanism.
  - Provide tax incentives for savings plans cashed out at retirement age.
  - Increase trust in private pension funds and private savings plans by closely regulating them.
  - Consider transforming closed pension providers into occupational savings plans.

3. Improve the governance of social protection:

3.1. Improve co-ordination of social assistance programmes and agencies:

- Re-establish the co-ordination at ministerial level through the Social Cabinet or assign to another agency the role of system co-ordinator.
- Facilitate exchange of information between agencies.
- Align targeting mechanisms.
- Have joint staff on the ground to ease the engagement with beneficiaries, referrals and reduce costs.
- Integrate the number of social assistance programmes with similar objectives, especially programmes supporting small entrepreneurs and farms.

3.2. Integrate monitoring and evaluation processes into the design of social assistance programmes and policies to ensure rigorous assessments of results and the identification of potential improvements.

3.3. Supervise and regulate pension providers:

- Create a supervisory body for pension providers:
  - Furnish the supervisory body with the necessary financial and human

resources.

  - Ensure impartiality of the supervisory body and auditors by detaching their payment from the audited institution.

- Set guidelines for investments of pension funds:
  - Set ceilings for levels of investment by category.
  - Enforce diversification of investments.

3.4. Improve the internal governance of pension providers:

- Digitalise the registry of contributions, contributors and beneficiaries in all pension funds.
- Standardise financial reports submitted to the Ministry of Finance (and other institutions).
- Clearly separate the management of the IPS pension and health branches.
- Revise the law limiting IPS's independence in managing its real estate investments.
- Transform the Caja Fiscal into an independent institution.

4. Establish a more coherent, fair and inclusive pension system

4.1. Improve equity in the pension system:

- Set the retirement age to be the same across all schemes: the retirement age should be periodically revised taking longevity, labour force participation and other socio-economic factors into account. This mechanism should set out the stepwise increase in the retirement age to be predictable for affiliates.
- Unify the basis for benefit calculation (earnings measure), including for independent workers.
- Standardise replacement and accrual rates.
- Ensure all pension benefits are indexed.

4.2. Strengthen the link between benefits and contributions:

- Raise number of years used to calculate the pension benefit (earnings measure).
- Set a uniform ceiling for any pension benefit:
  - This ceiling can be a multiple of the minimum wage and should take the financial soundness of the system into consideration.
- Revise the benefit level:
  - Adjust the pension benefit level to reflect the decreasing contributors-per-pensioner ratio.
  - Reduce incentives for early retirement. This can be achieved by significantly reducing benefit levels.

- Adjust contribution rates:
  - Contribution rates should be revised on a regular basis. The revision should be based on actuarial studies, demographic developments, the economic situation, the ratio between pensioners and contributors and the financial soundness of each scheme.
  - Collect contributions on end-of-year bonuses or cease to pay out end-of-year pension benefits. Every benefit payment has to be backed by a contribution.

4.3. Improve portability:

- Establish a mechanism to transfer contributions and entitlements between pension providers (as long as the system remains fragmented). This mechanism should grant a single pension, instead of the current procedure of granting partial pensions from all the systems the affiliate contributed to.

Notes

[1] The law creating *Adulto Mayor* (3728/09) only specifies a minimum for the benefit (25% of the minimum wage), but no maximum. This leaves the possibility of arbitrary and unfunded increases of the benefit amount.

[2] The direct taxes included in this analysis are IRP, IRPC, IRACIS and IRAGRO.

[3] The legislation does not stipulate a maximum number of years of contributions that can be settled with this method.

[4] The IPS pension scheme pays old-age, survivors and disability pensions. The IPS health scheme pays the sickness, maternity and occupational injury benefits.

[5] In recent years, pension benefits have been stable; the fluctuation in the replacement rate stems from changes in the net income of current workers.

[6] The benefit value of *Adulto Mayor* is equivalent to 20.9% of the economy-wide average earnings, if income from self-employment is included in the comparison.

[7] The efficiency in managing assets cannot be calculated for the IPS and Caja Fiscal. The IPS does not have a separate accounting between their management costs for the pension and health scheme. IPS's total administrative costs (pension and health) accounted for 5.6% of total contributions (pensions and health) in 2016. The Caja Fiscal is part of the Ministry of Hacienda and thus does not publish figures on its management costs.

[8] The Caja Bancaria is additionally supervised by the authority in charge of banking supervision (*Superintendencia de Bancos*).

[9] The 2003 reform of the Caja Fiscal separated programmes and funds and implemented parametric changes to avert its financial collapse.

References

Alaimo, V. and W. Tapia (2014), *Perspectivas del mercado de trabajo y las pensiones en Paraguay* [Perspectives on the labour market and pensions in Paraguay], Nota técnica #772, Inter-American Development Bank, Washington D.C.

Aristy-Escuder, J. et al. (2018), "Fiscal Policy and Redistribution in the Dominican Republic" *in Commitment to Equity Handbook. Estimating the Impact of Fiscal Policy on Inequality and Poverty*, Brookings Institution Press and CEQ Institute, Tulane University, New Orleans.

Beneke, M., N. Lustig and J. A. Oliva (2018), "The Impact of Taxes and Social Spending on Inequality and Poverty in El Salvador" in *Commitment to Equity Handbook. Estimating the Impact of Fiscal Policy on Inequality and Poverty*, Brookings Institution Press and CEQ Institute, Tulane University, New Orleans.

Borda, D. and M. Caballero (2018), *Una Reforma Tributaria para Mejorar la Equidad y la Recaudación*, Centro de Análisis y Difusión de la Economía Paraguaya, Asunción, http://paraguaydebate.org.py/wp-content/uploads/2018/03/Reforma-Tributaria-2018.pdf (accessed on February 2018).

Bosch, M., D. Fernandes and J. Villa (2015), *Nudging the Self-employed into Contributing to Social Security. Evidence from a Nationwide Quasi Experiment in Brazil*, IDB Working Paper Series N° IDB-WP-633, Washington D.C.

Bosch, M., A. Melguizo and C. Pagés (2013), *Mejores Pensiones, Mejores Trabajos. Hacia la Cobertura Universal en América Latina y el Caribe*, Inter-American Development Bank, Washington D.C.

Bruno, S. (2017), *Evaluación de impacto redistributivo de la pensión alimentaria para adultos mayores en situación de pobreza. Un abordaje desde la Encuesta Permanente de Hogares 2016*, Ministerio de Hacienda de Paraguay, Asunción.

Bucheli, M. et al. (2014), "Social Spending, Taxes and Income Redistribution in Uruguay" in *The Redistributive Impact of Taxes and Social Spending in Latin America*, Public Finance Review 42, no. 3, pp. 413-433, http://dx.doi.org/10.1177/1091142113493493.

Caja Ande (2017), *Memoria y Balance*, Caja de Jubilaciones y Pensiones del Personal de la Administración Nacional de Electricidad, Asunción, www.cajaande.gov.py/formularios/MEMORIA%20Y%20BALANCE%202016%20para%20WEB.pdf (accessed on Janaury 2018).

Carranza, L., A. Melguizo and D. Tuesta (2017), "Funcionan los incentivos monetarios para el ahorro en pensiones? A propósito de los esquemas matching contributions" in *Ideas para una Reforma de Pensiones*, Universidad de San Martin de Torres.

Carranza, L., A. Melguizo and D. Tuesta (2012), "Matching Defined Contribution Schemes in Colombia, Mexico and Peru: Experiences and Prospects for Coverage Expansion" in *Matching Contributions for Pensions: A Review of International Experiences*, World Bank, Washington D.C., https://doi.org/10.1596/978-0-8213-9492-2.

Casalí, P. and M. Velásquez (2016), *Paraguay. Panorama de la protección social: diseño, cobertura y financiamiento*, International Labour Organization, Santiago.

CELADE - Population Division of ECLAC (2013), *Long-term Population Estimates and Projections 1950-2100. The 2013 Revision*, Economic Commission for Latin America and the Caribbean, Santiago, www.cepal.org/celade/proyecciones/basedatos_bd.htm.

CEQ (2017), Commitment to Equity Institute Data Center on Fiscal Redistribution (database), Tulane University, New Orleans, www.commitmentoequity.org/datacenter (accessed on February 2018).

Cetrángolo, O. et al. (2014), *Monotributo en América Latina: Los casos de Argentina, Brasil y Uruguay*, International Labour Organization, Lima.

CIAT/SET/GIZ (2015), Estimación de los Gastos Tributarios en la República del Paraguay 2013 -2016.

Colpensiones (2018), *Los BEPS, programa para que millones de colombianos del Sisbén 1, 2 y 3 tengan un ingreso en la vejez, es una realidad*, Colpensiones, Bogotá, www.colpensiones.gov.co/beps/Publicaciones/noticias_beps/los_beps_programa_para_que_millones_de_colombianos_del_sisben_1_2_y_3_tengan_un_ingreso_en_la_vejez_es_una_realidad (accessed on March 2018).

DGEEC (2017), *Encuesta Permanente de Hogares* [Permanent Household Survey] (database), Dirección General de Estadística, Encuestas y Censos de Paraguay, Fernando de la Mora, www.dgeec.gov.py/datos/encuestas/eph (accessed on August 2017).

DSD/SASSA/UNICEF (2016), Removing barriers to accessing Child Grants: Progress in reducing exclusion from South Africa's Child Support Grant, UNICEF South Africa, Pretoria.

Durán-Valverde, F. (2015), *Monotax: Promoting formalization and protection of independent workers*, International Labour Organization, Geneva, www.social-protection.org/gimi/gess/RessourcePDF.action?ressource.ressourceld=48020 (accessed on March 2018).

ECLAC (2017), *Panorama Social de América Latina 2017*, Economic Commission for Latin America and the Caribbean, Santiago.

FAO/STP (2018), Documento técnico sobre el estado del arte de las necesidades de los mecanismos de gobernanza y coordinación del PSO existentes, Food and Agriculture Organization, Asunción.

Gabinete Social (2018), *Nota Sectorial de Protección Social 2.0: La Oportunidad de implementar un sistema de protección social*, Gabinete Social de Paraguay, Asunción, www.gabinetesocial.gov.py/archivos/documentos/documento-consolidad-VF-NSPS_xbirna9z.pdf (accessed on May 2018).

Gabinete Social (2017), *Nota Sectorial de Protección Social*, Gabinete Social, Asunción, www.gabinetesocial.gov.py/archivos/documentos/NotaSectorialParalevantarenlapagina08112017_qfljwixj.pdf (accessed on December 2017).

Giménez, L. et al. (2017), *Paraguay: Análisis del sistema fiscal y su impacto en la pobreza y la equidad*, Commitment to Equity (CEQ) Working Paper Series 74, Tulane University, New Orleans.

González, D. (2006), *Regímenes Especiales de Tributación para Pequeños Contribuyentes en América Latina*, IDB Working Paper Series N° IDB-WP-2302, Inter-American Development Bank, Washington D.C.

Higgins, S. and Claudiney Pereira (2014), "The Effects of Brazil's Taxation and Social Spending on the Distribution of Household Income" in *The Redistributive Impact of Taxes and Social Spending in Latin America*, Public Finance Review 42, 3, pp. 346–67, http://dx.doi.org/10.1177/1091142113501714.

Icefi (2017a), *Incidencia de la política fiscal en la desigualdad y la pobreza en Guatemala*. CEQ Working Paper 50. CEQ Institute, Tulane University, IFAD and Instituto Centroamericano de Estudios Fiscales, New Orleans.

Icefi (2017b), *Incidencia de la política fiscal en la desigualdad y la pobreza en Honduras*, CEQ Working Paper 51, CEQ Institute, Tulane University, IFAD and Instituto Centroamericano de Estudios Fiscales, New Orleans.

Icefi (2017c), *Incidencia de la politica fiscal en la desigualdad y la pobreza en Nicaragua*, CEQ Working Paper 52, CEQ Institute, Tulane University, IFAD and Instituto Centroamericano de Estudios Fiscales, New Orleans.

ILO (2018), SECSOC Social Security Department, Geneva, www.ilo.org/dyn/ilossi/ssimain.home (accessed on February 2018).

ILO (2017), *World Social Protection Report 2017–19: Universal social protection to achieve the Sustainable Development Goals*, International Labour Organization, Geneva.

ILO (2014), *Cadastro Único: Operating a registry through a national public bank*, Building Social Protection Floors Series No. 001/2014, International Labour Organization, Geneva.

ILO (2010), *World Labour Report: Income security and social protection in a changing world*, International Labour Organization, Geneva, www.ilo.org/public/english/standards/relm/gb/docs/gb279/pdf/esp-7.pdf (accessed on February 2018).

IMF (2017), *Paraguay's Pension and Health System*, IMF Country Report No. 17/234, International Monetary Fund, Washington D.C.

IPS (2018), Datos TABLEAU-AOP (database), Instituto de Previsión Social, Asunción (accessed on January 2018).

IPS (2017), *Anuario Estadístico Institucional IPS 2016*, Instituto de Previsión Social, Asunción, https://portal.ips.gov.py/sistemas/ipsportal/archivos/archivos/1513090445.pdf (accessed on March 2018).

IPS (2014), *Estudio y Proyecciones Actuariales del Régimen de Jubilaciones y Pensiones del Instituto de Previsión Social*, Instituto de Previsión Social, Asunción, http://servicios.ips.gov.py/Informe%20Actuarial%20JyP%202012-62%20Resumen%20Ejecutivo.pdf (accessed on December 2017).

IOPS (2013), *Good Practices for Governance of Pension Supervisory Authorities*, International Organisation of Pension Supervisors, Paris, www.iopsweb.org/principlesguidelines/IOPS%20%20Good%20Practices%20on%20Governance%20of%20Pension%20Supervisory%20Authorities.pdf (accessed on March 2018).

Jaramillo, M. (2014), "The Incidence of Social Spending and Taxes in Peru" in *The Redistributive Impact of Taxes and Social Spending in Latin America*. Public Finance Review 42, no. 3, pp. 391-412, http://dx.doi.org/10.1177/1091142113496134.

Lindert, K. et al. (2007), The nuts and bolts of Brazil's Bolsa Família Program: implementing conditional cash transfers in a decentralized context, Social Protection Discussion Paper No. 709, World Bank, Washington D.C.

Law 5.508 (2015), Ley No. 5508 Promoción, Protección de la Maternidad y Apoyo a la lactancia Materna, Gaceta Oficial, Asunción.

Law 4.933 (2013), Ley No. 4933 Que autoriza la incorporación voluntaria de trabajadores independientes, empleadores, amas de casa y trabajadores domésticos al seguro social – Fondo de Jubilaciones y Pensiones del Instituto de Previsión Social, Gaceta Oficial, Asunción.

Law 4.290 (2011), Ley No. 4290 Que establece el derecho a solicitar reconocimiento de servicios anteriores en el Instituto de Previsión Social y modifica parcialmente el artículo 59 del Decreto-Ley N◦ 1.860/50, aprobado por Ley N◦ 375 del 27 de agosto de 1956, modificado por el artículo 2◦ de la Ley N◦ 98 del 31 de diciembre de 1992, y aclara el alcance de la Ley N◦ 3.404 del 7 de diciembre del 2007 – De continuidad en el beneficio, Gaceta Oficial, Asunción.

Law 3.404 (2007), Ley No. 3404 que modifica el artículo 25 de la Ley N° 430, de fecha 27 de diciembre de 1973, modificado por el artículo 4° de la N° 98, de fecha 31 de diciembre de 1992, Gaceta Oficial, Asunción.

Law 2.345 (2003), Ley No. 2345 de reforma y sostenibilidad de la caja fiscal. Sistema de jubilaciones y pensiones del sector público, Gaceta Oficial, Asunción.

Law 375 (1956), Ley No. 375 por el cual se aprueba el decreto-ley N° 1.860 del 1 de diciembre de 1950 por el cual se modifica el decreto-ley N° 17 071 de fecha 18 de febrero de 1943 de creación del Instituto de Previsión Social, Gaceta Oficial, Asunción.

Llerena Pinto et al. (2015), *Social Spending, Taxes and Income Redistribution in Ecuador*, CEQ Working Paper 28, Center for Inter-American Policy and Research and Department of Economics, Tulane University and Inter-American Dialogue, New Orleans.

Martinez- Aguilar et al. (2018), "The Impact of Fiscal Policy on Inequality and Poverty in Chile" in *Commitment to Equity Handbook. Estimating the Impact of Fiscal Policy on Inequality and Poverty*, Brookings Institution Press and CEQ Institute, Tulane University, New Orleans.

Medina-Giopp, A. and S. Codas Salinas (2018), *Lessons on the use of online dashboards to monitor government plans in Paraguay*, Poverty and Equity Notes N° 5, World Bank, Washington D.C.

Melendez, M. and V. Martinez (2015), *CEQ Master Workbook: Colombia 2010*, CEQ Data Center on Fiscal Redistribution, CEQ Institute, Tulane University and Inter-American Development Bank, New Orleans.

MH (2018), Sistema Integrado de Administración Financiera (SIAF [database]), Ministerio de Hacienda de Paraguay, Asunción, http://isdatabank.info/boost_paraguay (accessed on March 2018).

MH (2017), *Balance Anual de Gestión Pública 2016* [*Annual Public Management Report 2016*], Ministerio de Hacienda de Paraguay, Asunción, www.hacienda.gov.py/web-presupuesto/index.php?c=279.

MH (2016), *Evaluación de Impacto del programa Tekoporã*, Ministerio de Hacienda de Paraguay, Asunción, www.economia.gov.py/application/files/9514/7939/4429/Evaluacion_de_Impacto_del_Programa_Tekopora_07062016.pdf (accessed on January 2018).

Molina, E. (2016), *CEQ Master Workbook: Venezuela (2012)*, CEQ Data Center on Fiscal Redistribution, CEQ Institute, Tulane University, New Orleans.

MTESS (2016), *Boletín Estadístico de Seguridad Social 2015*, Ministerio de Trabajo, Empleo y Seguridad Social de Paraguay, Asunción, www.mtess.gov.py/application/files/2314/7765/9442/boletin-estadistico-2016-dgss.pdf (accessed on January 2018).

MTESS (2017), *Boletín Estadístico de Seguridad Social 2016*, Ministerio de Trabajo, Empleo y Seguridad Social de Paraguay, Asunción.

National Government of Paraguay (2014), *Plan Nacional de Desarrollo: Paraguay 2030* [National Development Plan: Paraguay 2030], Asunción, www.stp.gov.py/pnd/wp-content/uploads/2014/12/pnd2030.pdf.

Navarro, B. and E. Ortiz (2014), *El Sistema de Pensiones de Paraguay. Debilidades que Exhibe y Perspectivas de la Reforma*, Centro de Análisis y Difusión de la Economía Paraguaya, Asunción.

Navarro, F. (2016), *La nueva ola de reformas previsionales y la igualdad de género en América Latina*, Economic Commission for Latin America and the Caribbean, Santiago.

OECD (2018a), *Multi-dimensional Review of Paraguay. Vol I: Initial Assessment*, OECD Publishing, Paris, https://doi.org/10.1787/9789264301900-en.

OECD (2018b), *Public Governance Review of Paraguay: Pursuing National Development through Integrated Public Governance*, OECD Publishing, Paris, https://doi.org/10.1787/9789264301856-en.

OECD (2017), *Pensions at a Glance 2017: OECD and G20 Indicators*, OECD Publishing, Paris, http://dx.doi.org/10.1787/pension_glance-2017-en.

OECD (2016a), *Multi-dimensional Review of Peru: Volume 2. In-depth Analysis and Recommendations*, OECD Development Pathways, OECD Publishing, Paris, http://dx.doi.org/10.1787/9789264264670-en.

OECD (2016b), *Core Principles of Private Pension Regulation*, OECD Publishing, Paris, www.oecd.org/finance/private-pensions/Core-Principles-Private-Pension-Regulation.pdf (accessed on March 2018).

OECD (2015), *Social Protection System Reviews: Concept Note*, OECD Development Centre, Paris (unpublished).

OECD (2011), *Chile: Review of the Private Pensions System*, OECD Publishing, Paris, www.oecd.org/finance/private-pensions/49497472.pdf (accessed on March 2018).

OECD/ECLAC/CIAT/IDB (2017), *Revenue Statistics in Latin America and the Caribbean 2017*, OECD Publishing, Paris, http://dx.doi.org/10.1787/rev_lat_car-2017-en-fr.

OECD/IDB/World Bank (2014), *Pensions at a Glance: Latin America and the Caribbean*, OECD Publishing, Paris, http://dx.doi.org/10.1787/pension_glance-2014-en.

Ortiz, I., M. Cummins and K. Karunanethy (2017), *Fiscal Space for Social Protection and the SDGs: Options to Expand Social Investments in 187 Countries*, ESS Working Paper N° 48, International Labour Organization, Geneva.

Ovando, F. (2017), Análisis longitudinal de las transiciones de status laboral en la población juvenil urbana de Paraguay, Ministerio de Trabajo, Empleo y Seguridad Social, Asunción.

Paz Arauco et al. (2014), "Explaining Low Redistributive Impact in Bolivia" in *The Redistributive Impact of Taxes and Social Spending in Latin America*, Public Finance Review 42, no 3, pp. 326-345, http://dx.doi.org/10.1177/1091142113496133.

Rossignolo, D. (2018), "Taxes, Expenditures, Poverty, and Income Distribution in Argentina" in *Commitment to Equity Handbook. Estimating the Impact of Fiscal Policy on Inequality and Poverty*, Tulane University, New Orleans.

Ruppert Bulmer, E. et al. (2017), *Paraguay Jobs Diagnostic. The Dynamic Transformation of Employment in Paraguay*, Jobs Series N° 9, World Bank, Washington D.C., http://documents.worldbank.org/curated/en/500641499411206696/Paraguay-jobs-diagnostic-the-dynamic-transformation-of-employment.

Santoro, M. (2017), *Pension Reform Options in Chile: Some Tradeoffs*, Working Paper WP/17/53, International Monetary Fund, Washington D.C.

Sauma, P. and J. D. Trejos (2014a), *Gasto público social, impuestos, redistribución del ingreso y pobreza en Costa Rica*, CEQ Working Paper 18, Center for Inter-American Policy and Research and Department of Economics, Tulane University and Inter-American Dialogue, New Orleans.

Scott, J. (2014), "Redistributive Impact and Efficiency of Mexico's Fiscal System" in *The Redistributive Impact of Taxes and Social Spending in Latin America*, Public Finance Review 42, no. 3, pp. 368-390, http://dx.doi.org/10.1177/1091142113497394.

Serafini, V. (2016), Paraguay: Inversión en Protección Social No Contributiva. Avances y desafíos una década después, Centro de Análisis y Difusión de la Economía Paraguaya, Asunción.

SISALRIL (2018), Superintendencia de Salud y Riesgos Laborales de la República Dominicana, Santo Domingo, www.sisalril.gov.do/RegimenContSubs.aspx (accessed on March 2018).

STP (2016), Encuesta Longitudinal de Protección Social [Longitudinal Survey of Social Protection] (database), Secretaría Técnica de Planeación de Paraguay, Asunción.

Stuart, E., E. Samman and A. Hunt (2018), I*nformal is the new normal. Improving the lives of workers at risk of being left behind*, ODI Working Paper 530, Overseas Development Institute.

UNDP (2016), Regional Human Development Report for Latin America and the Caribbean: Multidimensional progress: well-being beyond income, United Nations Development Programme, New York.

Van Panhuys et al. (2015), *ICROP: Reaching out to rural poor through mobile service units*, International Labour Organization, Geneva, www.social-protection.org/gimi/gess/RessourcePDF.action?ressource.ressourceId=51861 (accessed on March 2018).

World Bank (2018a), The Atlas of Social Protection – Indicators of Resilience and Equity (database), http://databank.worldbank.org/data/reports.aspx?source=1229.

World Bank (2018b), World Development Indicators (database), http://data.worldbank.org/data-catalog/world-development-indicators.

Annex 2.A. Overview of social security and pension schemes

Annex Table 2.A.1. Overview of social security schemes by eligibility group

Contingency	Benefit	Institution	Agency	Target group	Coverage (2016)	Participation	Introduced	Financed by
Government official								
Death	Death of income earner	General Directorate on non-contributory pensions	Ministry of Finance	Survivors of police and military personnel	237 228			General budget
Disability	Invalidity pension	Caja Fiscal	General Directorate on Pensions, Ministry of Finance	Public officials	237 228	Compulsory	1909	Contributions
Old age	Old-age pension	Caja Fiscal	General Directorate on Pensions, Ministry of Finance	Public officials	237 228	Compulsory	1909	Contributions
Health	Medical care	Health agencies of the Armed Forces and Police		Military personnel, police personnel and dependants		Universal		General budget
	Medical care	Pre-paid private insurance	Agencies with contracted plans	State employees and officials		Occupation-based		General budget
	Medical care	Private insurance	All other agencies	State employees and officials		Voluntary		Private contributions

Annex Table 2.A.1 *(cont.)*

Contingency	Benefit	Institution	Agency	Target group	Coverage (2016)	Participation	Introduced	Financed by
Formal sector workers								
Maternity	Maternity cash benefit	Social Security Institute (IPS) + small closed pension schemes	MTESS	Private sector employees	743 852[b]	Compulsory	1942	Contributions
Disability	Invalidity pension	Social Security Institute (IPS) + small closed pension schemes	MTESS	Private sector employees	555 844[b]	Compulsory	1943	Contributions
Sickness	Income in sickness	Social Security Institute (IPS) + small closed pension schemes	MTESS	Private sector employees	743 852[b]	Compulsory	1944	Contributions
Occupational injury	Occupational injury and sickness cash benefit	Social Security Institute (IPS) + small closed pension schemes	MTESS	Private sector employees	743 852[b]	Compulsory	1943	Contributions
Death	Survivor pension	Social Security Institute (IPS) + small closed pension schemes	MTESS	Children (minor or disabled) and partner of insured private sector employee	555 844[b]	Compulsory	1944	Contributions
Health	Medical care	Social Security Institute (IPS)	MSPBS	Private sector employees	743 852[b]	Compulsory	1943	Contributions
Old age	Pensions	Social Security Institute (IPS) + small closed pension schemes	MTESS	Private sector employees	555 844[b]	Compulsory	1943	Contributions
	Pensions	Private pension providers (e.g. Caja Mutual de Cooperativistas, Caja Médica, Caja de Profesores de la UCA)	MTESS		30 000[b]	Voluntary		Contributions

Annex Table 2.A.1 *(cont.)*

Informal sector workers								
Disability	Invalidity pension	Social Security Institute (IPS)	MTESS	Private sector employees	518c	Voluntary	2011	Contributions
Death	Survivor pension	Social Security Institute (IPS)	MTESS	Children (minor or disabled) and partner of insured private sector employee	518c	Voluntary	2011	Contributions
Health	Medical care	Public Hospitals	MSPBS, UNA	Universal		Universal		Tax revenues
Old age	Pensions	Social Security Institute (IPS)	MTESS	Private sector employees	518c	Voluntary	2011	Contributions

Annex Table 2.A.1 *(cont.)*

	People living in poverty							
Childhood	Allowance (*Tekoporã*)	Secretariat for Social Action (SAS)	Presidency	Children, adolescents, people with disability, indigenous people	685 578 people[d]	Means-tested (Ficha Hogar – SAS)	2005	Tax revenues
Childhood	Allowance (*Abrazo*)	National Secretariat for Children and Adolescents (SNNA)	Presidency	Working children, street children	10 784 children and adolescents	Means-tested (Ficha Social – SNNA)	2005	Tax revenues
Poverty	Productive investment (*Tenonderã*)	Secretariat for Social Action (SAS)	Presidency	Tekoporã beneficiaries with family businesses	5 856 families	Means-tested (Ficha Hogar – SAS)	2014	Tax revenues
Poverty	Productive investment (*Familia por Familia*)	Secretaría Técnica de Planificación (STP)	Presidency	Families with agricultural businesses	776 families	Means-tested (Ficha Social)	2014	Tax revenues
Poverty	Productive investment (Proyecto de Inclusión de la Agricultura Familiar en Cadenas de Valor)	MAG	MAG	Families with agricultural businesses in selected regions, vulnerable farmers, indigenous population	14 500 families (goal)	Targeted	2012	Loan (IFAD)
Poverty	Productive investment (Proyecto de Desarrollo Rural Sostenible)	MAG	MAG	Small or indigenous farmers	29 600 (2016)	Regional targeting	2008	Loan (World Bank)
Health	Medical care	Public Hospitals	MSPBS, UNA	Universal		Universal		Tax revenues
Old age	Allowance (*Adulto Mayor*)	General Directorate on non-contributory pensions	Ministry of Finance	Poor elderly aged 65 or above	162 130[e]	Means-tested (FIcha Hogar – Adultos Mayores)	2010	Tax revenues
Food	Programa Alimentario Nutricional Integral (PANI)	Direccion de Nutricion y Programas Alimentarios, Instituto Nacional de Alimentacion y Nutricion (INAN)	MSPBS	Children and mothers	113 709 (2016)	Means-tested	2005	Tax revenues
Food	Seguridad Alimentaria Nutricional	Secretaría Técnica de Planificación (STP)	Presidency	Indigenous population, for mothers with children below age 5	20 000	Means-tested (Ficha Social)		Tax revenues

Note: MTESS = Ministry of Labour and Social Security. MSPBS = Ministry of Health and Social Well-being. MAG = Ministry of Agriculture.
Source: Own elaboration a. b. IPS (2017), c. Data received by IPS, d. OECD (2018), e. MH (2017).

Annex Table 2.A.2. Public contributory pension schemes in Paraguay

		IPS	Caja Fiscal: Military	Caja Fiscal: Police	Caja Fiscal: Teachers and university professors	Caja Fiscal: Central Administration and judicial personnel	Caja Bancaria	Caja Municipal	Caja Parlamentaria	Caja Ferroviaria	Caja de la ANDE[b]	Caja de Itaipu Binacional
Target group		Private sector	Public sector employees				Banking sector	Local government	Members of Parliament	Railways	Electricity utility	Itaipu
Contributors		531 725	36 350		93 529	107 349	12 762	7 629	125	4	3 914	348
Pensioners		52 532	15 472		24 842	15 141	2 741	1 500	196	471	1 634	442
Contribution rate (% of salary)	Employers'	14	0	0	0	0	17	10	7	10	5+12	15
	Employees'	9	16	16	16	16	11	10	20	10	5+6	6
Standard pension	Benefit (% of salary)	100	Starting at 50[a]	Starting at 30[a]	Starting at 83[a]	Starting at 47[a]	100	Starting at 45[a]	80	100	66.7+42.5	80
	Earnings measure (nominal)	Last 3 years			Last five years		Last 4 years	Last 2 years	Last month	Last 2 years	Last 3 years	Last 3 years
	Retirement age	60	no	no	no	62	60	55	55	50	60	60
	Min. annuities	25	15	10	25[c]	20	30	15	15	25	20	10
Proportional retirement	Benefit (% of salary)	60	n.a	n.a.	n.a.	Starting at 20	n.a.	Starting at 40	60		Proportion of standard pension	Proportion of standard pension
	Retirement age	65				62		50	55	40	60	60
	Min. annuities	15				10		20	10	15	15	5

Note: Contributors and Pensioners: 2016 data for IPS, Caja Fiscal, Caja Bancaria, Caja Ferroviaria, Caja ANDE and Caja Itaipu; 2013 data for Caja Parlamentaria; 2011 data for Caja Municipal. a. The pension benefit increases with annuities, reaching a maximum of 100%; b. The Caja de la ANDE is a complementary system, Employers and employees contribute each 5% to the Caja de la ANDE and respectively 12% and 6% to the IPS; c. Each child counts as an additional annuity for female teachers

Source: Navarro and Ortiz (2014), MTESS (2017), MTESS (2016), Caja ANDE (2017), Dirección General de Jubilaciones y Pensiones (Ministry of Finance) www.hacienda.gov.py/web-hacienda/jubilaciones (accessed on february 2018).

Chapter 3. Reforming to foster healthier lives in Paraguay

Paraguay has set ambitious targets to improve the health of its citizens. The country faces a double burden. The weight of non-communicable diseases is growing, fuelled by longer lives but also less healthy lifestyles. At the same time, unresolved issues remain in communicable diseases, maternal, neonatal and nutritional diseases. The health system in Paraguay suffers from fragmentation and the weaknesses of its stewardship institutions. To measure up to the challenge, the country has undertaken a series of reforms, starting with a landmark law passed in 1996. The reforms have succeeded in setting the stage for a new approach to healthcare based on primary care. However, they have not altered significantly the foundations of the health system and its fragmentation into multiple subsystems. This chapter describes the health challenges that Paraguay faces and focuses on challenges in financing healthcare and in achieving universal health coverage.

The statistical data for Israel are supplied by and under the responsibility of the relevant Israeli authorities. The use of such data by the OECD is without prejudice to the status of the Golan Heights, East Jerusalem and Israeli settlements in the West Bank under the terms of international law.

Ensuring that all citizens have access to appropriate, pertinent and quality health services, without anyone being pushed to financial hardship because of health payments, is of critical importance in fostering citizen well-being. It is also a means of breaking the intergenerational transmission of poverty, as children with ill health have worse learning outcomes than healthy children. Adults in poor health have lower income generation potential than healthy adults. Universal healthcare access and coverage are therefore central tenets of a strategy to reduce poverty and inequality (PAHO/WHO, 2014).

Achieving its ambitious goals will require Paraguay to intensify efforts in the development of its national health system. This chapter begins by presenting the development objectives in the health sector that Paraguay has set and the progress achieved so far. It goes on to analyse the healthcare needs of the population, as they emerge from the burden of disease, and the progression of the demographic and epidemiological transitions in the country. It then describes the key features of the Paraguayan health system and offers avenues for pursuing ongoing reforms and options for intensifying the pace of reform, focusing first on financing functions and then on the need to expand health coverage along its three dimensions, namely population coverage (breadth), financial protection (height), and health service coverage (depth).

Paraguay has set ambitious targets to improve the health of its citizens

Paraguay has made ambitious commitments to improve the health of its citizens. The National Development Plan (PND) sets ambitious targets to increase life expectancy and to reduce maternal mortality, child mortality, undernutrition, obesity as well as deaths by non-communicable diseases. More broadly, the National Health Policy sets out to advance towards universal access to health and achieving universal health coverage by 2030 (MSPBS, 2015).

To deliver on this commitment and on the right to health enshrined in the Constitution, the country has undertaken major reforms of the governance and approach of the national health system. The adoption of law 1032 in 1996, which created the National Health System, is a major milestone in this reform process. However, it has only been partially successful. The system remains very fragmented and stewardship is challenging. However, significant progress has been achieved in terms of access to health, in the process of decentralisation of the health system, and in the adoption of an approach to universal health coverage based on primary healthcare.

Demographic trends are favourable but as the transformation of the health system will require time, it should start now. Paraguayans are young and live relatively long lives. Life expectancy at birth in Paraguay is 73.6 years (70.8 years for men and 76.5 years for women) according to the most recent projections (DGEEC, 2015). The Paraguayan population is eminently young. By 2017, 30% of the population was 15 years old or less, while only 6% were 65 years or older. The relatively large young population is a key advantage of the health system in Paraguay. It gives Paraguay a window of opportunity to reform the health system before demand for health increases significantly while offering the country some leeway for pre-paid contributions to finance the health system and social protection more generally (see Chapter 2). However, the demographic dividend will gradually decline over the coming decades. The structure of the population has become less expansionary in recent decades and is stationary in the under-20 age group. The population is currently growing at an annual rate of 1.3%, while women have 2.5 children on average. Projections suggest that the growth rate will stabilise with fertility falling to just below 2 children per woman by 2040.

Figure 3.1. Paraguay's progress towards health SDG indicators is mixed

Progress from 2005 to 2015, in percentage of distance to target in 2005, selection of SDG health indicators

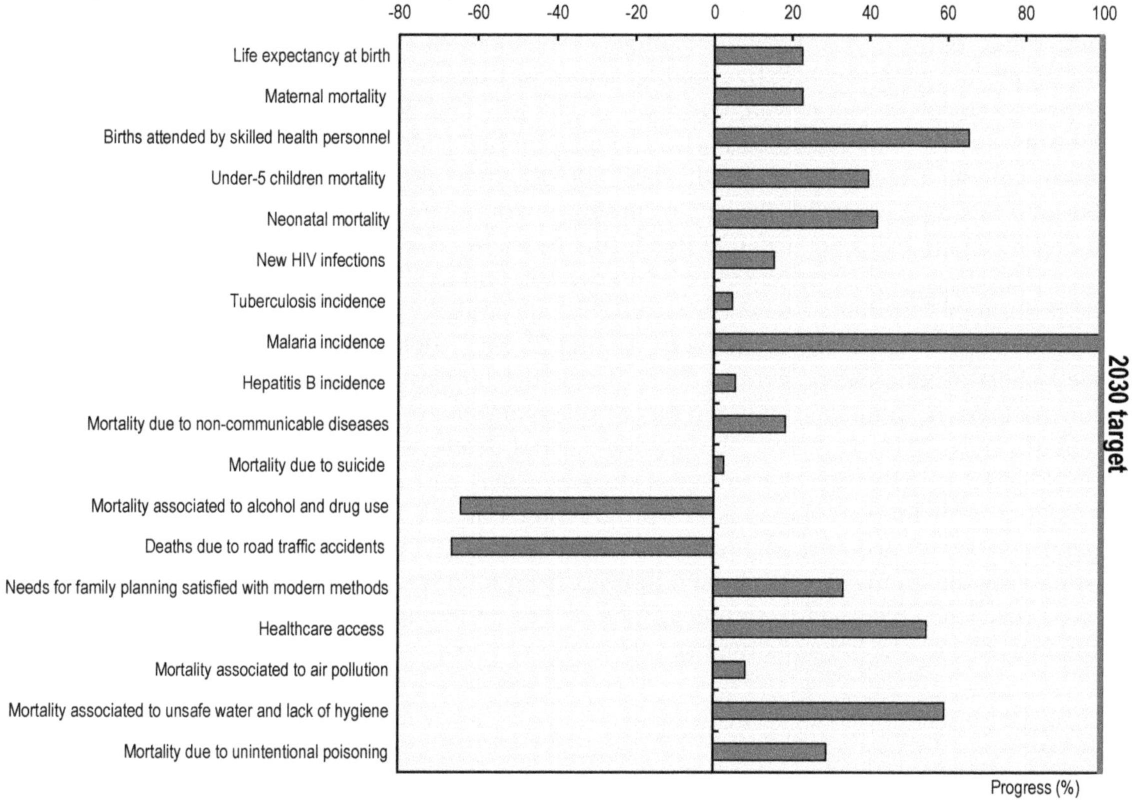

Notes: 1. Blue bars show progress of Paraguay in a selection of SDG indicators between 2005 (0 axis) and 2015. The 100 axis represents SDG targets by 2030. All figures are normalised to provide an accurate comparison.

2. National targets may differ from UN official targets. For child mortality ratios, the UN's official target is estimated at 25 per 1 000 live births; however, the national target, set by the National Development Plan, is 9 per 1 000 live births (reduction of 70%). For the neo-natal mortality ratio, the UN's official target is estimated at 12 per 1 000 live births; however, the national target, set by the National Development Plan, is 5 per 1 000 live births (reduction of 70%). For maternal mortality ratios, the UN's official target is estimated to be below 70 per 100 000 live births; however, the national target is 39.8 per 100 000 live births (reduction of 75%). The National Development plan set the goal of a 50% reduction in the suicide mortality rate, the mortality rate attributed to cardiovascular disease, cancer, diabetes or chronic respiratory disease and for deaths due to road traffic accidents. When the baseline year is not specified in official documentation, authors used 2005 as a year of reference to allow comparisons with official SDG targets.

3. Data related to the proportion of women of reproductive age (aged 15-49 years) using modern birth control methods are dated back from 2004 and 2008. The latest data related to mortality rate attributed to unintentional poisoning are from 2012.

4. Data are not available to measure national performance in the following official SDG indicators: 3.5 (*Strengthen the prevention and treatment of substance abuse, including narcotic drug abuse and harmful use of alcohol*) and 3.8 (*Achieve universal health coverage, including financial risk protection, access to quality essential health-care services and access to safe, effective, quality and affordable essential medicines and vaccines for all*). As an alternative, authors used similar indicators to measure progress in these SDG indicators, namely: *Mortality rate attributed to alcohol and drug use* (Global Burden of Disease Study) and *Health care access* (sick and injured that received skilled healthcare) (Paraguay Permanent Household Survey).

Source: Authors on the basis of official national data when available, and alternatively, international data; (National Government of Paraguay, 2014); United Nations, SDG Indicators, Global database, https://unstats.un.org/sdgs/indicators/database (United Nations, 2018); World Bank, World Development Indicators, http://databank.worldbank.org/data/reports.aspx?source=world-development-indicators, (World Bank, 2018); Global Burden of Disease Study (Global Burden of Disease Collaborative Network, 2016); Global Health Observatory (database) (WHO, 2018b); DGEEC (2017).

StatLink https://doi.org/10.1787/888933822957

In this context, performance on key health outcomes has been mixed. In terms of the Sustainable Development Goals (SDG), Paraguay has progressed in several indicators over the last decades, but progress has not always been at the pace needed to achieve the targets set by the SDGs or by the National Development Plan. SDG 3 gathers a series of indicators to ensure healthy lives and promote well-being for all, at all ages (Figure 3.1). Life expectancy has improved, but faster progress is needed in order to meet the target of 79 years by 2030, as set in the PND. The maternal mortality ratio has decreased by 17%, from 159 to 132 estimated deaths per 100 000 live births, between 2005 and 2015. Despite this positive trend, the rate of progress would be insufficient to achieve the SDG target of less than 70 per 100 000 live births by 2030. The national official target is even more ambitious with a set objective of 40 per 100 000 live births. On the other hand, rates of preventable deaths of newborns and children under 5 years of age are already well below the SDG target of respectively, 12 and 25 per 1 000 live births. But, they still fall well short of national objectives. In terms of the burden of specific diseases, HIV and tuberculosis has remained stable in recent years, and there have been no endemic cases of malaria since 2010. However, the prevalence and death rate of dengue and other tropical diseases have increased over the past decade. Rates of satisfaction of needs for family planning with modern methods are progressing but are not yet universal. Finally, the death rate associated to road injuries increased between 2005 and 2015, making the target of halving the number of deaths and injuries from road traffic accidents by 2020 unlikely to be reached. This trend is similar for the rate of premature mortality (YLL, i.e. years of life lost) due to alcohol and drug use.

Health and health care needs in Paraguay

Paraguay has been going through a marked demographic and epidemiological transition. Non-communicable diseases have risen sharply, whereas communicable, maternal, neonatal and nutritional diseases have not decreased as expected. The epidemiological transition has been accompanied by changes towards sedentary lifestyles and poor dietary habits among the population, deteriorating risk factors and the social determinants of health. Furthermore, disability and death rates associated to external injuries have been rising over the last decades, mostly due to traffic accidents and interpersonal violence (Figure 3.2).

Figure 3.2. Epidemiological transition Paraguay and Peru, 1990-2016

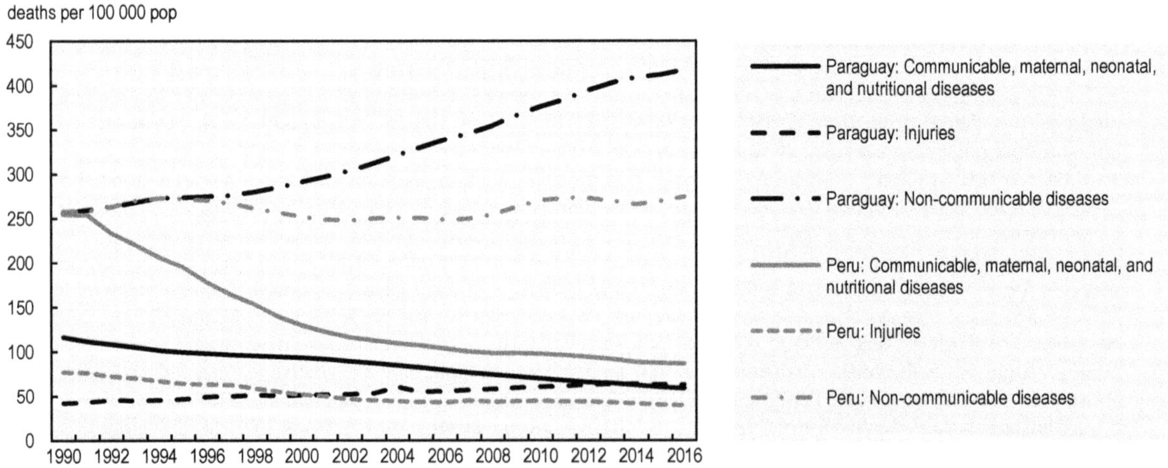

Source: Global Burden of Disease Study (database) (Global Burden of Disease Collaborative Network, 2016).

StatLink https://doi.org/10.1787/888933822976

The unresolved agenda of communicable, maternal, neonatal and nutritional diseases

Although communicable, maternal, neonatal and nutritional diseases (CMNN) tend to decrease alongside economic and social development, Paraguay still faces high rates of prevalence and associated deaths. Currently, CMNN represent around 11% of total deaths per year. Death rates have reduced by 37.6% over the last two decades, falling from 97.8 to 58.7 deaths per 100 000 people, between 1996 and 2006. Contrastingly, Latin America and the Caribbean region saw a faster reduction (46.6%) over the same period, falling from 125.4 to 66.9 deaths per 100 000 people. Despite the relatively slow progress, death rates due to CMNN are lower than in some neighbouring countries like Ecuador (63.6), Uruguay (68.9) and Brazil (69.21), but higher than in Panama (57.4), Chile (44.8) and Costa Rica (23.4). Among the major causes of death, pneumonia causes 20.5 deaths per 100 000 people (3.8% of total deaths) and neonatal disorders cause 15.1 deaths per 100 000 people (2.8% of total deaths). These two main causes of death are followed by HIV/AIDS and tuberculosis, nutritional deficiencies and diarrhoeal diseases (6.6, 4.8, and 3 deaths per 100 000 people respectively).

A high share of Paraguayan women still die from preventable causes related to pregnancy and childbirth. Estimations suggest that the maternal mortality ratio fell from 158 to 132 deaths per 100 000 live births between 2000 and 2015 (Figure 3.3 Panel A). Compared to the benchmark countries, Paraguay registered the highest maternal mortality ratio (Figure 3.3 Panel B). The leading causes were preeclampsia, haemorrhage and complications from abortions. An increased access to higher-quality health care during pregnancy and childbirth can prevent many of those maternal deaths, as well as improve pregnancy and childbirth, particularly for adolescent girls. By 2015, 77.4% of pregnant women had at least four prenatal check-ups and 97% of deliveries took place in health facilities (PAHO, 2017). The recent increase in the number of births attended by skilled health staff had a positive impact on the decrease in maternal mortality rates. In ten years, the number of births attended by skilled health staff increased from 87% to 95% in 2015. Moreover, 56.6 births were to adolescent mothers per each 1 000 women aged between 15 and 19 in 2017. Adolescent mothers face higher risks of eclampsia, puerperal endometritis, and systemic infections than adult mothers. Similarly, the babies born to adolescent mothers face higher risks (e.g. low birthweight, preterm delivery, and severe neonatal conditions) than those born to adult mothers (Ganchimeg, 2014).

Figure 3.3. Maternal mortality rate 2015

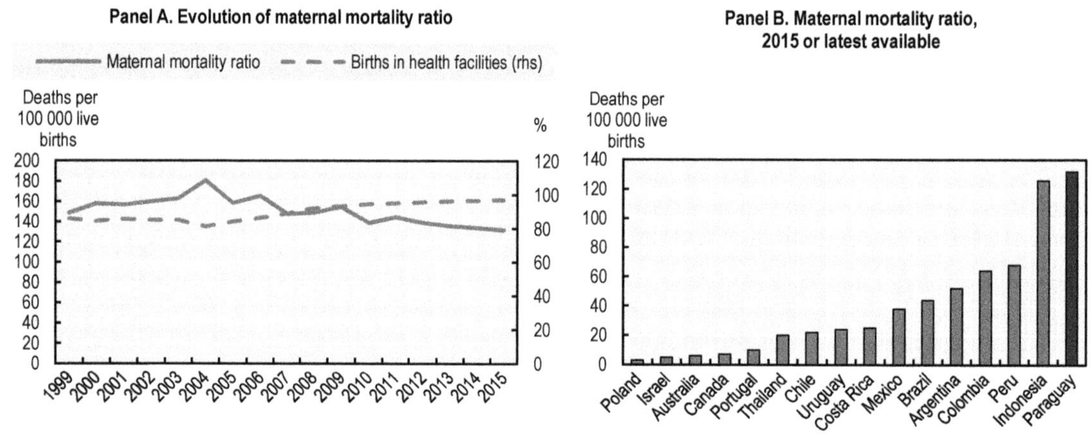

Source: Panel A: World Bank (2018), World development Indicators (WHO, UNICEF, UNFPA, World Bank Group, and the United Nations Population Division. Trends in Maternal Mortality: 1990 to 2015. Geneva, World Health Organization, 2015), births in health facilities from (PAHO/WHO/MSPBS, various years). Panel B: World Bank (2018), World development indicators (database).

StatLink https://doi.org/10.1787/888933822995

Neonatal, infant and child mortality is highly associated with the lack of quality and skilled care of common diseases. By 2015, reported mortality in children under 1 and children under 5 was 14.2 and 16.4 deaths per 1 000 live births, respectively (MSPBS, 2016a). Compared to the benchmark countries on the basis of internationally comparable estimates, Paraguay still registers high child mortality rates, well above those registered in OECD countries (Figure 3.4 Panel B). The leading causes of death were pneumonia, influenza, and diarrheal diseases. On the other hand, by 2015, neonatal mortality reached 9.7 deaths per 1 000 live births; its leading causes were preterm birth complications, encephalopathy due to birth injuries, pneumonia, infections and sexually transmitted diseases. Skilled health care during pregnancy, childbirth and in the postnatal period prevents complications for both mother and newborn and problems can be detected in their early stages and treated accordingly.

Figure 3.4. Child mortality rates

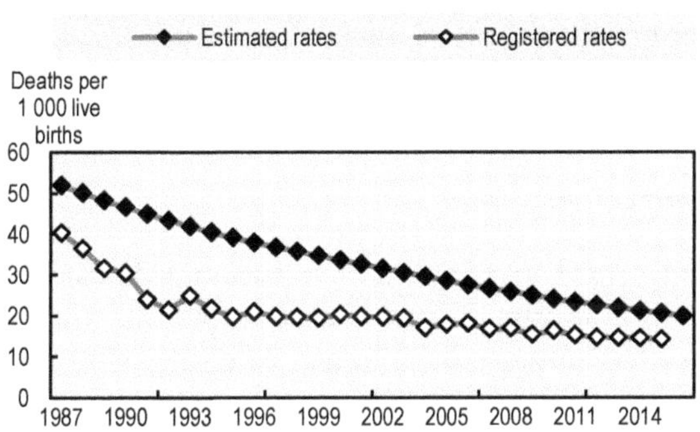

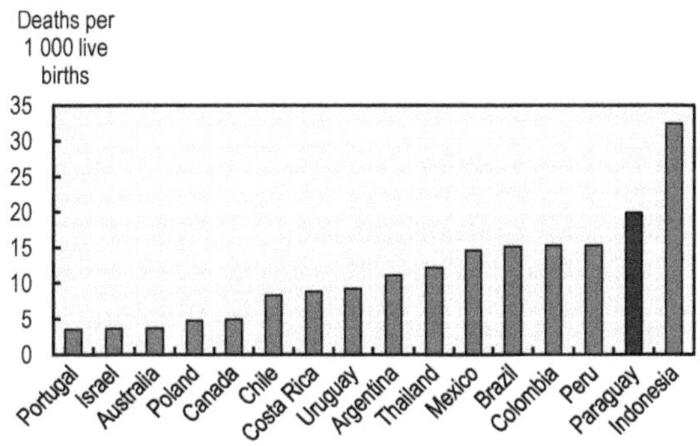

Source: Panel A: Registered rates are from National Health Indicators (Indicadores básicos de salud). Estimated rates are from the UN Inter-agency Group for Child Mortality Estimation [UNICEF, WHO, World Bank, UN DESA Population Division]. Panel B: World Bank (2018), World development Indicators (Estimates Developed by the UN Inter-agency Group for Child Mortality Estimation [UNICEF, WHO, World Bank, UN DESA Population Division].

StatLink https://doi.org/10.1787/888933823014

Nutritional deficiencies are particularly high among children. Better nutrition is related to improved infant, child and maternal health, stronger immune systems, safer pregnancy and childbirth, lower risk of non-communicable diseases (such as diabetes and cardiovascular disease) and longevity (WHO, 2017). The overall prevalence of nutritional deficiencies in Paraguay was 20.1 cases per 100 000 people in 2016. Contrastingly, the prevalence among children under 5 was 37.8 cases per 100 000 people, out of which 33.5 were due to iron-deficiency anaemia and 4.2 due to vitamin A deficiency. Nutritional deficiencies produced 3.1% of total deaths among children under 5 in 2016, most of them being associated to protein-energy malnutrition (Global Burden of Disease Collaborative Network, 2016).

Infectious diseases mostly affect people who face social and economic vulnerability, including indigenous persons and children. Pneumonia and diarrheal diseases still list among the most common causes of death in Paraguay. By 2016, the former was the seventh biggest cause of death, leading to 3.8% of total deaths across all ages, while among children under 5, it lead to 7.4% of total deaths. The prevalence of tuberculosis was 21 272.7 cases per 100 000 people in 2016, with a mortality rate of 3.8 deaths per 100 000 people. The most vulnerable population to tuberculosis are the indigenous communities, inmates and people living with HIV. An estimated 17 564 people were living with the human immunodeficiency virus in 2015; more than half of them were between the ages of 20 and 34.

Although immunisation coverage has progressed and prevalence of infectious diseases has decreased, Paraguay has not yet attainted Universal Immunization Coverage. A strong investment was made to strengthen the vaccination program between 2009 and 2010, increasing the budget of the Expanded Immunization Program (PAI for its acronym in Spanish) by 56% over a two-year period. The new resources made it possible to guarantee operational resources and the introduction of new vaccines to the national vaccination schedule to prevent rotavirus, chickenpox, influenza, hepatitis A, whooping cough, pneumococcal infections, and the human papilloma virus (among others). The country has seen progress in the elimination of malaria, measles, congenital rubella syndrome, and other communicable diseases over the last years. Vaccination coverage reached 80% for the pentavalent vaccine (DPT-3) and 91% for the measles, mumps, and rubella vaccine by 2016. However, immunisation coverage for the BCG vaccine is 10 percentage points lower in Paraguay than in the southern cone, 8 percentage points lower for the polio virus vaccine and 11 percentage points lower for the DTP3 vaccine (WHO, 2017).

A fast-growing burden of non-communicable diseases

The concomitant presence of communicable, maternal, neonatal and nutritional diseases is aggravated by the growing burden of non-communicable diseases (NCD). Late epidemiological transition in Paraguay has resulted in a sharp increase in cases of non-communicable diseases. NCD are the main cause of death in the country and have been increasing, strikingly so, over the last few decades, rising from 65.2% of total deaths in 1996 to 77.5% in 2016. Most common conditions were cardiovascular diseases (31.1% of total deaths); neoplasms (tumours) (17.5% of total deaths); diabetes, urogenital, blood, and endocrine diseases (13% of total deaths); and neurological disorders (5.6% of total deaths). Among the top 10 causes of death in 2016, seven were associated to non-communicable diseases (Figure 3.5). In order to advance towards achievement of the SDG, Paraguay should aim to reduce by one-third premature mortality from non-communicable diseases by 2030 through prevention and treatment, as well as through the promotion of mental health and well-being.

Figure 3.5. Top 10 causes of death

2006 and 2016

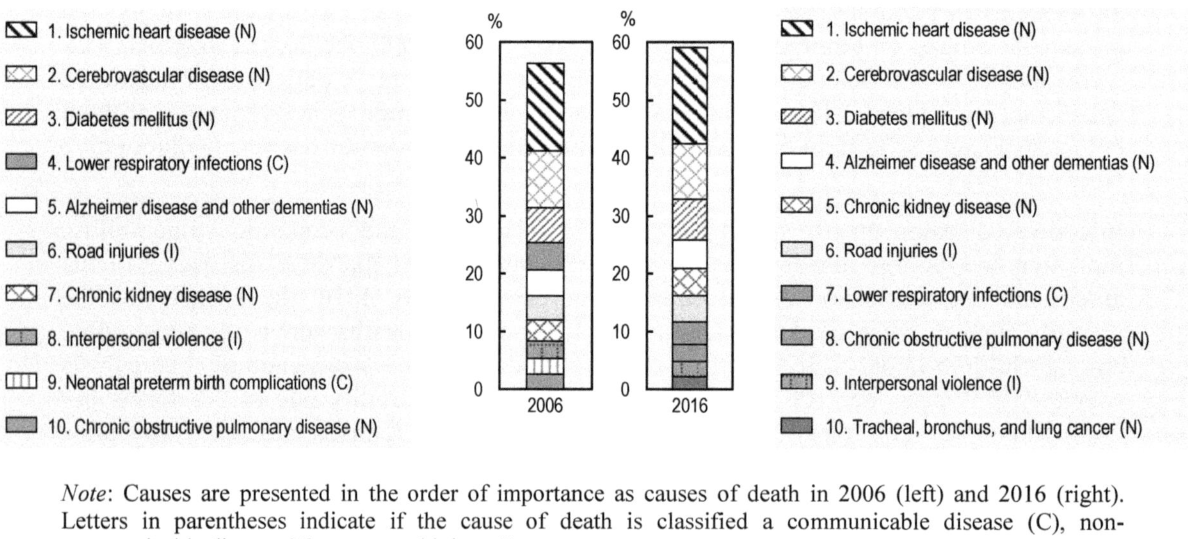

Note: Causes are presented in the order of importance as causes of death in 2006 (left) and 2016 (right). Letters in parentheses indicate if the cause of death is classified a communicable disease (C), non-communicable disease (N) or external injury (I).
Source: Global Burden of Disease Study (database) (Global Burden of Disease Collaborative Network, 2016).

StatLink https://doi.org/10.1787/888933823033

Diabetes and chronic kidney diseases impose a large death burden in Paraguay. Diabetes mellitus is the most common within this disease family, producing a prevalence of 5 011 cases per 100 000 people and 38 deaths per 100 000 people; around 0.76% of diabetes patients die in Paraguay. Although Latin America and the Caribbean region has on average a higher prevalence of diabetes (5 214.4 cases per 100 000 people), death rates are lower than in Paraguay (31.4 deaths per 100 000 people). Accordingly, a diabetes patient is more likely to die in Paraguay than in the average LAC country. In the same way, while around 0.94% of patients suffering from chronic kidney disease eventually die from it in Paraguay, 0.64% of patients die on average in Latin America and the Caribbean (Global Burden of Disease Collaborative Network, 2016).

Table 3.1. Comparison of Paraguay's top 10 causes of premature death in 2016

Age-standardised premature death rates (Years of Life Lost) per 100 000 people

	Ischemic heart disease	Cerebrovascular disease	Road injuries	Diabetes mellitus	Chronic kidney disease	Interpersonal violence	Lower respiratory infections	Neonatal preterm birth complications	Congenital birth defects	Alzheimer disease and other dementias
Paraguay	2 255	1 400	1 177	1 038	745	696	695	694	681	459
Benchmark countries' average	1 432	768	610	410	375	401	542	332	425	337
Argentina	1 802	786	646	362	374	300	936	503	541	251
Australia	905	351	289	159	118	62	129	109	194	286
Brazil	1 811	1 068	1 049	564	363	1 446	862	487	653	520
Canada	1 084	335	336	193	117	79	174	203	255	258
Chile	938	699	497	250	290	213	311	303	511	252
Colombia	1 560	539	629	308	360	1 677	453	500	571	365
Costa Rica	1 186	353	620	149	463	372	228	416	619	362
Indonesia	3 299	2 556	742	1 118	479	89	784	837	505	463
Israel	858	348	309	338	292	108	223	94	212	347
Mexico	1 604	547	742	1 272	1 313	791	559	442	666	380
Peru	944	459	581	298	411	163	1 427	356	473	259
Poland	2 333	876	448	194	128	71	312	232	285	269
Portugal	856	741	378	231	163	61	351	77	167	351
Thailand	1 050	919	1 195	441	524	324	872	171	229	429
Uruguay	1 243	941	691	270	231	259	503	248	486	257

Note: YLL refers to the years of life lost due to premature mortality. Age-standardization involves a statistical technique used to compare populations with different age structures, in which the characteristics of the populations are statistically transformed to match those of a reference population.
Source: Global Burden of Disease Study (*database*) (Global Burden of Disease Collaborative Network, 2016).

Half of the main premature causes of death are due to non-communicable diseases. Rates of premature death are higher in Paraguay than in most of the benchmark countries. After adjusting for different age structures, Paraguay loses 1 038 years of life (YLL) due to diabetes per 100 000 people, whereas benchmark countries lose around 410 years of life on average due to the same cause (Table 3.1). Similarly, premature death rates due to cerebrovascular and chronic kidney diseases are close to doubling the average of those in benchmark countries. Regarding external causes, road injuries and interpersonal violence produce very high premature death rates compared with other countries. Lastly, among the main communicable, maternal, neonatal and nutritional diseases, the main causes of premature death in Paraguay are pneumonia (lower respiratory infections), neonatal preterm birth complications and congenital birth defects.

Risk factors are on the rise partly driven by social determinants of health

Non-communicable diseases are strongly associated with risk factors related to lifestyle. Most of them are generally preventable through interventions on the key risk factors related with people's lifestyle and habits. Such interventions might not only reduce morbidity but also reduce the high socio-economic costs for both people and the health system. The Ministry of Health implemented the First National Survey on Risk Factors of Non-Communicable Diseases in 2011. It analysed the main risk factors in the country, such as tobacco and alcohol consumption, dietary habits, physical activity, overweight and obesity, high blood pressure and glucose and cholesterol, among others.

Metabolic and behavioural risks lead the causes that contribute to disability and deaths in Paraguay. In particular, risks associated with high fasting plasma glucose, high blood pressure, high blood body mass index, dietary risk and malnutrition are among the top 10 main contributors to premature deaths. Most of the deaths associated with these risks could be prevented by encouraging people to adopt better habits (Figure 3.6).

Figure 3.6. Top 10 risks contributing to DALYs (Disability-Adjusted Life Years lost) in 2016

Change 2006-16

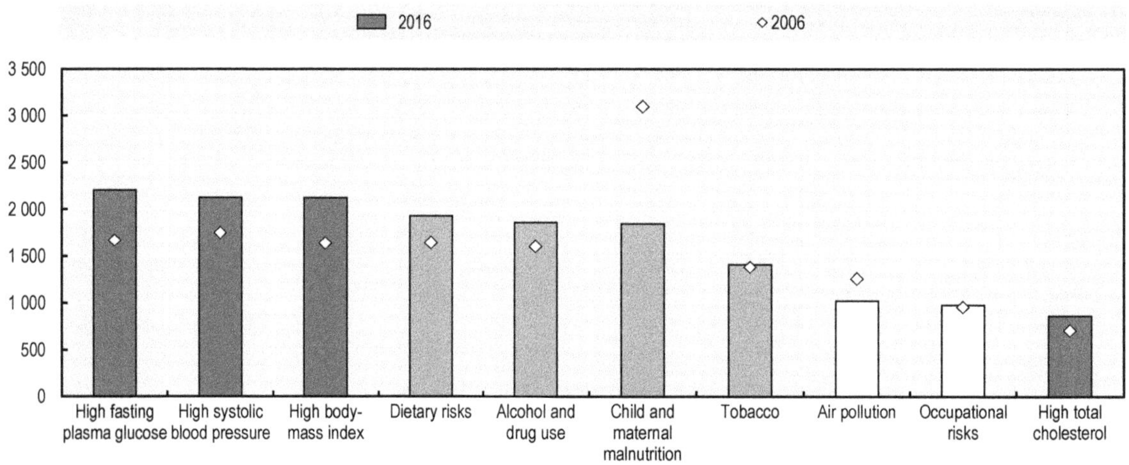

Note: Metabolic risks are indicated by the blue bars. Behavioural risks are indicated by the grey bars. Environmental and occupational risks are indicated by the white bars.
Source: Global Burden of Disease Study (database) (Global Burden of Disease Collaborative Network, 2016).

StatLink https://doi.org/10.1787/888933823052

Metabolic and behavioural risks are the main contributors to cases of non-communicable diseases in Paraguay. Among metabolic risks, the main contributors are high fasting plasma glucose, high blood pressure and high mass index. In 2016, these risks factors were associated to 20.17%, 17.16% and 13.03% of total deaths respectively. Similarly, among behavioural risks, the main contributors are dietary risks, malnutrition, alcohol and drug use and tobacco. More than half of adult males (51.5%) and of adult women (51.3%) were overweight or obese in 2014, while 24.6% of adults did not get enough physical activity in 2010. Contrastingly, 39% of adults in the world aged 18 years and older were overweight and 13% were obese in 2016 (WHO, 2017). Furthermore, 28.3% of male adults and 7.9% of female adults in Paraguay smoked tobacco in 2015.

Environmental and occupational risks significantly contribute to prevalence of non-communicable diseases. Air pollution and occupational risks are among the main risks that contribute to increasing the incidence of these conditions. Deforestation in Paraguay continues with severe implications for climate regulation (Da Ponte et al., 2017). The rapid expansion of the agricultural frontier and deforestation caused the loss of around 90% of the original[1] forest cover between 1945 and 2007, in the eastern region of the country, where the Atlantic Forest is located (Fleytas, 2007). In 2016, more than 3 000 deaths were associated to air pollution, which represents around 8.47% of total deaths in the country. Furthermore, Paraguayans are very vulnerable to the impact of major natural disasters and the consequences of environmental degradation. The worst natural disasters have been related to floods and droughts, especially due to El Niño, in some areas of the Paraguayan Chaco.

Universal access to sexual and reproductive healthcare services has a crosscutting positive impact on health. Services include family planning, information and education, and the integration of reproductive health into national strategies and programmes. Around 15% of women who do not want to become pregnant are not using contraception. Likewise, only 68% of women of reproductive age (aged 15-49 years) use modern methods to meet their needs in terms of family planning. In 2016, around 588 deaths were associated with unsafe sex (Global Burden of Disease Collaborative Network, 2016).

Poverty restricts access to basic services such as sewage treatment, garbage collection, medical services and education. In Paraguay, 98% of households had access to clean drinking water but only 12.3% had access to sewer systems in 2015. Moreover, 42.8% of homes had a septic tank and drainage well, 26.7% had a pour-flush pit latrine, and 18% had some other latrine system. In 2016, almost 200 deaths were associated with unsafe water, sanitation and handwashing. Nearly 52% of households have refuse collection services, 76% in urban areas and 16.3% in rural areas, while 15% of urban municipalities have an authorised dump (PAHO, 2017).

A first and fundamental way of achieving sustainable Universal Health Coverage is investing more in health promotion and disease prevention. Investments in public health can improve health outcomes at a relatively low cost (OECD, 2016d). Within the context of primary health care, health promotion is critical for improving outcomes in the prevention and control of both chronic and communicable diseases, and for meeting the health-related Sustainable Development Goals, particularly among poor and marginalised groups (WHO, 2017). In Paraguay, health promotion and disease prevention actions are undertaken mostly by community agents within the Family Healthcare Units (USF). The country had 801 such units as of 2017 but there is still a significant unmet need. Between 2014 and 2016, only 46 new USFs were incorporated into the system (MSPBS, 2017a) whilst estimates of need suggest 1400 USFs would be needed (Ríos, 2014). This shows that health promotion and disease prevention needs to be strengthened and receive more attention and resources.

Tackling strategic risk factors is a challenging but worthwhile investment and is often more cost-effective than waiting to treat people in poor health. Paraguay needs to invest more in health campaigns and programmes to address effectively the most harmful risk factors. To this end, the country needs to reinforce the capacity of its health promotion and disease prevention mechanisms. Some of the key actions include discouraging tobacco smoking and the consumption of harmful substances (including alcohol), encouraging physical activity and more healthy diets, and improving the provision of clean water and sanitation services. Additionally, there are strong economic incentives for the country to address the risk factors associated to mental diseases, harmful environments and road safety (OECD, 2016d).

Among prevention measures, a package of fiscal, regulatory measures and primary care interventions can reduce the entire burden of disease associated with harmful alcohol use. Such strategies would yield yearly savings in health expenditures of between USD PPP 4 and 8 per person (OECD, 2015). Effective policies against harmful drinking include minimum pricing laws and taxation, advertising restrictions including regulations on the labelling of alcohol products, laws restricting driving under the influence, regulations restricting access to alcohol (minimum age, regulation on outlets), pharmacological and psychosocial treatments for alcohol dependence,, education policies on the dangers of harmful drinking, and public-private collaborations to discourage harmful drinking practices.

Box 3.1. Preventive health care: The case of Mexico

Mexico is at the leading edge of what OECD countries are doing in terms of health promotion and public health activities. Its vast array of public health campaigns, advertising restrictions, food labelling and changes to school nutrition programmes are unparalleled and provide a model for other OECD countries to follow. Indeed, Mexico is widely heralded for its ambitious and comprehensive approach to tackling diabetes, high blood pressure and other chronic diseases through public health programmes and public policy. Initiatives have all captured international interest including the Acuerdo Nacional por la Salud Alimentaria, the Consejo Nacional para las Enfermedades Crónicas, the Estrategia Nacional para la Prevención y el Control del Sobrepeso, la Obesidad y la Diabetes (including its most well-known campaign, Chécate Mídete Muévete) as well as constitutional reforms prohibiting unhealthy foods in schools alongside other norms and regulations, clear food labelling and most recently restrictions on advertising unhealthy foods during children's typical television and cinema viewing times.

Source: OECD Reviews of Health Systems: Mexico (OECD, 2016c).

External injuries produce unusually high death rates

Road injuries create a large social and economic burden in Paraguay. Paraguay has the second highest death rate due to traffic accidents in the Americas. This cause has gone from being the third cause of death producing more premature causalities in 2005 to be the second one by 2016, with an increase of 5.8 deaths per 100 000 over that period. By 2016, Paraguay had 24.6 deaths per 100 000 people due to road injuries, while neighbouring countries like Peru and Chile had 13 and 12.7 deaths per 100 000 people, respectively. More than half of the deaths associated to road injuries were due to motorcycle accidents (53.6%), followed by car accidents (24.2%), (MSPBS, 2018).

Although prevalence of road injuries is in line with the average of the region, Paraguay has a higher death rate due to this cause. In particular, in 2016 prevalence of road injuries reached 1 813 cases per 100 000 people and produced 24.6 deaths per 100 000 people.

Latin America and the Caribbean region had a quite similar prevalence of 1 825 cases on average per 100 000 people; but road injuries only produced 19.08 deaths per 100 000 people. This suggests that, although there is a similar prevalence of road injuries, people are more likely to die due to this cause in Paraguay than in the average LAC country.

Interpersonal violence also causes a large number of causalities in Paraguay. It ranks as the ninth main cause of death in the country. Interpersonal violence produced 14.11 deaths per 100 000 people in Paraguay in 2016. This is 8.63 deaths per 100 000 people higher than the average of its neighbouring countries, Argentina, Chile and Uruguay (5.48). Gender violence and in particular domestic violence, remains a challenge in Paraguay. While 4.12% of intentional homicides of men were perpetrated by the victim's partner in 2014, 46.37% of intentional homicides of women were perpetrated by the victim's partner (ONU Mujeres/Ministerio de la Mujer, 2016; Ministerio del Interior, 2015).

The health system in Paraguay is segmented and suffers from weak stewardship

Paraguayan law establishes the right to health. The Paraguayan Constitution of 1992 enshrines the right to health. It states that "*no one shall be deprived of public assistance to prevent or treat illness, pests or plagues*" (Art. 68) and calls for the establishment of a National Health System (Art. 69). This constitutional provision has real effects. Indeed, court orders are regularly sought and often obtained to force specific health service providers to provide care. The national health policy (MSPBS, 2015) sets the objective of *advancing towards universal access to health and achieving universal health coverage at the highest possible level to reduce inequalities in health and improve the quality of life of the population in the framework of sustainable human development".*

The health system consists of the public subsystem, the social security subsystem and the private subsystem. The three subsystems are largely vertically integrated, that is they raise revenue, pool funds and deliver service independently. The public subsystem comprises the Ministry of Health (MSPBS, Ministerio de Salud Pública y Bienestar Social), occupational schemes for the Armed Forces and the Police, the *Hospital de Clínicas* (the teaching hospital of Asunción National University, UNA), and health service provision by local governments, with the MSPBS covering a much larger share of the population than the other providers. Each of these segments of the public subsystem is largely independent of the others. The social security system comprises health insurance and service provision by the social security institute (IPS). Although IPS is a public institution, its governance, funding and coverage are different from that of the public subsystem, which is why it is considered as a separate subsystem. The private subsystem comprises private providers, private insurance companies and private pre-paid medicine firms, most of which deliver care in their own facilities. The various subsystems cover different population groups, mainly based on their employment status and ability to pay. The set of services they provide is not the same and each population segment receives different benefits and quality standards.

Provision of health services has improved in recent years, driven by the increase in public health expenditure. Past governments have made a great effort to increase progressively the allocated public budget to health, with funds to government programmes (excluding social security) going from 1% to 2.7% of the GDP between 2002 and 2015 (WHO, 2018a). New resources have been invested mainly in more hospital infrastructure, equipment and human resources. New vaccines have been incorporated into the basic plan and several programmes have been implemented to improve maternal and neonatal health, improve nutritional outcomes, and intensive therapies (Giménez Caballero, 2013).

There are not enough health facilities to meet the needs of the population. Despite the increased public expenditure in health, the provision of some essential health facilities remains relatively limited, as in the case of hospital beds in the public subsystem. In 2002, the MSPBS had 0.8 hospital beds per 1 000 people. By 2015, this figure remained unchanged (MSPBS, 2016b). Currently, the public subsystem has 5 569 available hospital beds in the country in establishments of the MSPBS, 822 in the teaching hospital of the UNA and 284 in the hospitals of the armed forces and the police, while the IPS and the private subsystem sum 2 076 and 1 914 respectively. The national aggregate is equivalent to a rate of 1.582 hospital beds per 1 000 inhabitants. This is lower than the regional average of two beds per 1 000 inhabitants (Casalí, Cetrángolo and Goldschmit, 2017).

Figure 3.7. Hospital bed density, 2015 or most recent data available

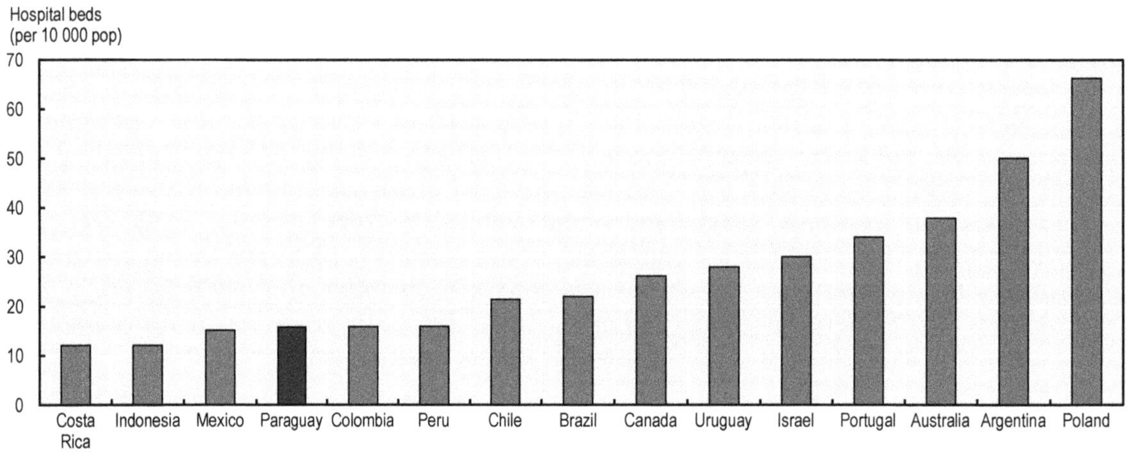

Note: Data relate to 2016 for Paraguay, 2014 for Argentina, Australia, Brazil, Colombia, Peru and Uruguay.
Source: Data for Paraguay is calculated based on PAHO/WHO/MSPBS (2017), DGEEC (2015) and information provided by the health superintendence. Data for Brazil, Costa Rica, Peru, Uruguay and Argentina are from Global Health Observatory (database) (WHO, 2018b). Data for Colombia, Mexico, Chile, Canada, Israel, Portugal, Australia and Poland are from OECD Health Statistics 2017 (database).

StatLink https://doi.org/10.1787/888933823071

There are significant asymmetries across regions in the range of services that are available to meet the health needs of the population. While in Asunción there were 2.1 hospital beds per 1 000 people in 2015, regions such as Alto Paraná or Canindeyú had only 0.3 hospital beds per 1 000 inhabitants. Around 43.8% of the total hospital beds from the private subsystem are located in Asunción, 13.58% are in the Central region, 12.9% in Alto Paraná and 8.6% in Boquerón (Figure 3.8).

Figure 3.8. Available hospital beds in 2016, per region

Hospital beds per 1 000 population

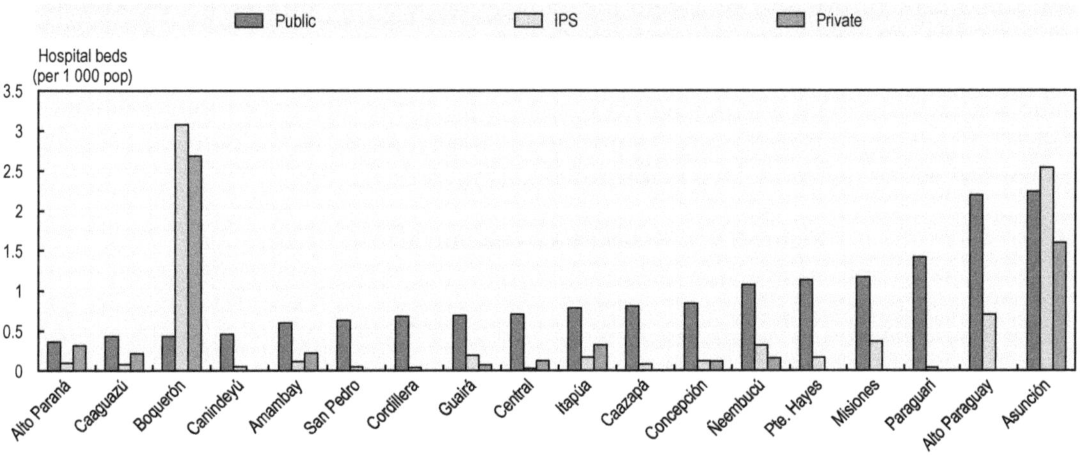

Note: Public subsystem includes only the hospital beds from the Ministry of Public Health and Social Wellbeing. Subsystems can establish agreements to make use of the beds of another subsystem in some regions; therefore, some beds may be counted more than once. Notably, the IPS does not have its own beds in the Boquer6n region, but has agreements with the public and private subsystems to make use of their hospital beds.
Source: Ministry of Public Health and Social Wellbeing (2017).

StatLink https://doi.org/10.1787/888933823090

The health system is segmented and uncoordinated

The social security system provides health insurance to just under 20% of the population.[2] The Social Security Institute (IPS) is a public yet financially autonomous institution in charge of covering active formal workers and their dependants. The IPS is financed through employee and employer contributions. It provides medical attention, as well as recovery and rehabilitation services (Casalí, Cetrángolo and Goldschmit, 2017). Additionally, it is responsible for supplying medicines and prostheses to its beneficiaries and paying social security subsidies related to health (i.e. due to work leaves and accidents). Most contributors to IPS are also covered by IPS for old age and disability. Around 18.46% of the population respond that they rely primarily on the coverage of IPS as their main health services provider when asked in the main national household survey (DGEEC, 2017). IPS faces some uncertainty regarding its actual coverage due to dependants not being systematically enrolled and enrolling only when requesting services. Nevertheless, in practice only around 13% of the population resorts[3] to medical attention provided by the IPS (Figure 3.9).

The private subsector offers health insurance to wealthier households but private services are also used by the middle class. In the private subsector, there are medical insurance companies and health services providers that deliver mostly services related to recovery and rehabilitation (Casalí, Cetrángolo and Goldschmit, 2017). The private subsystem is made up of for-profit entities and non-profit entities. The latter include the Red Cross, which receives financial support from the Ministry of Health, as well as cooperatives, which operate hospitals in the Chaco region and the department of San Pedro. Among the for-profit entities, there are pre-paid medical insurance companies, clinics, institutes and private laboratories that provide health services and independent professionals. For-profit entities comprise more than 150 institutions that provide health services (medical centres, sanatoriums, hospitals) and more than 70 health provision units from pre-paid medicine companies (Oficina Comercial de Chile en Paraguay – ProChile, 2017; Superintendencia de Salud, 2017). Around 6.1% of the population rely on private health insurance. Beneficiaries of the private subsector are mainly formal and informal workers who pay for health insurance, including employees of the state, who cannot be covered by IPS. In practice, around 15% of the population resorts to private medical attention. Although the better off are more likely to rely on private medical care, there are users of the private subsystem across the entire income distribution (Figure 3.9).

Figure 3.9. Last health service provider by deciles

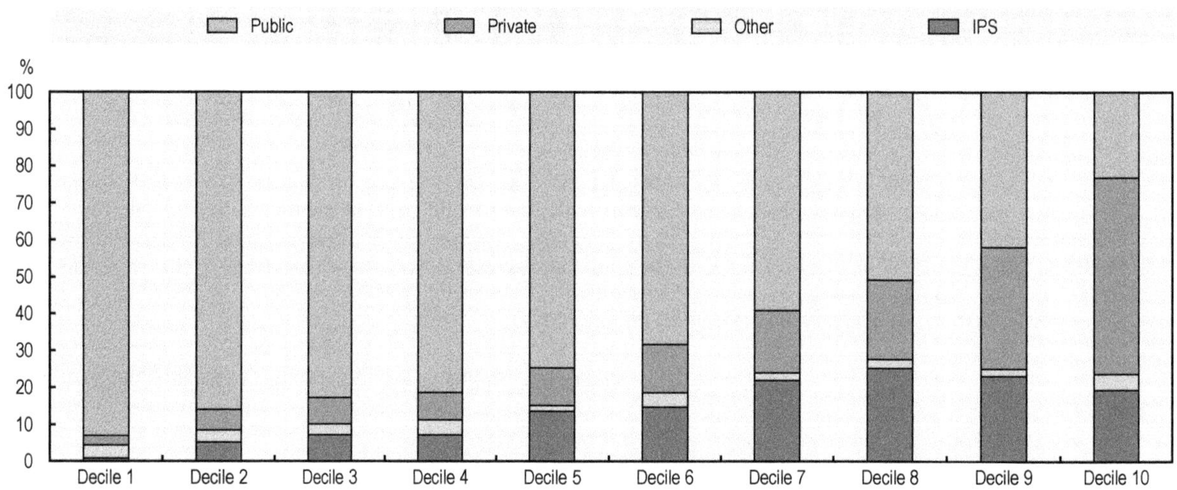

Note: Service providers based on the declared health provider that attended the illness or injury in the past 90 days.
Source: Paraguay Permanent Household Survey 2016 (DGEEC, 2017).

StatLink https://doi.org/10.1787/888933823109

The public subsystem is the largest health service provider in the country. The public subsystem is in charge of two different population segments. Firstly, the hospitals and other service provision units of the Ministry of Public Health and Social Welfare and the hospital of the National University of Asunción are in charge of covering the general population, homeless, some informal workers, unemployed people, and their dependants. Secondly, the hospitals of the Public Forces (Military, and Police Hospitals) are in charge of covering military and police workers and their dependants. Around 74% of the population is not covered by any health insurance and therefore rely entirely on the services provided by the public subsystem. Public health services institutions not only provide recovery and rehabilitation services but also most of the actions towards health promotion and protection in the health system (Casalí, Cetrángolo and Goldschmit, 2017). In practice, around 66.77% of the population resorts[3] to medical attention provided by the public subsystem.

The public subsystem also covers procedures and conditions not covered by other subsystems. In Paraguay, all citizens have the right to medical attention. The public subsystem must provide services without any type of discrimination, and based on the principles of equity, quality, efficiency and social participation. This means that the public subsystem must provide services to any person, including individuals covered primarily by other subsystems. For this reason, the public subsector incurs additional residual expenditures for providing medical procedures not covered by private insurance, which are generally related to pre-existing and congenital conditions, psychiatric diseases, accidents and sexually transmitted infections, among other coverage exemptions (Figure 3.10). In practice the public subsystem also provides care to people insured by IPS (Figure 3.10). The two institutions have agreements at the local level for joint provision of care in certain localities.

Figure 3.10. Insurance coverage and last health service provider, 2016

Service provider used, by main insurance held

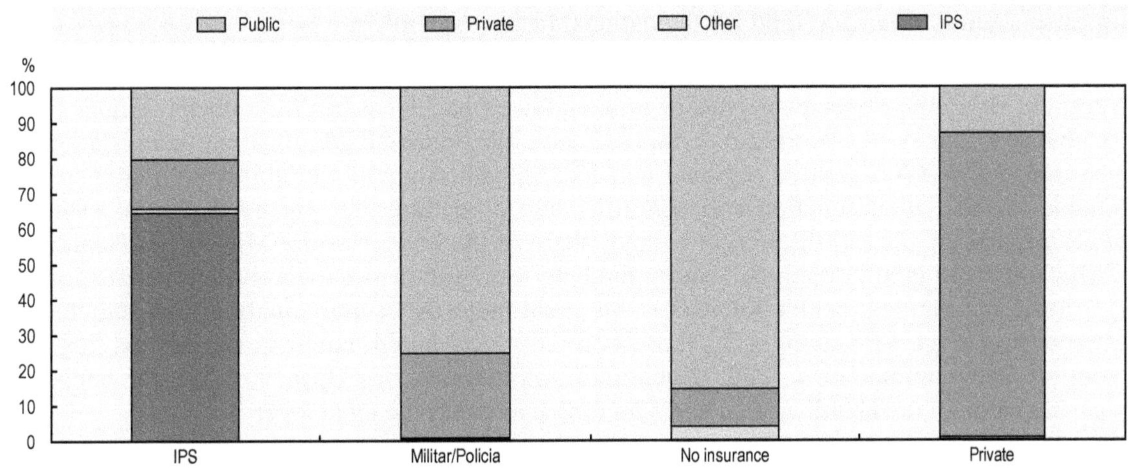

Note: Insurance coverage refers to the main insurance held, while service providers indicate the service provider to which they went. This graph is based on individuals that received healthcare during the last 90 days.
Source: Paraguay Permanent Household Survey 2016 (DGEEC, 2017).

StatLink https://doi.org/10.1787/888933823128

A series of reforms failed to usher in a meaningful transformation of the health system

The adoption of Law 1032 in 1996 was a landmark in the formation of the health system in Paraguay. Law 1032 stipulated that the health sector would be organised as a National Health System and provided the legal basis for a series of governance institutions to ensure health service delivery. According to the law primary healthcare programmes and strategies are the foundation for extending coverage. The law also establishes decentralisation as a key principle, and calls for the implementation of total quality control throughout the system.

According to the law, the governance of the health system rests on the shoulders of the National Health Council. The National Health Council (*Consejo Nacional de Salud*) is a consultation and co-ordination body with representatives from across the sector and is responsible for promoting the national health system, design health programmes, participate in policymaking in the health domain and monitor the implementation of health policy. It is assisted by a smaller Executive Committee that is responsible for managing the national health system and its budget. The Executive Committee is supported by a Medical Directorate responsible for regulation of services, a national health fund responsible for financing policy and a Health Superintendence responsible for accreditation, certification and quality control. Law 1032 also set the basis for the creation of regional and local councils mirroring the national council to take on systemic functions at the local level.

The implementation of the reform has been partial even to this day. The National Health Council has not met in ordinary sessions since its creation. The technical and financial bodies to support the national council were never created, nor was the National Health Fund established in practice (Giménez Caballero, 2013). Indeed, the law creating FONACIDE allocates 10% of FONACIDE resources to the national health fund. However, it also redefines the purpose of the fund, giving it much narrower scope than the original law and establishing project finance logic, whilst the original intent was to create a central financing fund for the national health system[4].

Law 1032 and subsequent reforms have achieved greater decentralisation of the health system. By 2008, fewer than 10% of municipalities had local health councils (Giménez Caballero, 2013). A reform of Law 1032 and of financial administration legislation carried out in 2006 granted regional and local health councils the ability to administer funds to fulfil their function and simplified the procedures for financial control. This reform, and the decentralisation of a small share of the budget of the Ministry of Health, which is distributed through an "equity fund" to local authorities incentivised the creation of local and regional health councils in the great majority of municipalities and regions. According to MSPBS authorities, there were 250 local health councils at year-end 2017 out of 260 municipalities. This decentralisation process has opened space for social participation in the health system and for co-ordination at the local level.

The full implementation of the reforms undertaken since 1996 requires a broad agreement on a future vision for the health sector in Paraguay. Although there has been progress in setting up integrated health networks in certain areas, a number of key governance provisions in the 1996 reform and subsequent reforms face strong opposition. The fact that the Paraguayan health system is a mixture of models, with different values and with significant vested interests makes reform difficult without a national consensus on the way forward. More recently, the emphasis on primary healthcare and the integration at the local level have garnered support and could serve as the basis for a national dialogue on the future of health.

Stewardship and quality control remain weak

The stewardship of the health authority in Paraguay needs to be reinforced. The stewardship role fall to the Ministry of Public Health and Social Welfare (MSPBS). However, its stewardship role is weak in practice. The fragmentation of the health system, with different modalities for financing, regulation, enrolment, and service delivery makes stewardship particularly challenging. For example, the framework for the oversight of the market for pharmaceutical products is relatively well developed (MSPBS/OPS/WHO, 2014). Centralised purchasing allows the MSPBS to obtain medicines at just under double the international reference price, but citizens pay 13 times the international reference price despite the existence of price controls (MSPBS/PAHO/WHO, 2015). Another example is the regulatory framework for pricing medical services in the private and pre-paid sector, which is outdated and has *de facto* been taken over by associations of medical practitioners.

The organisation and functions of the MSPBS are very broad, which can contribute to diluting its leadership. The MSPBS's primary function is as steward of the national health policy. However, it also has functions in social welfare and citizen's environment. These stem from a holistic view of public health, but in practice result in the MSPBS undertaking functions that overlap with other institutions or that could be located elsewhere in the executive, allowing the MSPBS to concentrate on the difficult task of managing a fragmented system with very many actors. For example, the Ministry is tasked with implementing a national social services system for the most vulnerable segments of the population, an area where multiple institutions act and where stewardship and co-ordination are also weak (see Chapter 2). The Ministry also oversees the sanitation agency (SENASA), and its relatively large investment budget. In practice, while the organisation of the ministry (Decree 21376 of 1998) contemplates a vice-minister overseeing co-ordination and administrative tasks, while the Minister is tasked with the political direction role, most administrative units (human resources, administration and finance) report directly to the minister while the programmatic elements are under the vice-ministry.

The regulatory framework and bodies are weak. The Superintendence of Health is in charge of verifying that the entities providing health services are duly registered and authorised by the MSPBS and that they adequately grant the health and healthcare services regulated by the legislation in force. Furthermore, it is in charge of establishing preventive and systematic monitoring to verify the conditions under which health entities manage their benefits and ensure compliance. In practice, the Superintendence of Health has scarce economic and human resources and little autonomy to undertake its role. As a consequence, regulation on private and public services providers is weak, resulting in asymmetries in the quality across providers and arbitrary clauses of coverage (Giménez Caballero, 2013). There is no regulation specifying, for example, the standard or minimum levels of coverage for private plans or for pre-paid plans provided to state employees, which increases the variability in offers and makes procurement processes more difficult.

Weak stewardship has limited Paraguay's potential in terms of healthcare access and quality. According to the Healthcare Access and Quality Index, the Paraguayan health system scored 60.4 in a scale from 0 (lowest) to 100 (highest) in 2015. However, considering the resources and development status of the country, Paraguay has an untapped potential of 13.6 points in this index for improving personal healthcare access and quality, i.e. the country's target should be 74 (Figure 3.11). This gap has widened in recent decades (8.7 in 1990 to 13.6 in 2015). Overall, Paraguay ranks among the lowest versus benchmark countries. Other international studies also suggest that the population is unhappy with the quality of health services. Fewer than half of Paraguayans (43%) reported being satisfied with the health system, a figure that is below what could be expected given the country's level of economic development. In addition, this satisfaction index has hardly budged relative to its value ten years ago (48% – OECD, 2018). Increasing the profile of quality of care in the institutional framework will be critical to address this growing gap.

Figure 3.11. Personal healthcare access and quality (HAQ) against "best possible", 1990 vs. 2015

HAQ Index is measured on a scale from 0 (lowest) to 100 (highest).

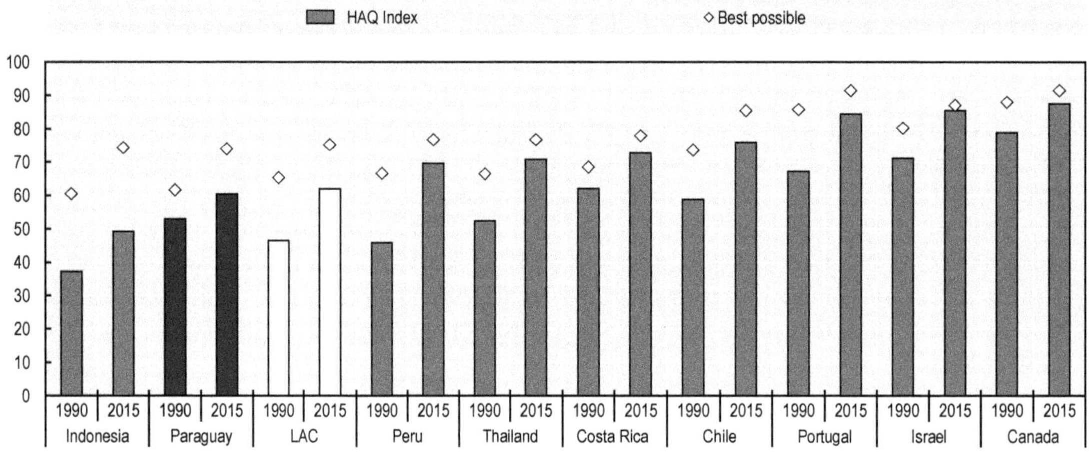

Notes: 1. The Healthcare Access and Quality (HAQ) Index provides a summary measure of personal healthcare access and quality on a scale from 0 (lowest) to 100 (highest). This measure is based on risk-standardised mortality rates from causes that, in the presence of high-quality healthcare, should not result in death.
2. "Best possible" represents the highest personal healthcare and access achieved at a given level of development. The gap between the HAQ Index and "best possible" represents how much untapped potential exists for improving personal healthcare access and quality given a location's resources and development status.
Source: Healthcare Access and Quality Index 2015 (GBD 2015 Healthcare Access and Quality Collaborators, 2017).

StatLink https://doi.org/10.1787/888933823147

A lengthy transition towards an integrated health network based on Primary Healthcare

Integrated health services delivery networks aim to tackle the major challenges posed by the fragmentation of Paraguayan health services. Fragmentation is a major cause of poor performance of health services and systems, since it has a rash of consequences: limited access to services, delivery of services of poor technical quality, irrational and inefficient use of available resources, unnecessary increases in production costs, and low user satisfaction with services received (PAHO, 2010). Furthermore, fragmentation in the financing schemes often lead to insufficient financing that impedes the effective delivery of health services. In this regard, the concept of 'integrated health services delivery networks' intends to reshape health systems to ensure the provision of equitable, comprehensive, integrated, and continuous health services to the entire population. This concept seeks to promote, preserve and/or restore the health of individuals and the community as a whole (PAHO, 2010).

Paraguay has undertaken reforms to shift from a pyramidal structure to a network model based on primary healthcare, but the change has not yet fully materialised. Past legal reforms have introduced new norms to gradually reshape the system towards an integrated health services network based on primary healthcare. In a network model, vertical relationships based on technological densities or levels of care are replaced by horizontal polycentric networks (Vilaça Mendes, 2011). This adjustment implies that, despite the different levels of healthcare and of technological complexity amongst actors in the health system, each one plays an essential role in providing adequate healthcare. Consequently, the size of the allocated budget in a network model is not necessarily proportional to the level of complexity of the services offered by each healthcare institution. Quite the opposite, primary healthcare plays a central role in the network since it is the gateway to the health system and manages the continuity of care (i.e. co-ordinating health service bodies that provide more complex care). In practice, the new legal framework in Paraguay has not managed to effectively transform the health system.

The role of primary healthcare is essential for ensuring the continuity of care throughout the system. The role of primary healthcare units within the network includes creating the links and transfers with specialised, emergency and hospital healthcare, depending on the complexity required. In a nutshell, the different actors within the healthcare network in Paraguay are primary healthcare (family health units); specialised healthcare (specialist outpatient centres); hospital healthcare (basic, general and specialised hospitals); complementary services (pharmaceutical assistance, health surveillance, rehabilitation and diagnostic support); and the subsystem of medical regulation, communication and transportation (*Sistema de Emergencias Médicas Extrahospitalarias*, SEME) (Instituto Suramericano de Gobierno en Salud, 2012). SEME is responsible both for emergency response and for the referral of patients to higher levels of care. The latter enables in practice the interaction of all actors in the network. Health facilities offering high complexity care are mostly concentrated in Asunción and the Central Department, while primary healthcare units are intended to be located across the entire national territory and cover all Paraguayans.

Paraguay has made efforts to strengthen primary healthcare provision through the creation of Family Health Units. Primary healthcare in Paraguay is mostly provided through the Family Health Units (USF) and through health centres of the IPS. USFs are intended to be the entry point to the health system and rely on a community-based approach. They are responsible for providing services to address and resolve most health problems in their assigned social territory (covering 3 500 to 5 000 people). The system thus provides free access to health services to a larger share of the population (Instituto Suramericano de Gobierno en Salud, 2012).

The development of USFs has led to a significant increase in access to health and better integration of health service delivery within the public sector. The establishment of USFs was originally guided by geographical targeting of the most underserved areas. This resulted in a significant increase in access to health. The establishment of USFs also led to a more integrated approach to care, instead of a vertical approach where different staff members are in charge of specific programmes (vaccination, reproductive health, specific diseases, etc.). This integration has been found by evaluations of the USF programme to be more difficult where USFs are larger (Monroy Peralta et al., 2011).

The process of reorganising the health system around primary care is still ongoing and should be accelerated. Between 2008 and 2016, the Ministry of Public Health and Social Wellbeing built around 800 new Family Health Units (USF) under the primary healthcare strategy (MSPBS, 2017a). However, estimations suggest that Paraguay needs around 1 400 Family Health Units (Ríos, 2014), which points to the sizeable gap that needs to be addressed in the upcoming years. In terms of financial resources, the share of the health budget distributed to regions for primary healthcare has remained stagnant, from 26% of the total budget of the MSPBS in 2006 to 27% in 2014 (MH, 2018). However, the primary healthcare strategy relies on a network approach and therefore budgetary information by area may understate actual resources available for primary care. For example, significant resources channelled through programmes rather than functions are also devoted to primary care. However, the lack of political leadership, as well as the lack of tools and institutional mechanisms for the decided implementation of the reorganisation of the health system has resulted in the stagnation of this overhaul.

Inefficient information management limits the available evidence base and continuity of care

A thorough record of the country's vital statistics is essential for identifying health needs and outlining assertive policies. A well-functioning civil registration and vital statistics (CRVS) system should register all births and deaths, issue birth and death certificates, and compile and disseminate vital statistics, including cause of death information. Ideally, it should also contain breakdown information of data by sex, age, place of residence, ethnic origin, and other relevant variables. This information is an essential tool for governments to respond to the healthcare needs of the population.

Figure 3.12. Under-registration of vital statistics, 2001-16

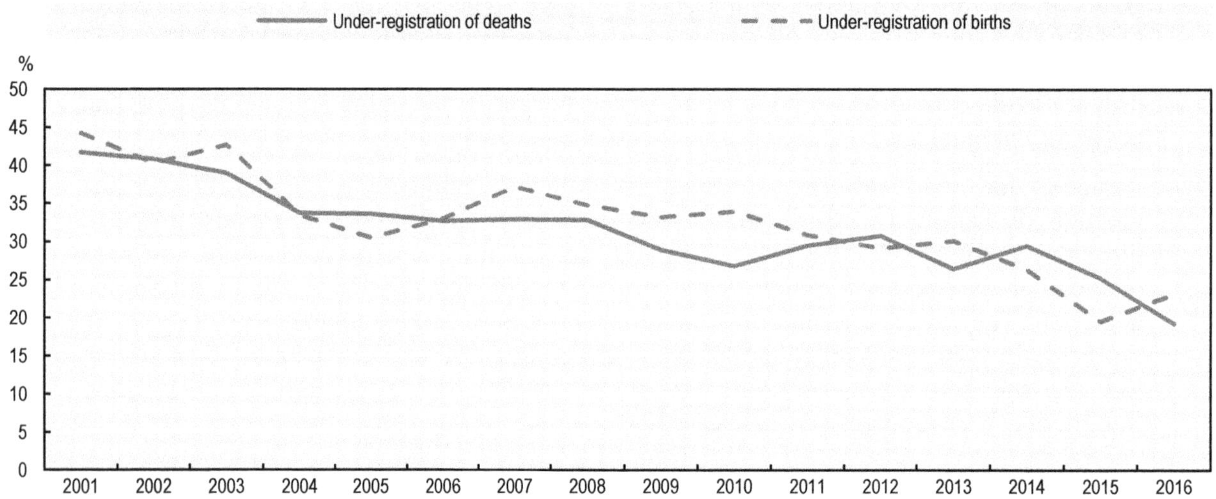

Note: Under-registration is calculated as estimated minus reported values divided by estimated value.
Source: Paraguay Vital Statistics Information Subsystem (MSPBS, 2018).

StatLink https://doi.org/10.1787/888933823166

Although under-registration has been addressed over the last decade, it remains high. In 1991, the Ministry of Health created a database containing vital statistics and information on provision of services. The vital statistics system is the most developed, as it covers the entire health system. This system has been going through a modernization process that aims to provide a computerized system based on internet networks (Dullak et al., 2011). In particular, the Biostatistics Department has worked in co-ordination with the Civil Registry and the Directorate General of Statistics, Surveys and Censuses (DGEEC) to reduce under-registration of deaths and births as part of the redesign of vital statistics (Mancuello and Cabral de Bejarano, 2011). A specific effort to identify maternal deaths has also contributed to reducing under-registration of both maternal deaths and live births.

As a result, under-registration of births has fallen remarkably (from 44.2% to 23.1% between 2001 and 2016). In addition, under-registration of deaths fell significantly over the same period (Figure 3.12). Nevertheless, both indicators reflect that around one fifth of births and deaths are not documented in Paraguay. In contrast, countries such as Argentina, Brazil and Chile register 99.5%, 95.9% and 99.4% of births respectively (WHO, 2018).

Most statistical information systems in health are scattered and segmented. In the Ministry of Health, information is collected separately by different programmes, which leads to duplication and increases the administrative burden on health professionals. According to officials from the Ministry of Health, doctors in USFs spend as much as a quarter of their working time filling out reporting forms. While an electronic recording system exists, limited connectivity makes online access to databases impractical and often counterproductive. Increasing the connectivity of health facilities by purchasing internet services through public tender would help alleviate this problem. In the short term, methods that allow for offline information provision would be more adapted to the current circumstances. In the private sector, the Superintendence of Health receives a significant amount of information from private providers but lacks the capacity to produce statistics on the basis of that information.

An efficient management of health information is necessary to ensure continuity in healthcare. Medical records form an essential tool for the continuity of patients' care, as they contain key information about their health and treatment. Moreover, medical records can potentially be used in the management and planning of healthcare facilities and services, for medical research and the production of healthcare statistics. In Paraguay, the management of patient information is undertaken independently by each health service provider using mostly non-electronic procedures. Within the ministry of health, records are not systematically shared between primary and other levels of care. These mechanisms hinder the transfer of patients' information between one institution and another. This is mainly reflected in the hundreds of transfers made from primary healthcare institutions to institutions that offer greater healthcare complexity.

Box 3.2. Taking stock of the evidence – from data use to health system improvement

There is a very large and growing body of evidence of the importance of the collection, analysis, linkage and reporting of results from personal health data assets for health care quality monitoring and improvement, population health policy, and health system performance measurement and evaluation. Many countries are benefiting from the linkage of personal health data to follow the pathway of care and understand health outcomes of care in order to evaluate the quality and effectiveness of health care treatments.

The PERFECT study in Finland monitors the content, quality and cost-effectiveness of treatment episodes in specialised medical care and thus contributes to monitoring health system performance. The methodology developed for PERFECT is now having an impact on monitoring among other countries throughout Europe.

Korea's quality assessment of medical services includes assessment of the clinical appropriateness and cost effectiveness of health care by reporting on quality and inducing service providers to make improvements in response to the evidence. It aims to identify underuse, overuse and misuse of therapies and to reduce variation in care practices through the regular reporting of quality indicators.

There are also quality and efficiency assessments of clinical care guidelines in Sweden. For areas of care subject to national guidelines, such as cardiac and stroke care, care for selected cancers, dental care, diabetes care and mental health care, data linkages are undertaken to develop indicators in order to evaluate the effectiveness of recommended therapies. The evidence contributes to revisions of care guidelines.

To monitor and study health care consumption and expenditures, Belgium has developed a permanent sample of socially insured persons via the linkage of health care reimbursement invoice data to create longitudinal histories of health care encounters. Results inform policy decisions to manage health care expenditures.

Source: Strengthening Health Information Infrastructure for Health Care Quality Governance: Good Practices, New Opportunities and Data Privacy Protection Challenges (OECD, 2013).

Funding for health has increased but significant challenges remain

Financial resources for health insurance and provision in Paraguay come from multiple sources. Financial flows largely mirror the fragmentation of the health service provision system. Revenues for the care of different population groups are raised through separate systems, including public funding, social security contributions, pre-paid health plans and out-of-pocket expenditure. Funds are held in separate pools, with little or no potential for pooling risk and cross-subsidies across segments. Despite ongoing efforts to increase public spending on health, funding remains insufficient and inequitable. Furthermore, given that out-of-pocket expenditure represents a primary source of funding, a significant portion of the population in Paraguay is at risk of catastrophic health expenditure.

Despite a remarkable increase in public funding, challenges for financing health remain sizeable

Spending on health in Paraguay is relatively high as a share of GDP. Total health expenditure in Paraguay stood at 7.8% of GDP in 2015 (WHO, 2018a). This is lower than the OECD average of 8.9% of GDP but markedly higher than health expenditure in more developed countries in the Latin America region. Health expenditure per capita in 2015 was USD 724 PPP. While this is much smaller than the OECD average of USD 3 851 PPP, it is higher than expenditure in richer countries, like Peru or Thailand (Figure 3.13).

Health expenditure has increased considerably in the past 15 years, driven by the increase in public health expenditure. Expenditure on government health programmes grew from 1% to 2.7% between 2002 and 2015 (WHO, 2018a). This period coincides with the strengthening of primary care within the MSPBS and with the elimination of co-payments and user fees in the MSPBS' provision of services. In spite of this, out-of-pocket payments' growth rate is on par with that of GDP (Figure 3.14).

Figure 3.13. Health expenditure per capita in 2015

Current USD PPP

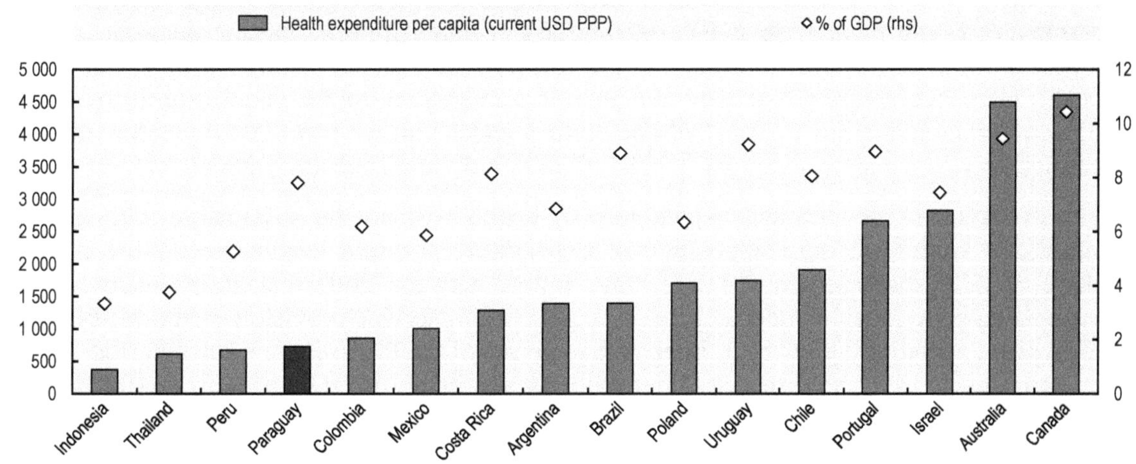

Source: Global Health Expenditure Database (database) (WHO, 2018a).

StatLink https://doi.org/10.1787/888933823185

Figure 3.14. Current health expenditure by financing scheme

Percentage of GDP

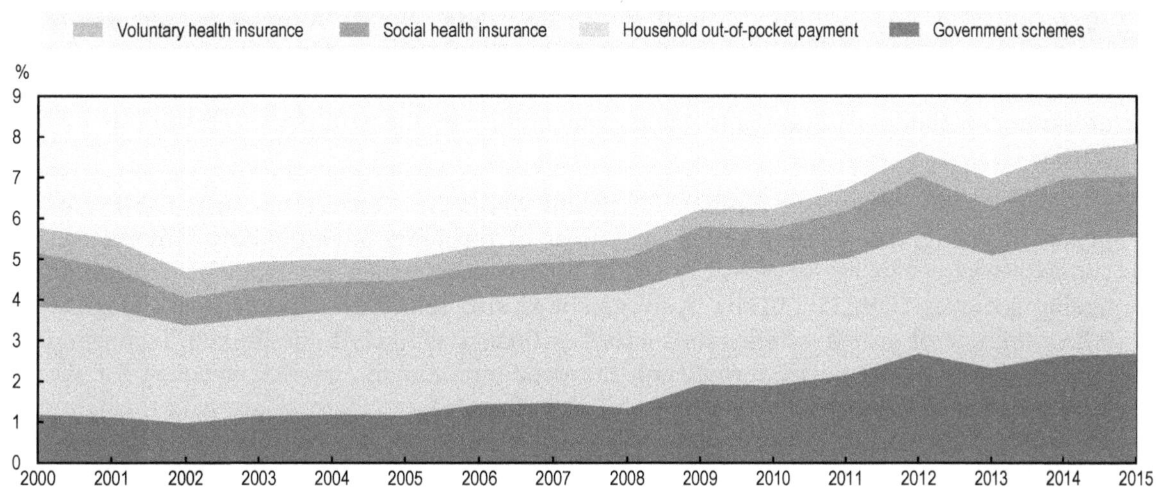

Source: Global Health Expenditure Database (database) (WHO, 2018a).

StatLink https://doi.org/10.1787/888933823204

Prepayment schemes are sizeable in Paraguay due in part to the reliance of civil servants on private health provision. Indeed, according to its charter, the IPS cannot cover civil servants.[5] Instead, the budget reserves a subsidy of PYG 300 000 (EUR 44.19) per month for each civil servant and employee of the state to finance a private prepaid plan (National Government of Paraguay, 2018). Public bodies can instead pool these funds and offer their staff a pre-agreed plan selected through public tender. This system fosters demand in a sizeable market for private prepaid health insurance. Considering public employees in the central administration alone and excluding those for whom special regimes allow coverage by IPS, potential demand stemming from public institutions and their employees would be as high as PYG 450 billion or about EUR 67 million per year.[6] On the basis of procurement information, the Ministry of Finance estimates the value of health insurance contracts for civil servants and employees of the state to be just over PYG 400 billion for the Central Administration and a further PYG 70 billion for other entities, to which can be added PYG 126 billion in individual subsidy payments.[7]

The evolution of government expenditure in health will not be sustainable without a significant change in the composition of expenditure. Current health expenditure as a share of GDP increased by 2.8 percentage points between 2002 and 2015, led by the increase in government-funded schemes (largely health service provision by the MSPBS) for which expenditure grew by 1.5 percentage points of GDP. During the same period, tax revenues excluding social security contributions as a share of GDP grew from 10.8% to 13.2% (OECD/CIAT/IDB/ECLAC, 2018). Therefore, a continuation in the uptick in health expenditure would imply a significant increase in the share of public expenditure and in the share of public expenditure devoted to health.

Income from the binational dams earmarked for health contributes to finance public health expenditure. The National Fund for Public Investment and Development (FONACIDE) earmarks 10% of the income generated from operating the Itaipú dam for a National Health Fund. In practice, these funds are managed by the Ministry of Health in their entirety. The Ministry of Health also receives funds from FONACIDE directly, which finance both health and sanitation expenditure. The resources channelled through FONACIDE are a relatively small fraction of the Ministry of Health's budget (7.2% in 2016, up from 2.4% in 2015 [Ministerio de Hacienda, 2018]). Moreover, their use is limited to a series of objectives. However, these include purchasing medicines and strengthening facilities. In practice, FONACIDE's funds constitute a significant proportion of the funds devoted to capital expenditure by the Ministry of Health (56% in 2016).

Diversifying the sources of funding for health would help ensure the sustainability of health financing. The diversification in sources of financing is particularly important in contexts where existing sources are likely to decrease, which is certainly the case in ageing societies (OECD, 2016d). However, it is also relevant in the case of Paraguay where the rate of growth of existing sources of finance is likely to be limited. Increasing social security coverage by formalising the economy and by creating avenues for the incorporation of independent workers to the IPS is one way to increase pre-paid financing of health. However, as formalisation typically progresses slowly, raising funds from general taxation for health financing should also be contemplated. Possibilities to be considered in the case of Paraguay also include increasing taxes on goods that generate risks or costs for public health, including tobacco and alcohol, and earmarking part of revenues from these taxes for health financing. Indeed, taxes on tobacco are low in Paraguay compared to the region, representing 18 to 22% of the final price (Giménez Caballero, 2013). In all OECD countries (except the United States), the tax burden on tobacco products is above 50% of the retail price and it is above 80% in ten countries (OECD, 2016a). A recent reform has increased the tax burden on tobacco albeit to levels that remain well below those prevalent in OECD countries. Taxation of alcoholic beverages is also relatively low in Paraguay. They are subject to an 8% to 10% excise tax.

In this case, an increase could be contemplated, possibly reflective of alcohol content, and bearing in mind fiscal practices in commercial partners, especially within Mercosur.

Health financing relies heavily on out-of-pocket expenditure

Funding for health expenditure in Paraguay comes in large part from private sources. Expenditure relies substantially on out-of-pocket expenditure. According to WHO data, out-of-pocket expenditure represented 2.9% of GDP in 2015, accounting for 36% of total health expenditure. Compulsory contributory schemes represented 19% of total health financing. In Paraguay, the bulk of contributory health financing is represented by the IPS, which relies almost exclusively on employee and employer social security contributions.[8] Of these, 9% of declared wages are committed to the Health Fund, which covers health expenditure, maternity and sick leave (Figure 3.15).

Figure 3.15. Health expenditure in Paraguay relies heavily on out-of-pocket payments

Health expenditure by financing scheme, as a percentage of GDP, 2015

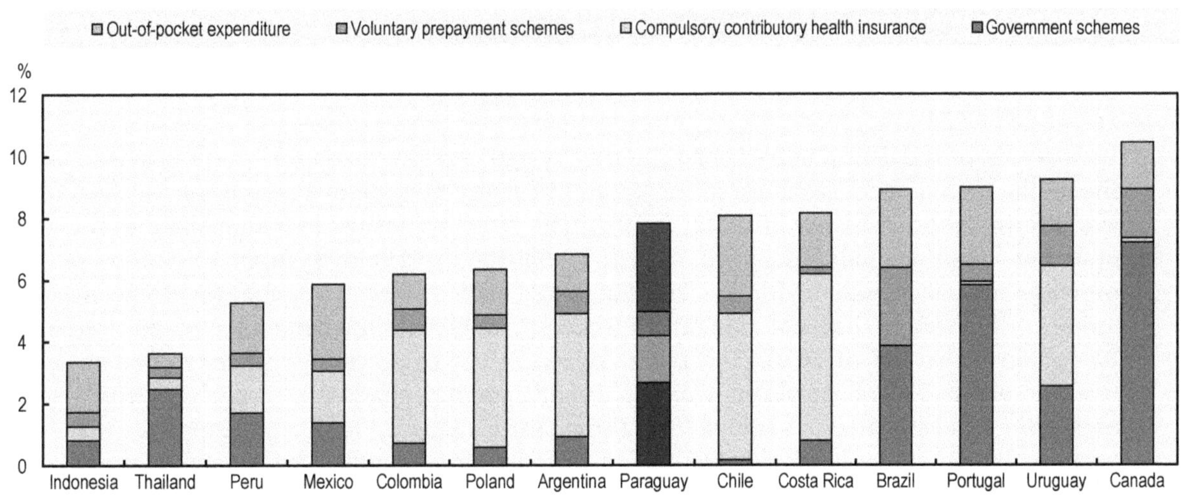

Source: Global Health Expenditure Database (database) (WHO, 2018a).

StatLink https://doi.org/10.1787/888933823223

The large share of out-of-pocket expenditure further tilts the health system towards wealthier individuals. In Paraguay, the poorest decile of the population pays around 7% of the total out-of-pocket expenditure in the system, while the richest quintile spends 15% of total out-of-pocket expenditure (Figure 3.16 Panel A). Although most out-of-pocket expenditures are paid by people not covered by any health insurance (60.8% of total OOP expenditure), significant fractions are paid by people insured by the IPS (21.1%) and by people holding private insurance (17.2%) (Figure 3.16 Panel B). In this regard, the National Development Plan 2030 establishes the reduction of out-of-pocket payments in health as a strategy to combat social exclusion and poverty, by integrating the public and private subsectors to advance towards Universal Health Coverage (National Government of Paraguay, 2014).

Figure 3.16. Payers of the aggregate out-of-pocket health expenditure

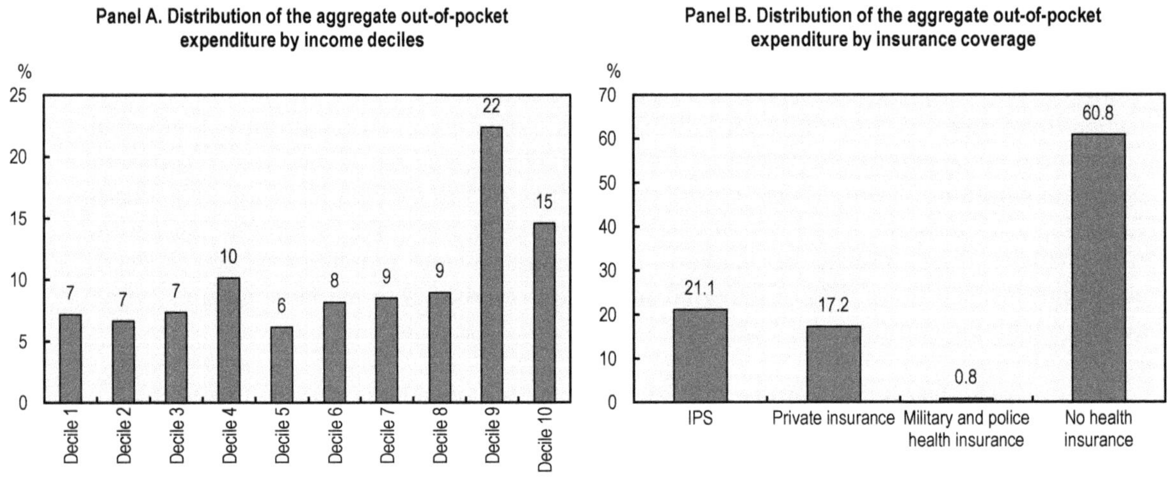

Source: Paraguay Permanent Household Survey 2014 (DGEEC, 2017).

StatLink https://doi.org/10.1787/888933823242

The inability of the contributory social security system to raise funds for health provision reflects the employment structure in Paraguay. As many as 64% of Paraguayan workers have informal jobs. A highly informal employment structure results in a high share of the population being excluded de facto from the contributory health system. IPS offers a voluntary insurance regime for the self-employed and a special regime for domestic workers. The former has not had much success in generating demand and covered 504 people at the end of 2016. The latter covered 19 161 domestic workers as of end-2016, or about 7% of domestic workers in the country. Evasion of social security contributions is estimated to stand at 70% (Giménez Caballero, 2013). IPS estimates that it covers 38.6% of the target population. In this regard, encouraging formalisation and tackling evasion may bring important financing flows to the system.

Paraguay should consider ways of channelling out-of-pocket expenditure to mandatory pre-payment regimes. This step is critical in sustaining health financing and in moving towards Universal Health Coverage in a way that is fairer and more efficient. In OECD countries, this is achieved by the use of significant publicly-funded, pre-payment pools: 6.5% of GDP on average (OECD, 2016d). Indeed, the high level of out-of-pocket expenditure implies limited and inequitable financial protection (see next section). It also implies imbalanced finance and limitations in the degree to which larger expenditures can be planned in advance. Voluntary enrolment leads to self-selection and, as exemplified in Paraguay, is ultimately ineffective. Making enrolment mandatory is a critical step, but must be accompanied by the design of a contribution system that ensures contributions are paid from the public purse for those unable to pay and appropriate means are available for those with the ability to pay to contribute.

Fragmented pooling contributes to systemic inefficiency and inequity

Financial flows reflect the fragmentation of the health system. The public health subsystem, social security and the private subsystem have largely separate revenue raising, pooling and purchasing functions. The public subsystem is financed by the general budget (including earmarked transfers from non-tax income originating from the binational dams) and user fees. Its financing sources coming from the internal public funds (government schemes) are estimated to account for around 34.3% of total health financing. The Social Security Institute (IPS) is entirely financed by social security contributions, mostly made by formal workers. They are estimated to be 19.3% of total health financing. The private subsector is financed by voluntary contributions and co-payments to insurance companies and users' direct payment of specific services. These include pre-paid plans for employees of the state, whether purchased directly by employees, or purchased through public procurement and provided to all staff of a state institution. Voluntary healthcare payments in Paraguay are estimated to account for 9.9% of the total health financing sources. Finally, and crosscutting to all subsystems, out-of-pocket expenditure is estimated to account for around 36.5% of the total financing sources of health in Paraguay (Table 3.2).

The fragmentation of finance pools leads to unequal financing of health needs. The private health insurance subsystem, which covers 6.9% of the population through pre-paid plans, raises 15.5% of prepaid revenues. Social security covers 19.7% of the population but raises 30% of prepaid revenues. Finally, the public subsystem, which covers personnel insured through occupational schemes (policy and military in particular) and those without other coverage, covers the remaining 74% of the population which is uninsured, but only obtains 54% of total prepaid revenues (Table 3.2). Out-of-pocket payments made by the groups covered by the different parts of the health system do not balance finances. In Table 3.2, out-of-pocket payments are calculated as a share of total finance for each group by health coverage. In practice, out-of-pocket payments go largely to the private system, given the elimination of user fees in the Ministry of Health's facilities.

Finance and risk pools are further segmented within systems. Within the public subsystem, the budget for the Ministry of Health is centralised, with a small fraction devolved to departmental and municipal health councils. However, these financing flows are in separate budgets from the military and police systems and from the teaching hospital of the University of Asunción (*Hospital de Clínicas*). IPS pools funds from its beneficiaries (contributing members, their dependants and retirees). The private system is dominated by a few players that own their health provision facilities and which pool pre-payment funds across each firm's client base.

The segmentation of finance leads to unequal, installed capacity to manage health provision. According to available data for 2015, the occupation rate for hospital beds in the public subsystem was 66% across specialised hospitals and 45% in other facilities. The largest facilities of the Ministry of Health and the IPS (respectively the *Hospital Nacional* and *Hospital Central*) had occupation rates of 88% and 85% respectively. In practice, this means certain services were operating at full capacity. For example, the general internal medicine service, the neonatology service and the urology service were operating at full capacity through 2014 in the IPS Central Hospital (DGEEC, 2015). In contrast, the occupation rate in the Armed Forces Hospital was 26%, and that of the Police Hospital was 46%. This imbalance is also visible in intensive care units, where private health facilities have 241 beds while the Ministry of Health had 307 beds at end-2016 even though to the latter provides services to about ten times as many people (MSPBS, 2017b).

The imbalance in funding also reinforces territorial inequality in health service provision. All parts of the health system have a significant proportion of their installed capacity in

Asunción and the surrounding Central department, and in Ciudad del Este, the country's second largest city. However, this concentration is even higher for IPS and the private subsystem than for the Ministry of Health.

Table 3.2. Sources of health financing, 2015

Millions of PYG (share of total health financing in parenthesis)

	Segment of population		Prepaid revenues		Out-of-pocket payments
Public subsystem	People without health insurance	72.6%	Government financing schemes (public funds)	3 812 610 (34.3%)	2 465 854 (22.2 %)
	Beneficiaries of military and police health service	1.4%			33 809 (0.3%)
Social security subsystem	People insured by the social security health scheme	19.7%	Compulsory contributory health insurance schemes	2 143 121 (19.3%)	856 143 (7.7%)
Private subsystem	People insured by private health insurance	6.3%	Voluntary health care payment schemes	1 097 122 (9.9%)	697 286 (6.3%)
		100%		**7 052 853 (63.5%)**	**4 051 509 (36.5%)**
			Total health financing	**11 104 362 (100%)**	

Note: The out-of-pocket payments presented in the right column correspond to any payment to health service providers made by the population segment identified in the column to the left (most of these payments are made to private health service providers). Distributions of population and aggregate out-of-pocket expenditure have been calculated based on the individually-declared main health service provider in 2014 (DGEEC, 2017).
Source: Global Health Expenditure Database (WHO, 2018a) and Paraguay Permanent Household Survey 2014 (DGEEC, 2017).

Risk pooling ensures equity and protects individuals from the financial risk associated with their healthcare needs. By pooling risk the high-cost, infrequent health expenditures can be funded and the cost of high frequency, low cost events can be spread across individuals. It therefore has two key roles: spreading the financial burden between high-risk and low-risk individuals and between high-income and low-income individuals (Gottret and Schieber, 2006). In Paraguay, there are no cross-subsidies among subsystems and pools since the revenues for the healthcare of different population groups are held in separate pools. In practice, coverage by one system or another is largely determined by income levels, with the wealthy opting for pre-paid private insurance, the IPS covering some of them and a fraction of the middle class, while the others are left to the residual coverage of the Ministry of Health.

Shifting health insurance for civil servants and employees of the state to IPS would contribute to consolidating service and finance. At present, IPS can only cover civil servants under special regimes, which exist for teachers in the Ministry of Education and Culture and for personnel of the Office of the Public Prosecutor. The capacity of IPS to provide service to a significantly larger fraction of the population would have to be considered. To that end, the transition could be gradual and be of course accompanied by the relevant contribution transfers.

In the long run, Paraguay should consider options to merge risk pools or create a system that allows for transfers across risk pools. The current system in Paraguay presents characteristics of several models. Health financing models can be broadly classified into national health services, social insurance and private insurance (Gottret and Schieber, 2006). In practice, each of the three main subsystems in Paraguay follows one of these models. Countries with success in advancing universal health coverage have used one of these models as the basis for reform, as the examples of Colombia, Costa Rica, Korea or Thailand show.

In the short run, Paraguay can establish financing mechanisms to cover key contingencies. Certain contingencies are insufficiently covered by existing insurance pools and could benefit from a pooling system that allows the separation of funds' pooling and purchasing functions. The coverage of high complexity treatment, for example, is limited to certain pre-paid private plans. Moreover, pre-paid private health insurance typically does not cover pre-existing conditions and in some cases does not provide continuous coverage for chronic conditions (e.g. dialysis). In 2016, IPS established a system to exclude new affiliates with pre-existing conditions in an attempt to curb the enrolment of individuals with costly conditions under fictitious employment contracts. Coverage for treatment and rehabilitation of victims of road accidents could also be financed by a pooled fund. In both cases, such a fund would receive contributions from both the general budget (to cover those individuals who are unable to pay) and contributions channelled through their insurance (for those individuals covered by IPS or private insurance).

A fund for high-complexity care was created on paper but never implemented. The National Fund of Solidarity Resources for Health (FONARESS, *Fondo Nacional de Recursos Solidarios para la Salud*) was created by law 4392 in 2011. It established a fund to finance treatments for high-complexity conditions (renal insufficiency, transplants, heart disease and cancer) for those without "*the necessary cover from a private, public or mixed insurance scheme*". The fund is to be financed by a transfer from the firms that manage the two binational dams (Yacyretá and Itaipú), an annual contribution from the general budget, a share of taxes on alcoholic beverages and tobacco products and a share of unclaimed lottery winnings. The regulations for the fund created a number of bodies to oversee its implementation in particular an Executive Committee for the Fund, but the fund was never implemented.

The implementation of FONARESS with a diversified revenue source could establish a pooled fund for high-complexity care. The current wording of the law is open to interpretation as to who would benefit from financing, and the resources for the fund are all from the public purse. In practice, private insurers and IPS could act as revenue collectors and feed the fund, while adjusting their financial provisions as cover for the specific set of conditions would be financed through FONARESS, however that would require a legislative reform.

Ultimately, adequate financing for health will require Paraguay to establish financing mechanisms with broader service coverage, which could be achieved by reforming FONARESS if it is implemented. In order to fund a well-defined, comprehensive benefit package, FONARESS could be reformed or replaced by a fund that also covers primary and secondary care. As it currently stands, the implementation of FONARESS risks maintaining and even reinforcing segmentation in risk pools, as FONARESS does not allow pooling of the most common risks. Indeed, the analysis of health expenditures in the next section shows that hospitalisation and high-complexity treatment are not the main cause of financial hardship linked to health.

Purchasing should be separated from service provision to open pathways for greater efficiency

Service provision largely follows financing lines with a few exceptions. The majority of health services are provided within the various segments of the health system. The Ministry of Health and the UNA teaching hospital rely on public funds and provide service in their own facilities. Likewise, IPS delivers service primarily in its own health provision units. All large players in the private health insurance market also provide service in their own facilities or through doctors in their networks. This is in contrast with health systems where institutions raising revenue or pooling funds purchase health services for their beneficiaries, possibly from their own health provision units, but also from other private or public providers in the health system.

Institutional agreements between IPS and the Ministry of Health for the purchase of services from each other contribute to lowering fragmentation. One such agreement concerns the exchange of medicines and medical supplies whereby each institution provides medicines or supplies to the other on the basis of need, and the balance is cleared periodically. The amounts exchanged are relatively small: according to an audit by the Comptroller General's Office, in 2010, the exchanges amounted to about 0.1% of the IPS's budget for medical supplies (Contraloría General de la República, 2010). IPS and the Ministry of Health also have agreements for the provision of services in specific geographical areas. IPS lists 39 such agreements, most of which are for primary care and two for hospital care (IPS, 2016). One such case is the municipality of Ayolas, in the Misiones region. Services there are provided in a joint facility (owned by IPS). In practice, personnel from each institution is assigned to the facility and the director is employed by both institutions. Each institution maintains their own pharmaceutical stock and delivers drugs separately.

Both IPS and the Ministry of Health purchase services from the private sector. IPS outsources care through contracts with the private sector in certain areas, in particular in the Chaco and the department of Caaguazú. IPS and the Ministry of Health also use private providers for certain services, including dialysis, medical imaging and the referral of patients for emergency or intensive care when there are no available beds in the relevant area.

Differences in cost models are an obstacle to further integration at the point of delivery. Without a clear schedule of costs for compensation between institutions, interinstitutional agreements set compensation on an *ad hoc* basis, for example setting the compensation value at the price established before the elimination of co-payments in the Ministry of Health (see e.g. MSPBS/IPS [2013]). In practice these cost schedules are likely to be outdated, as user fees were eliminated in 2008, which would dissuade actors from cooperating. Costs for provision in the private sector are bound by a minimum per act set by law, which the Ministry of Health has the responsibility to update. The law sets minima in "medical units", but the price of a unit has not been updated since 1974 (República de Paraguay, 1974). In practice therefore, fees are set by specialists' associations in the medical profession, with private health providers effectively competing on the quality of their management and the diversification of the services offered.

Within the public sector, differences in the benefit package also limit integration at the point of delivery. For example, since IPS and the Ministry of Health use different lists of essential drugs that are provided free of cost, they manage separate stocks even when service provision is unified through interinstitutional agreements. Integrating service will require unifying benefit packages, possibly by identifying a common core package that can be extended over time or for certain categories.

Institutional agreements between IPS and the MSPBS need to be reviewed and a general framework established. On top of differences in cost management models, interinstitutional agreements also present practical problems linked to the difference in benefit schedules and the management of resources. These result in low levels of enforcement for these agreements in particular in terms of compensatory financial flows. Given that the list of medicines covered by IPS and the MSPBS are not identical and that procurement is done through separate channels, they typically have two pharmacies even in shared facilities. Human resource management is also an issue. Medical personnel in Paraguay often have multiple employers and in some cases it has been documented that personnel in shared facilities were being paid by both institutions, which raises issues of fairness and control.

Budgeting and purchasing do not provide incentives to increase efficiency, quality or value for money. In the largest providers of healthcare, namely the public and the social security subsystem, budgeting is established year on year on the basis of past commitments. As it is not linked explicitly to existing capacity, population coverage, costs or outputs, it does not provide incentives for cost-containment. In the Ministry of Health, in practice, a significant proportion of the budget for care provision (31%) is channelled through programmatic instruments rather than as a budget for specific units or health regions. Of these, 50% or PYG 376 million correspond to medicines and other inputs, which are purchased centrally.

In the short to medium term, generalising the use of interinstitutional agreements and introducing new methods of provider payment would help limit fragmentation at the point of delivery and rationalise the use of resources. A more intensive use of interinstitutional agreements would enhance prioritisation of capital expenditure in the expansion of service provision, by rationalising supply. This means that the providers of health services to the public from the public sector (IPS, Ministry of Health, Hospital de Clínicas) must agree on framework conditions for such agreements. In practice, better cost management within each of the service providers would help set reasonable compensation levels, whether they are fee for service, capitation payments for certain types of attention (e.g. primary care) or other mechanisms.

Box 3.3 Overcoming fragmentation: The case of Colombia

Overcoming fragmentation is a key challenge to increase health expenditure efficiency. Colombia has made important efforts to have a more integrated health system where all sectors of the population can have equal access to a common basket of health services.

Health insurance and health care services in Colombia were historically provided by a fragmented, poorly regulated set of social security institutes and private enterprises, which has largely benefited wealthier Colombians. By 1993, health coverage only extended to 24% of the population and was highly unequal: while 47% of the richest quintile had health insurance, only 4.3% in the poorest quintile enjoyed financial protection from excessive health expenditure.

In 1993, Law 100 brought about far-reaching reforms by creating the Sistema General de Seguridad Social en Salud (SGSSS, or General System of Social Security in Health). This was a big-bang reform that created a national health system by making health insurance mandatory for all those who could afford it, creating a single national pool for insurance contributions, splitting the purchaser and provider functions, and encouraging competition by allowing individuals to choose their insurer, and allowing insurers to selectively contract with providers. Responsibility for managing the financing and operation of health services was devolved locally, whilst steering and regulatory functions were retained and strengthened centrally, through the creation of new institutions. Crucially, under Law 100 healthcare became a legally enshrined right of citizens, rather than a service dependent on charitable supply.

Individuals become affiliated with the SGSSS through three regimes, namely the contributory regime (CR) for individuals in formal employment, the subsidised regime (SR) for individuals not in formal employment (which historically offered a less generous basket of services than the CR), and the much smaller Special Benefit Regime, which includes the armed forces, teachers, and a state-owned petroleum company. Risk equalisation and cross-subsidy exists both within and across the CR and SR, supporting efficiency and social solidarity. In the CR, employees pay 4% of their income and the employer 8.5% to a fund called the Fondo de Seguridad y Garantía (FOSYGA). Private insurance covers approximately one million individuals and has not increased significantly in the last five years.

Source: OECD Reviews of Health Systems: Colombia (OECD, 2016b).

The mechanisms for purchasing service from the private sector can be made fairer and more responsive. Currently, there is no specific channel for public procurement of medical supplies or services. In practice, this generates a number of problems in the processes. Procurement processes for medical supplies and drugs can take up to six months, which increases difficulties in the management of stocks. One of the reasons for the decentralisation of finance from the Ministry of Health to Local Health Councils is that the latter are not subject to public procurement legislation, which makes them able to purchase services (e.g. maintenance) more quickly. From the supplier side, actors in the private sector consider that the lack of regulation in terms of the benefit package can lead to differences in the quality of offers that are not properly accounted for in the awarding of contracts.

In the long run, the separation of purchasing and service provision can help establish a system in which there is more pooling of funds and risk and better accountability. This reform would imply that when a unit provides service to an individual, it receives payment from the relevant system, be it from the public system if the individual is uninsured or from the relevant social or private insurer if the act is covered by insurance. This payment system would also work within institutions, creating tools and incentives for cost control and management. Reforms to achieve universal health coverage in Colombia (Box 3.3) or Thailand, for example, separated purchasing and service provision functions to create incentives for service provision for all. In Thailand, for example, service delivery units from the public sector receive payments from the contracting authority – based on a closed end capitation payment for outpatient care and diagnostic-related group payment for inpatient care. The split of purchasing and provision helped increase accountability in the system (Tangcharoensathien et al., 2018).

Towards universal health coverage

Universal health coverage (UHC) strives to ensure that all individuals and communities in a country receive the health services they need without suffering financial hardship. Despite recent advancements, Paraguay faces major challenges to achieve UHC.[9] Population coverage (breadth of the coverage) is still very limited, especially in the poorest deciles of the population, in which only a tiny minority is covered by any health insurance at all. Financial risk protection (height of the coverage) leaves many people to face catastrophic health expenditures and exposes them to other financial risks. Lastly, health service provision (depth of the coverage) is very limited and strongly linked with people's ability to pay.

Access to healthcare has progressed in recent years, but current pace of progress is too slow to meet the country's ambitions

Paraguay has been increasing healthcare access based on primary healthcare units, but it has a large gap to cover the total population. Primary healthcare is the first level of multidisciplinary care that covers the entire population and serves as a gateway to the system. It should integrate and co-ordinate health services in the country, in addition to meeting most of the population's health needs. In terms of healthcare access, the progress has been significant. The share of sick or injured people who received skilled healthcare increased from 52.3% to 75.5% between 2003 and 2016. However, in terms of operating primary healthcare units, progress has slowed down. Between 2008 and 2011, 707 new primary healthcare units were established (176.7 per year on average). However, between 2012 and 2016, only 92 new units were put in place (18.4 per year on average). By 2016, Paraguay had 800 units in total, even though it would need have approximately 1 400 units to cover its entire population (Ríos, 2014).

The share of people covered by health insurance has increased slowly and remains low. While healthcare access has seen a remarkable increase of more than 23 percentage points between 2003 and 2016, health insurance coverage has increased by less than 7 percentage points over the same period, from 19% to 26% (Figure 3.18 Panel A). Around 99% of people do not have any health insurance in the poorest decile. Even in the richest decile, around 39.4% do not have health insurance. The social security scheme covers less than 1% of the population in the poorest decile and only around 34% of the population in the richest decile (Figure 3.17).

Access and coverage asymmetries are large across departments and municipalities, although the urban-rural gap has been narrowing over the last decade. The asymmetry in the supply of health services across departments and municipalities is substantial. In urban areas, access reaches more than 78%, while in rural areas it is below 73%. Similarly, while 34.3% of the population in urban areas is covered by some form of health insurance in rural areas only 12.67% of the population has coverage. Still, the urban-rural gap in access to healthcare has been narrowing in recent decades, from 18.1 percentage points in 2003 to 5.8 percentage points in 2016 (Figure 3.18 Panel B).

Figure 3.17. Health insurance coverage per decile in 2016

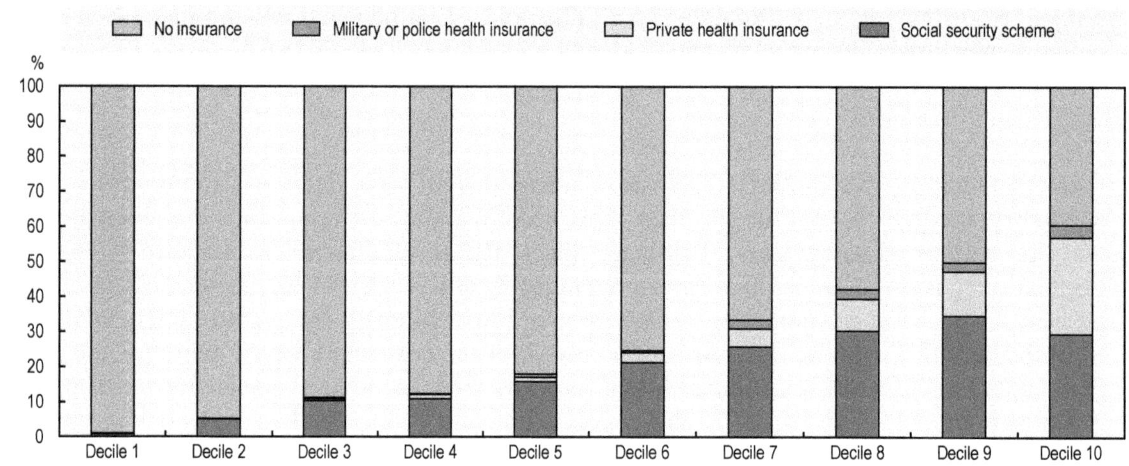

Source: Paraguay Permanent Households Survey 2016 (DGEEC, 2017).

StatLink https://doi.org/10.1787/888933823261

Figure 3.18. Healthcare access and insurance coverage 2003-2016

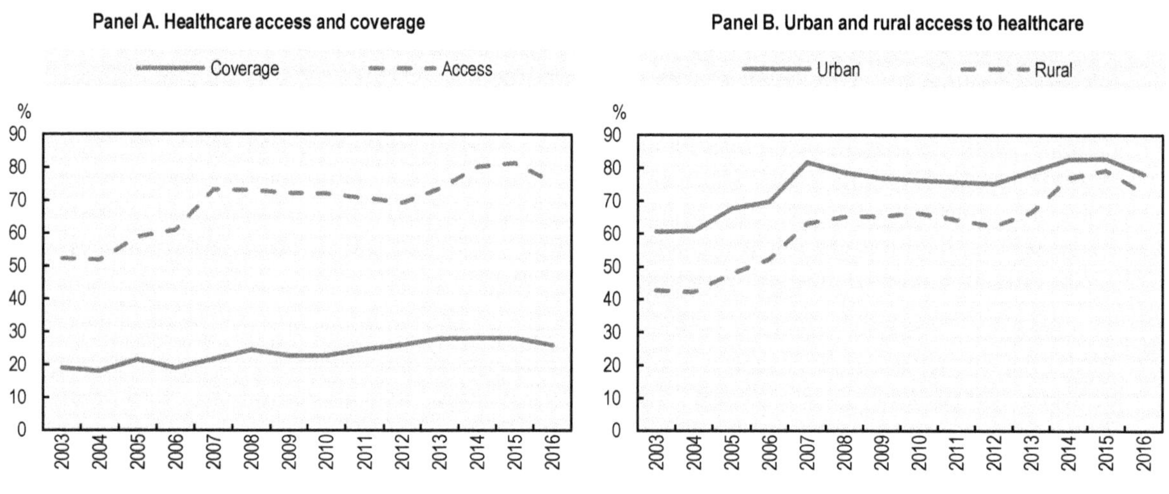

Note: Healthcare access includes the share of sick or injured who received skilled healthcare. Healthcare coverage includes the share of the population that has any form of health insurance.
Source: Paraguay Permanent Household Survey 2003-2016 (DGEEC, 2017).

StatLink https://doi.org/10.1787/888933823280

Although access has improved, primary healthcare quality is low, due in part to the difficulties in staffing primary care units. In terms of human resources, there is a gap of more than 20% of the required health professionals in the country. In theory, all primary healthcare units should be equipped with a team of health professionals (Family Health

Team) that includes a doctor, a nurse or obstetrician, a nursing assistant and between 3 to 5 community health agents (Ríos, 2014). In practice, a big share of primary healthcare units does not have a complete team of health professionals (Table 3.3). The country had 754 such units in 2014. However, the sum of community agents in all the country was only 414. Considering that Paraguay had a gap of around 646 missing USFs by 2014, there was a gap of around 5 186 community agents in Paraguay (Ríos, 2014) (See Table 3.3). Human resources tend to be more unstable and insufficient in remote and disadvantaged areas due mainly to the lack of economic incentives for health professionals to stay in these locations. In terms of physical resources, most USFs lack appropriate infrastructure; facilities are often in disrepair or too small. They also lack essential health equipment and the provision of medicines is insufficient to keep up with demand. In terms of their integration capacity within the whole health network, their communication and transportation systems are just in the development stage, which hinders the co-ordination for transferring patients to other health establishments (Ríos, 2014).

Table 3.3. Human resources gap in primary healthcare, 2014

Human resources	Operating primary healthcare: 754 units (USF)	Lacking primary healthcare: 646 units (USF)
Doctors	638	762
Nurses and/or obstetricians	742	658
Dentists	33	247
Nursing assistants	727	673
Community agents	414	5 186
Indigenous health promoters	40	380
Total	2 594	7906

Note: For every two Family Health Teams, there should be one Dental Team, made up of a Dentist and an assistant (Ríos, 2014). Primary healthcare figures above correspond to the Family Healthcare Units (USF) of the Ministry of Public Health and Social Welfare (MSPBS).

Box 3.4 Primary healthcare: The case of Costa Rica

Over recent decades, Costa Rica has had a clear national consensus on the role of the healthcare system. In particular, efforts towards increasing access to primary care were accelerated in the early 1990s, when Costa Rica opened up community clinics called Basic Comprehensive Health Care Teams (Equipos Básicos de Atención Integral de Salud, EBAIS). By 1995, there were 232 EBAIS in Costa Rica, mostly among underserved communities, which greatly improved rural access to primary care. Today over 1 000 EBAIS are present throughout the country; in effect, they constitute the basis of the national health care system. With at least one medical doctor, one nurse or nursing assistant and one health care assistant, EBAIS serve around 1 000 households each. Other personnel may include social workers, dentists, laboratory technicians, pharmacists and nutritionists, who may work across more than one EBAIS in clusters called Áreas de Salud, or health zones. Services include outpatient services, family planning and community medical services, health promotion and disease prevention, and management of (non-complex) chronic disease. When required, the EBAIS also refer patients to higher levels of healthcare.

Recently, Costa Rica's ambitious and innovative model of primary care has been further developed with the establishment of three Centres for Integrated Health Care (Centros de Atención Integral en Salud, CAIS). These centres constitute an extended network for the primary care system, offering maternity services, intermediate care beds (to avoid hospital admission or expedite early discharge), ambulatory surgery, rehabilitation, speciality clinics (such as pain management), and diagnostics such as x-rays. The CAIS also hold workshops in order to support typical local EBAIS by comparing and discussing their performance indicators, offering telemedicine and home-visits, and by keeping a focus on preventive care. In 2015, one of the CAIS established a local commission on domestic violence and most of its 15 000 home visits were for health promotion and preventive care. Upward integration with secondary care providers are established by the CAIS through the development of protocols and patients pathways for service networks in psychiatry, paediatrics, elderly care and other specialities. The Costa Rican primary healthcare model is thus of significant interest for OECD health systems looking to strengthen people-centred, integrated care.

Source: OECD Reviews of Health Systems: Costa Rica (OECD, 2017).

Although financial risks and barriers have been reduced, a share of Paraguayans incur in catastrophic health expenditures

User fees for the provision of basic health services by the MSPBS have been progressively eliminated. Avoiding direct payments and reducing out-of-pocket expenses is essential for increasing financial protection and preventing more people from falling into poverty. In this regard, recent OECD estimates show that cost-sharing (in the form of co-payments) leads to higher health spending in the long term, notably because it leads to a lower use of needed medical care with adverse consequences for health status (De la Maisonneuve, Moreno-Serra and Murtin, 2016). The government has made an effort to reduce rates charged for basic health services in Paraguay. In particular, colposcopy, cervical biopsy, Pap test, tubal ligation and provision of IUD have been free of charge since 2001. Basic supplies for childbirth and diagnosis of tuberculosis have been free of charge since 2005. Lastly and most importantly, the Ministry of Health eliminated all remaining charges for the use of basic services in 2008, as part of the gratuity policy to eliminate financial barriers for health in the country (Giménez Caballero, 2013).

The poorest people face a high risk of incurring catastrophic health expenditures (CHE). CHE occur when out-of-pocket payments for health services consume such a large portion of a household's available income that the household may be pushed into poverty as a result. Overall, there is a risk of falling into poverty if out-of-pocket expenditures in health exceed 30% of total income. In Paraguay, the households in the poorest decile of the population spend on average more than 12% of their total income to cover health expenditures, while households of the richest decile spend less than 1% (Figure 3.19 Panel A). Around 2% of households in Paraguay, and 7% in the poorest decile, incur catastrophic health expenditures (Figure 3.19 Panel B). Although no comparable figures exist for the region, catastrophic health expenditure is a problem common to most Latin American countries. However, countries such as Costa Rica have managed to keep the percentage of the population facing CHE quite low (0.4%), while in others, it is still very high, such as in Guatemala where 11.2% of households are concerned (Knaul et al., 2011).[10]

Figure 3.19. Out-of-pocket health expenditure by income deciles

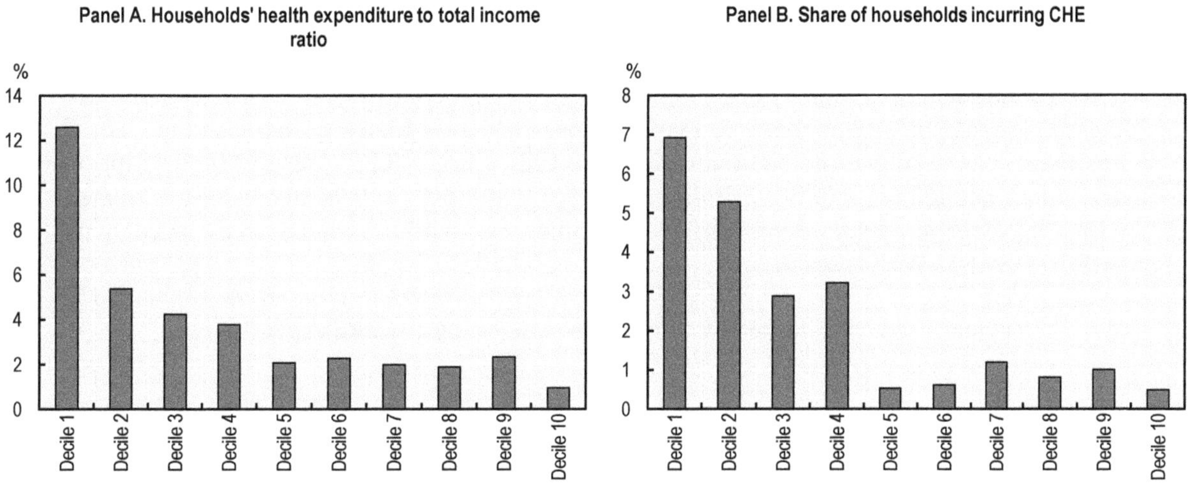

Note: Panel A indicates the health expenditure–to-total income ratio of those households that incurred health expenses during the last 90 days.
Source: Paraguay Permanent Household Survey 2014 (DGEEC, 2017).

StatLink https://doi.org/10.1787/888933823299

Most out-of-pocket health expenditures are due to medications, laboratory tests and transportation. Despite the policy to provide medicine free of charge, medication, rather than costly acute care, is the main source of out-of-pocket expenditure. Household expenditures for medication account on average for 62% of the total out-of-pocket expenditure, followed by transportation (17.7%) and medical tests (e.g. x-rays or laboratory tests – 8.4%). When it comes to catastrophic health expenditures, 50.7% are due to medications, 17.8% are due to laboratory tests, 10.5% are due to transportation and 6.5% are due to hospitalisation. The negative impact of medication expenditures is stronger among the poorest deciles of income. Contrastingly, catastrophic expenses due to hospitalisation cover a bigger share among the richest deciles of the population, reflecting the relatively low prevalence of health insurance even among the better off (Figure 3.20).

Ensuring adequate financial protection in Paraguay requires action to insure against expensive events that occur infrequently. This can be granted through the public sector or through a combination of free provision for those unable to pay and compulsory insurance in a regulated market for those able to pay – including in the social security and the private sector. The FONARESS fund intended to finance coverage for those without appropriate insurance for a number of such conditions, but was never implemented. Likewise, the Secretaria Tecnica de Planificacion and the Ministry of Health are piloting a scheme to guarantee a benefit package. The scheme, called Support service to child and maternal health (*Servicio de apoyo a la salud materno-infantil*), covers women of childbearing age and boys and girls under 18 years old (see Box 3.5). It relies on service provision by the Ministry of Health but constitutes a contingency fund to finance referral to the private sector in cases where the Ministry is unable to provide service. The project is being piloted with 150 000 households since October 2017. At of the end of 2017, the contingency fund had not disbursed any funds. By establishing a mechanism for service purchase for the Ministry of Health to fulfil the right to healthcare, the pilot contributes to setting the seeds for the necessary reform of purchasing in the health sector.

Ensuring adequate financial protection also implies a significant effort to improve the availability and accessibility of medicines. The insufficiency of stocks of medicines was a recurring conclusion of evaluations of USFs (Monroy Peralta et al., 2011). Improving on the availability of medicines in public health services is key, but the affordability of drugs in the private sector should also be monitored. Moreover, control over pharmaceutical use and sale should be strengthened to avoid misuse, which is likely to increase the cost of treatment. For example, the National Medicine Policy notes that 3 out of 10 prescription drugs are obtained without prescription and notes that most cases of diarrhoea are treated with rehydration salts combined with other, possibly unnecessary, treatments (MSPBS/PAHO/WHO, 2015).

Figure 3.20. Distribution of households' catastrophic health expenditures

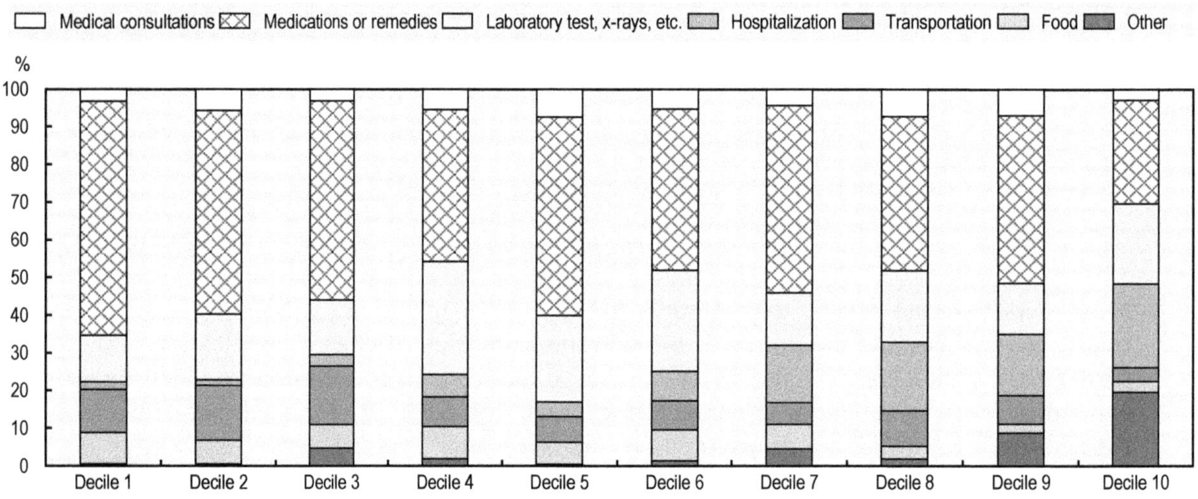

Source: Paraguay Permanent Household Survey 2014 (DGEEC, 2017).

StatLink https://doi.org/10.1787/888933823318

Moving towards a guaranteed health plan that is better defined

Most of the population is not guaranteed access to a comprehensive health service package. Although the public subsystem provides free inpatient and outpatient services, there is no specific benefit package. In Paraguay, only those who are insured by the Social Security Institute (IPS) or have private insurance are entitled to a specific and guaranteed set of benefits. They represent only 22.7% of the total population in Paraguay. The remaining majority is not insured and depends on the provision of services by the public subsystem. Such provision of services depends on the effective availability of services and resources at a given time, meaning that access to services often depends on people's ability to pay. This includes, for example, medicines that may not be available from the public subsystem. Moreover, private insurance and prepaid plans are subject to a number of exclusions.

A recently piloted programme has made progress in the definition of a guaranteed package of services and established a mechanism for financing the guarantee. The Support service to child and maternal health (Box 3.5) defined a package of services for beneficiary children and women of childbearing age and set up a contingency fund to finance the provision of intensive care in the private sector in cases when public sector facilities are not available. The definition of an explicit package of services contributes to empower citizens with respects to their rights to healthcare, and to make the cost of healthcare provision explicit. The package of services currently includes services defined by procedures or types of care and explicit inclusions based on pathologies or health problems (for example, pregnancy-related medical acts for women of childbearing age).To make the package of services more easily scalable, the criteria for inclusion in the package could be better defined. Initially, as in the case of Chile's Explicit Health Guarantees, it is desirable to base the inclusion of services upon a list of pathologies or health problems, possibly including areas of preventive care.

A reform to establish and finance a guaranteed package will require broad reach and financing. The contingency fund of the Support service to child and maternal health was not utilised during the 3-month implementation period. Project data have not been analysed yet, so the pattern of care of beneficiaries is not known. The protocol for the use of the contingency fund was limited to high complexity treatment. Moreover, the package did not specify waiting times as part of the guarantee (as is the case, for example in Chile [Bitrán, 2013]) so that the requirements of non-availability in the public subsystem may not have been met. Together these two elements may explain the lack of spending from the fund. Going forward, efforts to guarantee healthcare provision should include all necessary inputs and medicines for the treatment of health problems considered according to clinical guidelines, and include financing mechanisms for these as well as related diagnostics tests. Indeed, most catastrophic health expenditures among the poor stem from purchase of medicines and tests, rather than payments for hospitalisation (Figure 3.20). Finance will be all the more necessary given that a guarantee scheme can be expected to increase healthcare use by beneficiaries.[11] The randomisation elements in the pilot and the monitoring data collected should provide information on the impact of the guarantee on patterns of health service use and therefore potential financing needs. Depending on the quality of monitoring data available for non-beneficiaries in the catchment areas of the project, follow-up pilots should consider the establishment of a baseline.

Box 3.5. Piloting non-contributory insurance: the Support service to child and maternal health

The Support service to child and maternal health (*Servicio de apoyo a la salud materno-infantil*) was piloted between October and December 2017 with over 150 000 households. The programme was designed in the framework of the umbrella anti-poverty programme *Sembrando Oportunidades*.

The programme defines a schedule of guaranteed services for the beneficiaries. The beneficiaries are young men and women, and women of childbearing age. The schedule of services includes a broad range of services for children under 5, adolescents between 10 and 18, and of pregnancy-related services for women.

Programme participants receive a card that facilitates monitoring and provides a telephone number for complaints. The programme also set up a contingency fund of USD 1.5 million to guarantee service provision. In cases where the Ministry of Health is unable to provide service, the programme includes a protocol for service to be provided in the private system and financed through the fund; this protocol is linked to the Ministry of Health's referral system. The inter-institutional agreement governing the programme (MSBPS/STP, 2017) and its amendment specify such a protocol for the provision of intensive care. The fund was set up with Itaipú and managed by the United Nations Population Fund (UNFPA).

The STP and the MSPBS implemented the pilot in catchment areas of USFs with a full complement and levels of poverty above 20%. In those with poverty rates over 30%, all households were included, in those with poverty between 20% and 30%, half of household were randomly selected for inclusion.

Over the three months of the pilot, the contingency fund was not used. The project was implemented in a decentralised fashion which led to delays in the delivery of cards to some beneficiaries.

Source: MSPBS/STP (2017).

As private provision of health services is fairly limited, other subsystems incur residual expenditures to assume uncovered procedures. Health plans offered by private insurance companies usually do not cover protection against epidemics, congenital diseases, psychiatric illnesses, surgical treatment of sexually-transmitted infections and some accidents. Furthermore, they often do not include costly long-term treatments, such as chemotherapy and haemodialysis, and the provision of medications and other supplies is very limited (Mancuello and Cabral de Bejarano, 2011). When faced with those exclusions, patients opt to return to the public subsystem or take legal action to enforce their right to health and force private or public services to provide such care.

Many middle-income countries that guarantee citizens' right to health face difficulties in securing resources to deliver services. For example, Brazil, Colombia and Mexico guarantee a citizen's right to health but face difficulties in securing human resources and medical supplies. In Brazil, despite universal coverage of the public sector, 25% of the population resorts to private insurance to obtain timely diagnoses and consultations. In countries like Korea or Colombia, pharmaceuticals are not covered as well as hospital care and doctor's visits (OECD, 2016d).

Establishing appropriate breadth of cover is essential to ensure adequate financial protection for the whole population. It is important to clearly state which health services are covered and which are not in order to ensure that essential, cost-effective care is provided without financial barriers and that, on the other hand, cost-ineffective services and health services of questionable clinical benefit are excluded (OECD, 2016d). The determination of what services to cover needs to be based on critical assessment by agencies responsible for health technology assessment. This role could be played by the National Medical Directorate established by law 1032 in Paraguay, but it would have to be provided sufficient autonomy and resources.

Policy recommendations

To increase its chances of achieving Universal Health Coverage, Paraguay's health system requires systemic reform and a future vision. Maintaining the pace of growth in health financing, while increasing the equity and efficiency is a major challenge. The fragmentation of the health system into pre-paid private, general budget-based public and insurance-based social security systems is a significant hurdle to ensure effective stewardship and efficient allocation in the system. A national dialogue could determine what model the country chooses, in particular in terms of its financing – whether an insurance-based model in which coverage for those unable to pay is subsidised, preferably explicitly, by the public purse, or a national health service model in which a basic package of health services is provided for free to all citizens. In both cases, it is possible for the various segments that make up the system today to co-exist, but in a much more integrated fashion.

In the short-to-medium term, much can be done in order to increase the degree of integration and co-ordination in the national health system. This includes setting framework conditions that allow for inter-institutional agreements and the unification of care provision at the point of delivery, building on experience in the ground. Independently of the model chosen for the future, Paraguay should strengthen the shift towards integrated health provision networks based on primary care as a cost effective path to universal health coverage, and ensure sustainable health finance by diversifying sources of funds and shifting out-of-pocket payments towards pre-paid flows, be they in the form of taxation, social security contributions, or insurance premia.

Box 3.6. Main recommendations to reform the health sector

1. Establish a vision for the health system able to guarantee Universal Health Coverage with equity
2. Establish framework conditions favouring the integration of health service delivery across the public and potentially the private system
    a. Review existing inter-institutional agreements between public sector entities.
    b. Establish a framework to generalise the use of inter-institutional agreements for the provision of service across public sector entities
    c. Consider a reform to make public procurement of health services and supplies more responsive.
    d. Consider including civil servants and employees of the state under the social security health service.
    e. In the long run, separate purchasing and service provision functions across the health system.
3. Improve the governance of the national health system
    a. Strengthen the stewardship role of the Ministry of Health and Social Welfare by providing oversight institutions with the necessary autonomy, financial and human resources
    b. Pursue the implementation of the legal framework for the governance of the

national health system

c. Consolidate and streamline the legal and regulatory bodies pertaining to the health sector to:

- Ensure regulation applies to all relevant actors
- Remove inconsistencies
- Update or revoke outdated legislation

d. Further invest in the development of information systems in health to deliver better statistical information and support continuity of care

- Continue efforts to improve the accuracy of vital statistics
- Unify systems within institutions and, where relevant, across the public, private and mixed subsystems
- Increase capacity among stewardship bodies to generate health statistics for the entire health system, with the support of the National Statistical Office
- Develop the system for recording medical records and accessing them in order to ensure continuity of care

4. Ensure sustainable funding for health to support Universal Health Coverage

a. Diversify sources of finance for health

- Consider increasing taxes on consumption of goods harmful to health (e.g. tobacco, alcoholic beverages) and earmark part of revenues to health finance

b. Channel out-of-pocket expenditure towards pre-payment schemes

- Make enrolment in health insurance mandatory
- Reform contributory systems for independent workers to better adapt them to their circumstances
- Offer partly or fully subsidised health insurance for those unable to pay (through a means-tested subsidy)

c. Establish a pooled fund to cover key contingencies

- Implement FONARESS to cover high-complexity treatment for all Paraguayans, and include private and IPS funding in the pool of funds
- Reform FONARESS to cover a basic comprehensive care package, beyond high-complexity care, as a basis for pooled funding
- Consider the inclusion of other contingencies (e.g. traffic accidents)

d. Reform the provider payment system – in line with the separation of purchasing and service provision – ensuring that the new payment system provides incentives for quality service, cost control, and appropriate referral.

5. Deliver on Universal Health Coverage by expanding health services and insurance coverage, increasing financial protection, and ensuring the delivery of a well-defined benefit package
   a. Expand the coverage of Family Health Units (USF)
   b. Ensure adequate financial protection including through:
      - Universal coverage for high-cost conditions and treatments
      - Improving on the availability and affordability of medicines
   c. Define a set of guaranteed services and/or pathologies that can be provided to the population effectively and deliver on that guarantee.
   d. Build upon the pilot to guarantee a package of services for children and women of childbearing age.
6. Strengthen the orientation of the national health system towards integrated networks based on primary healthcare
   a. Strengthen Family Health Units (USF) by providing them with adequate human and financial resources
   b. Increase the pace of expansion of USFs to deliver on the objectives of universal coverage
7. Invest in health promotion and disease prevention
   a. A first and fundamental way of achieving a sustainable UHC is to invest more in health promotion and disease prevention
   b. Mitigating specific behavioural risk factors is potentially more cost-effective than waiting to treat poor health associated with these behaviours

Notes

[1] *Original* refers to the time when the area was mostly covered by pristine native forest vegetation. That time roughly corresponds to the late 15th and early 16th centuries, coinciding with the arrival of the first European immigrants and the beginning of the rapid process of transformation of the forest into agricultural land. Prior to this time, native people likely impacted the ecoregion as a whole to a relatively small or medium degree (Di Bitetti, Placci and Dietz, 2003).

[2] IPS coverage amounted to 1.37 million Paraguayans at the end of 2016 including dependants, special regimes and non-contributive regimes (ex-combatants and successors). On the basis of DGEEC projections for 2016, this corresponds to 19.93% of the population.

[3] Based on the individually-declared last health provider that attended the illness or injury in the past 90 days (DGEEC, 2017).

[4] In practice, the allocation of FONACIDE funds to the national health fund allows the Ministry of Health to tap a source of funds that is readily available and constitutes about 7% of the Ministry's total budget.

[5] Two special regimes are exceptions to this rule: civil servants and personnel under contract from the Office of the Attorney General (*Ministerio Público*) who can contribute to IPS and teachers in the public subsystem who can contribute to a special regime that covers health risks only (but not pensions).

[6] The number results from assigning a monthly allocation of PYG 300 000 to civil servants and employees of the Central Administration and financial entities of the state excluding the Ministry of Education and the Attorney General's office, as there are special regimes for teachers in the public subsystem and civil servants and employees in the Attorney General's office. This is therefore a conservative estimate.

[7] The figures provided based on procurement data do not necessarily correspond to actual payments as they are based on the capitation payment and the estimated number of beneficiaries.

[8] The Charter of IPS establishes a contribution from the general budget of 1.5% of the base (IPS, 2013). This contribution has never been paid, and the distribution of those funds according to the IPS charter itself is not feasible (as it plans in articles 23 and 34 a distribution that totals over 100% across funds).

[9] Health coverage can be measured based on the share of the population having access to health facilities (breadth of the coverage), based on the share of the total cost that is covered through pre-financing mechanisms (financial protection or height of the coverage) and based on the range of services that are available to meet the health needs of the population (depth of the coverage).

[10] Although the analysis of Knaul et al. (2011) provides a useful overview of catastrophic health expenditure in Latin America, shares have been calculated based on total household expenditures net of food spending, which makes values not entirely comparable with figures presented for Paraguay in this chapter.

[11] For example, in Chile, in 2009, four years after the implementation of the AUGE guarantees in 2005, the number of breast biopsies had doubled, surgical treatments for scoliosis had tripled and laparoscopic cholangiographies had quadrupled (Bitrán, 2013).

References

Bitrán, R. (2013), *Explicit Health Guarantees for Chileans: The AUGE Benefits Package*, Universal Health Coverage Studies Series N° 21, World Bank, Washington DC.

Casalí, P., O. Cetrángolo and A. Goldschmit (2017), *Paraguay. Protección social en salud: reflexiones para una cobertura amplia y equitativa*, International Labour Organization.

Contraloría General de la República (2010), R*esolución CGR N. 796/10: Examen especial al cumplimiento de convenios suscritos referentes a medicamentos e insumos del Instituto de Previsión Social (IPS), vigentes al ejercicio fiscal 2010*, Contraloría General de la República, Asunción.

Da Ponte et al. (2017), *Assessing Forest Cover Dynamics and Forest Perception in the Atlantic Forest of Paraguay, Combining Remote Sensing and Household Level Data*, Forests, 8(10), 389.

De la Maisonneuve, C., R. Moreno-Serra and F. Murtin (2016), *The drivers of public health spending: integrating policies and institutions*, OECD Working Papers N°1283, Paris.

DGEEC (2017), *Encuesta Permanente de Hogares* [Permanent Household Survey] (database, various years), Dirección General de Estadística, Encuestas y Censos de Paraguay, Fernando de la Mora, www.dgeec.gov.py/datos/encuestas/eph.

DGEEC (2015), *Anuario estadístico del Paraguay 2015* [Statistical Yearbook of Paraguay 2015], Dirección General de Estadística, Encuestas y Censos de Paraguay, Fernando de la Mora.

Di Bitetti, M., G. Placci and L. Dietz (2003), *A biodiversity vision for the Upper Paraná Atlantic Forest eco-region: designing a biodiversity conservation landscape and setting priorities for conservation action*, World Wildlife Fund, Washington, D.C.

Dullak, R. et al. (2011), *Atención Primaria en Salud en Paraguay: panorámica y perspectiva*, Ciência & Saúde Coletiva, 16(6), 2865-2875.

Fleytas, M. (2007). *Cambios en el paisaje. Evolución de la cobertura vegetal en la Región Oriental del Paraguay*, Fundación Moisés Bertoni, Asunción.

Ganchimeg, T. O. (2014), *Pregnancy and childbirth outcomes among adolescent mothers: A World Health Organization multicountry study*, BJOG: An International Journal of Obstetrics & Gynaecology, 121(s1), 40-48.

GBD 2015 Healthcare Access and Quality Collaborators (2017), *Healthcare Access and Quality Index based on mortality from causes amenable to personal health care in 195 countries and territories, 1990–2015: a novel analysis from the Global Burden of Disease Study 2015*, Lancet (390), 231–66.

Giménez Caballero, E. (2013), *Hacia un sistema de salud con garantías: Notas para nuevas políticas de salud en Paraguay*.

Global Burden of Disease Collaborative Network (2016), Global Burden of Disease Study 2016 (database), Institute for Health Metrics and Evaluation.

Gottret, P. and Schieber, G. (2006), *Health Financing Revisited: A Practitioner's Guide*, World Bank, Washington, D.C., https://openknowledge.worldbank.org/handle/10986/7094.

Instituto Suramericano de Gobierno en Salud (2012), *Sistemas de Salud en Suramérica: desafíos para la universalidad, la integralidad y la equidad*, Instituto Suramericano de Gobierno en Salud, Rio de Janeiro.

ILO (2017), *Paraguay: Protección social en salud: reflexiones para una cobertura amplia y equitativa*, International Labour Organization, Santiago, www.ilo.org/wcmsp5/groups/public/---americas/---ro-lima/---sro-santiago/documents/publication/wcms_566978.pdf.

IPS (2016), *Anuario Estadístico Institucional IPS 2016*, Instituto de Previsión Social, Asunción.

IPS (2013), *Carta Orgánica*, Instituto de Previsión Social, Asunción,

Knaul, F. et al (2011), *Household catastrophic health expenditures: a comparative analysis of twelve Latin American and Caribbean Countries*, Salud Publica Mex, 53(suppl 2), s85-95.

Mancuello, J. and M. Cabral de Bejarano (2011), *Sistema de Salud de Paraguay*. Revista Salud Pública Paraguay, 1 (1), 13-25, Asunción.

MH (2017), *Reporte Nacional de Inclusión Financiera del Paraguay 2017*, Ministerio de Hacienda de Paraguay, Asunción.

MH (2018), BOOST (database), Ministerio de Hacienda de Paraguay, Asunción.

Ministerio del Interior (2015), *Reporte Estadístico: Homicidio doloso 2015*, Observatorio Nacional de Seguridad y Convivencia Ciudadana, Asunción.

Monroy Peralta, G. et al. (2011), *Informe final de evaluación: Programa unidades de salud de la familia.* Ministerio de Hacienda de Paraguay, Asunción.

MSPBS (2018), *Vital Statistics Information Subsystem (SSIEV)* (database), Ministerio de Salud Pública y Bienestar Social de Paraguay, Asunción.

MSPBS (2017a), *Atención Primaria en Salud: Listado de Unidades de Salud de la Familia* (database), Ministerio de Salud Pública y Bienestar Social de Paraguay, Asunción.

MSPBS (2017b), *Promesa cumplida: Salud suma 111 nuevas unidades de terapia este año*, Ministerio de Salud Pública y Bienestar Social de Paraguay, Asunción, www.mspbs.gov.py/portal/7521/promesa-cumplida-salud-suma-111-nuevas-unidades-de-terapia-este-ano.htmlb (accessed on May 2018).

MSPBS (2016a), *Indicadores Básicos de Salud Paraguay 2016*, Ministerio de Salud Pública y Bienestar Social de Paraguay, Asunción.

MSPBS (2016b), *Indicadores de Recursos y Cobertura* (database), Ministerio de Salud Pública y Bienestar Social de Paraguay, Asunción.

MSPBS (2015), *Política Nacional de Salud 2015-2030*, Ministerio de Salud Pública y Bienestar Social de Paraguay, Asunción.

MSPBS (2013), *Indicadores Básicos de Salud Paraguay 2013*, Ministerio de Salud Pública y Bienestar Social de Paraguay, Asunción.

MSPBS/IPS (2013), *Convenio de Cooperación Interinstitucional entre el Ministerio de Salud Pública y Bienestar Social, El Instituto de Previsión Social - IPS y el Consejo Local de Salud de la Ciudad de Buena Vista - CLS*, Asunción.

MSPBS/PAHO/WHO (2014), *Perfil Farmacéutico de la República del Paraguay*, Asunción.

MSPBS/PAHO/WHO (2015), *Política Nacional de Medicamentos*, Asunción.

MSPBS/STP (2017), *Convenio marco de cooperación técnica interinstitucional*, Asunción.

National Government of Paraguay (2018), *Presupuesto General de la Nación para el Ejercicio Fiscal 2018* [General Budget of the Nation for Fiscal Year 2018], Asunción.

National Government of Paraguay (2014), *Plan Nacional de Desarrollo: Construyendo el Paraguay de 2030* [National Development Plan: Building the Paraguay of 2030], Asunción, www.stp.gov.py/pnd/wp-content/uploads/2014/12/pnd2030.pdf.

OECD (2018), *Multi-dimensional Review of Paraguay: Volume 1. Initial Assessment,* OECD Development Pathways, OECD Publishing, Paris. http://dx.doi.org/10.1787/9789264301900-en.

OECD (2017), *OECD Reviews of Health Systems: Costa Rica 2017*, OECD Reviews of Health Systems, OECD Publishing, Paris, https://doi.org/10.1787/9789264281653-en.

OECD (2016a), *Consumption Tax Trends 2016: VAT/GST and excise rates, trends and policy issues*, OECD Publishing, Paris, https://doi.org/10.1787/ctt-2016-en.

OECD (2016b), *OECD Reviews of Health Systems: Colombia*, OECD Publishing, Paris, https://doi.org/10.1787/9789264248908-en.

OECD (2016c), *OECD Reviews of Health Systems: Mexico*, OECD Publishing, Paris, https://doi.org/10.1787/9789264230491-en.

OECD (2016d), Universal Health Coverage and Health Outcomes, OECD Publishing, Paris, https://www.oecd.org/els/health-systems/Universal-Health-Coverage-and-Health-Outcomes-OECD-G7-Health-Ministerial-2016.pdf.

OECD (2015), *Tackling Harmful Alcohol Use: Economics and Public Health Policy*, OECD Publishing, Paris, https://doi.org/10.1787/9789264181069-en.

OECD (2013), Strengthening Health Information Infrastructure for Health Care Quality Governance: Good Practices, New Opportunities and Data Privacy Protection Challenges, OECD Publishing, Paris, https://doi.org/10.1787/9789264193505-en.

OECD/CIAT/IDB/ECLAC (2018), *Revenue Statistics in Latin America and the Caribbean 2018*, OECD Publishing, Paris, https://doi.org/10.1787/rev_lat_car-2018-en-fr.

Oficina Comercial de Chile en Paraguay – ProChile (2017), *Estudio de Mercado Servicios de Salud en Paraguay*, Santiago.

ONU Mujeres and Ministerio de la Mujer (2016), *Violencia contra las mujeres en Paraguay: Avances y Desafío*s, Oficina Comercial de Chile en Paraguay, Asunción.

PAHO (2010), *Redes Integradas de Servicios en Salud: Conceptos, Opciones de Politica y Hoja de Ruta para su Implementacion en las Americas*, Pan American Health Organization, Washington D.C.

PAHO (2017), *Health in the Americas+, 2017 Edition. Summary: Regional Outlook and Country Profiles*, Pan American Health Organization, Washington D.C.

PAHO/WHO (2014), *Estrategia para el acceso universal a la salud y la cobertura universal de salud*, World Health Organization, Washington, D.C.

PAHO/WHO/MSPBS (various years), *Indicadores Básicos de Salud Paraguay*, Asunción.

Republic of Paraguay (1974), *Ley 480 que actualiza el arancel médico-quirúrgico privado y de medicina pre-paga (Seguros)*, Asunción.

Ríos, G. (2014), *Mapeo de la Atención Primaria en Salud en Paraguay*, Instituto Suramericano de Gobierno en Salud, Río de Janeiro.

Superintendencia de Salud (2017), *Registro Nacional de Entidades Prestadoras de Servicios de Salud (RNEPSS)*, Superintendencia de Salud, Asunción.

Tangcharoensathien, V. et al. (2018), *Health systems development in Thailand: A solid platform for successful implementation of universal health coverage*, The Lancet, 391(10126), 1205-1223.

United Nations (2018), Global Indicators Database (database), https://unstats.un.org/sdgs/indicators/database/?area=PRY#footnotes.

Vilaça Mendes, E. (2011), *Las Redes de Atención de Salud*, Pan-American Health Organization, Brasilia.

WHO (2018a), Global Health Expenditure Database (database).

WHO (2018b), Global Health Observatory (database).

WHO (2017), Health Situation in the Americas: Basic Indicators 2017, Washington D.C.

World Bank (2018), World Development Indicators (database), http://data.worldbank.org/data-catalog/world-development-indicators

Chapter 4. Towards an education and skills system that fosters inclusiveness and employability in Paraguay

Paraguay has made substantial progress in various dimensions of its education system in recent years as highlighted in Volume I of the Multidimensional Review of Paraguay. However, major challenges remain and reforms are unfinished. Access to the education system has expanded markedly, but is still a challenge in pre-primary and secondary education and for some socioeconomic groups. Schooling has improved, but learning outcomes are poor. And the relevance of the education and skills provided by the system is questionable, as illustrated by the problematic transition from school to work, with many young people leaving the education system too early to enter inactivity or informality. This chapter analyses these challenges in depth, and provides recommendations to improve the education and skills system in Paraguay in order to foster inclusiveness and employability.

The statistical data for Israel are supplied by and under the responsibility of the relevant Israeli authorities. The use of such data by the OECD is without prejudice to the status of the Golan Heights, East Jerusalem and Israeli settlements in the West Bank under the terms of international law.

Transforming the education and skills system in Paraguay is vital to foster inclusiveness and better access to good quality jobs. Education is widely recognised as a critical area of public policy to support an equitable society and good quality opportunities for all. It is also a key driver of social mobility, enabling citizens to participate in society and the economy, and ensuring that future generations have access to better opportunities and increased well-being. More developed and cohesive societies have higher levels of education and more educated individuals report higher levels of self-confidence, civic participation and health. In addition, access to good quality jobs is strongly associated with the level of education of individuals and with the overall available pool of skills (OECD/CAF/ECLAC, 2016; OECD/CAF/ECLAC, 2014; OECD/Hanushek/Woessman, 2015). In sum, education and development go hand in hand, and Paraguay's success in achieving its main development objectives, as set out in the National Development Plan (*Plan Nacional de Desarollo* – PND) 2030, will heavily depend on its capacity to improve the education and skills system.

Paraguay has made substantial progress in various dimensions of its education system in recent years, but significant challenges remain. Volume I of this Multidimensional Review (MDCR) of Paraguay highlights that education outcomes have improved but reforms are unfinished, as illustrated by international comparisons with both OECD countries and with countries of a similar level of development. Access to the education system has expanded markedly, particularly at the primary level, but still remains a challenge in pre-primary and secondary education. And socioeconomic status is still a predictor of progression once within the education system, strongly determining enrolment and completion rates. Learning outcomes remain poor, reflecting the low quality of education, and are directly linked to deficiencies in teaching, inadequate resources, and poor management. And the pertinence of education is limited, as illustrated by the problematic transition from school to work, with many young people leaving the education system too early to enter inactivity or informality. This is also observed from the demand side, where a large number of firms claim that they struggle to find workers with the skills they need. In a country with a prevailing demographic bonus and in a global economy where knowledge and skills are keys to success, overcoming these challenges and strengthening education must be a priority in the public policy agenda.

This chapter analyses these challenges in depth, and provides recommendations to improve the education and skills system in Paraguay in order to foster inclusiveness and employability. It is structured as follows. First, it analyses the political momentum and the opportunity to reach a national agreement to transform education, where the expertise brought by international organisations can be of critical relevance. Second, it reviews the main education challenges in the country in terms of access and learning outcomes. Third, it analyses the transition from school to work. And fourth, it presents the main conclusions and provides a summary of the policy recommendations that are detailed throughout the chapter. The structure reflects a lifecycle approach, and university education is intentionally left aside to focus on previous levels of education and earlier stages of life, where a large share of the inequalities and the transitions to the labour market are already prevalent.

Major education challenges in Paraguay must be faced with strong political commitment and ambition

Improving education is at the core of Paraguay's ambition to become a knowledge economy with equal opportunities for all by 2030, as set out in its PND. Paraguay's PND was adopted in 2014 and established three key priorities: (i) poverty reduction and social development; (ii) inclusive economic growth; and (iii) inserting Paraguay into the world. Education appears as a cross-cutting dimension to support these three priorities, and specific education targets are included in the plan. The PND provides a mid-term horizon focusing on the development and implementation of education policies that go beyond the duration of a particular political cycle.

The ambition to transform Paraguay's education system and make it a driver of inclusion, economic progress and greater well-being for all is reflected in the current quest to develop a National Plan for the Transformation of the Education Sector for 2030 (*Plan Nacional para la Transformación Educativa 2030*, or PNTE following its acronym). The aim is to reach a national agreement on education that sets key strategic policy objectives with a well-established, mid-term horizon. This must be the result of a collaborative effort that guarantees that all actors in society have a voice in the discussion and in the definition of priorities, and that national and international expertise is mobilised in order to guarantee analytical rigour and that lessons learned and best practices are taken into account (MH, 2017) (Box 4.1).

Box 4.1. Towards a national agreement on education: the *Plan Nacional para la Transformación Educativa 2030*

The Ministry of Finance, the Ministry of Education and Science, and the planning authority (*Secretaría Técnica de Planificación* – STP), are currently engaged in a joint effort to promote the design of an ambitious *Plan Nacional para la Transformacion Educativa 2030* (PNTE). The funding comes from the *Fondo para la Excelencia de la Educación y la Investigación* (FEEI), which is a fund for education and research that is financed by royalties obtained from the hydroenergy plant of Itaipú. The main motivation behind this process is the acknowledgement that the education system must be transformed in order to achieve greater development and inclusion for all.

The discussion to develop a PNTE takes the National Development Plan 2030 as the framework of reference, and thus must be aligned with its priority areas. The PNTE also builds on the objectives of the previously adopted *Estrategia de Educación* 2024, which inspired the *Agenda Educativa* 2013-2018 that was embraced by the Cartes administration. These will be taken into account in the design of the PNTE, which ultimately aims to integrate the priorities of the existing national commitments on education.

The end goal is to develop an education plan that sets out priority areas and specific objectives for the mid-term horizon of 2030. A more concrete outcome of this process will be the development of a roadmap covering 2018-24 to guide the implementation of the PNTE in its first years, where specific targets and policy proposals will be included.

One of the main features of this PNTE is that it is intended to emerge from a participatory process where all relevant stakeholders and actors in society can have a role in the definition of the main priorities and objectives. To guarantee this, the process will constitute *mesas de trabajo*, i.e. working groups where discussions will be held among various actors, including civil society, academia, education experts, and international organisations, to come up with proposals to feed the PNTE. Another tool to incorporate citizens in the discussions will be a digital platform to carry out online consultations. Finally, regional fora are being planned to bring the discussions to the rural areas of the country.

The ongoing process should lead to the final signature of the PNTE 2030 as a national agreement on education by early 2019.

The global development agenda grants education a prominent role, and national efforts should be aligned with this broader international framework. The United Nations (UN) Sustainable Development Goals (SDG) set, as part of 'Goal 4', the goal of ensuring inclusive and quality education for all and promoting lifelong learning by 2030. This Goal includes various specific targets on areas related to equal opportunities in access to the education system and effective learning outcomes. On a regional scale, the *Metas Educativas 2021* (Education Targets 2021) signed in 2010 by the Organization of American States, the UN Economic Commission for Latin America and the Caribbean (UN-ECLAC) and the Iberoamerican General Secretariat (*Secretaria General Iberoamericana*) also represent a relevant background of reference to assess the progress achieved in recent years and the pending educational challenges for the 2030 milestone.

The national discussion on education, which is an ongoing process, is fertile ground for bringing to the table analytical support, policy recommendations and best practices from domestic and international experience and research. The focus of this chapter on education and skills will provide substantive content to the discussions around the process of defining the PNTE, and will provide input for the roadmap 2018-2023. The areas of focus of the PNTE are the financing of education, teachers' career and training, school management, early childhood education and care, and teaching and learning in primary and secondary education. The focus of this chapter is very much aligned with most of these topics – the financing of education is left aside – and adds the education-to-work transition as a fundamental dimension so that education can foster inclusion. In this respect, the chapter is intended to support the ongoing PNTE definition process as well as the subsequent stages to reach the 2030 landmark.

Expanding access to the education system and improving learning outcomes for all are key objectives to promote inclusion and equal opportunities

Access to the education system has improved but critical challenges remain for certain levels of education and socioeconomic groups

One of the greatest educational achievements in recent decades in Paraguay has been the broad expansion of access to the education system, supported by strong political will and the corresponding institutional transformations. Law 1264/98, which in 1998 established the current structure of the education system, was bolstered in 2010 by a law that made education free and compulsory until 14 years of age, with the mandatory age for entry lowered to pre-school level (age 5) in 2011. These landmarks define the formal education system in Paraguay today, which is structured as follows. First, initial education (*educación inicial*) from ages 0-5, which includes all pre-primary education and corresponds to level 0 of the International Standard Classification of Education (ISCED). Only the year of pre-school (age 5) is compulsory at this level. Second, basic education (*educación escolar básica*), which is compulsory and comprises three three-year cycles from ages 6 to 14: the first-two (*primer ciclo* and *segundo ciclo*) make up primary education, and are equivalent to level ISCED 1; the third one (*tercer ciclo*), corresponds to lower secondary education and is equivalent to level ISCED 2. Third, a three-year cycle from ages 15-17 known as middle education (*educación media*), which corresponds to upper secondary education (ISCED level 3). Finally, higher education with its different modalities (Elías, Walder and Sosa, 2016).

Access to the education system has improved for all levels of education, as shown by increasing enrolment rates. Efforts to expand access have paid off and enrolment in primary school is virtually universal today, on par with Latin America and Caribbean (LAC) and OECD levels. Access to secondary education has also been largely expanded and net enrolment rates reached almost 80% in 2015. While this places the country close to LAC levels of secondary enrolment, it is still below OECD levels (85% in 2014). Exclusion from the education system takes a toll particularly in remote areas and among disadvantaged groups. Enrolment rates in tertiary education have caught up with LAC levels, but remain poor when compared with OECD standards (Figure 4.1).

Years of education of the population in Paraguay have expanded as a result of the increases in coverage. The population aged 25-65 had on average 9.3 years of education in 2015, up from a level of 7.8 years in 2005. A focus on younger cohorts illustrates the significant progress achieved in recent years: the population aged 21-30 accumulated on average 11.4 years of education in 2015, up from an average of 9.5 years of education in 2005; and those aged 10-20 had on average 7.7 years of education in 2015, versus 6.7 in 2005 (CEDLAS and World Bank).

Figure 4.1. Enrolment rates by level of education in Paraguay, Latin America and the OECD

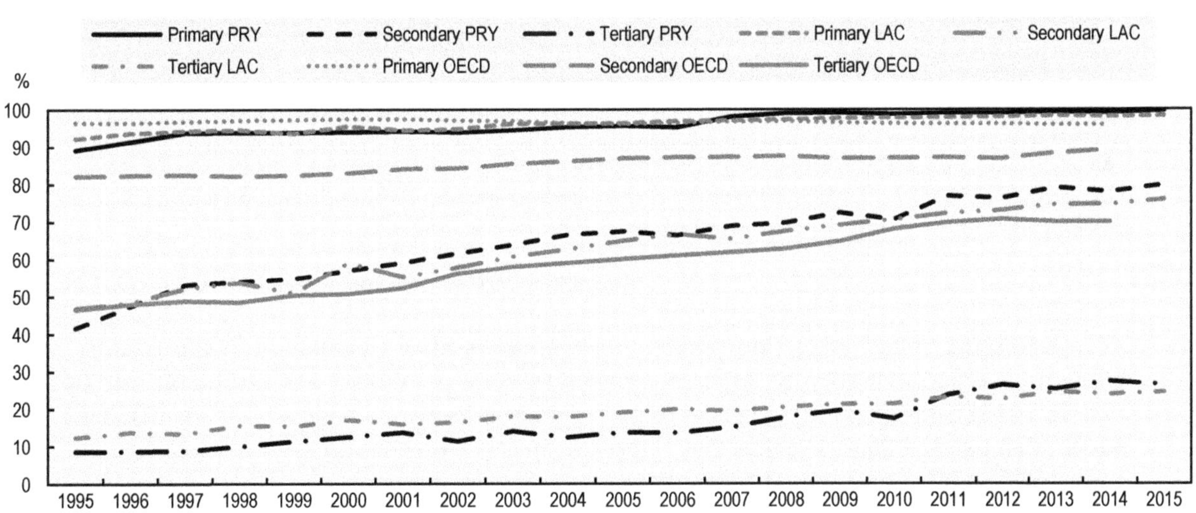

Note: Enrolment rates are net for all education levels and geographic areas, except for tertiary enrolment rates in the OECD which are gross. LAC includes the benchmark countries defined in MDCR Volume I: Argentina, Brazil, Chile, Colombia, Costa Rica, Mexico, Peru and Uruguay.
Source: Authors' calculations based on CEDLAS and World Bank (2017) for Paraguay and Latin America, and based on World Development Indicators for the OECD.

StatLink https://doi.org/10.1787/888933823337

After having achieved virtually universal enrolment in primary education, the challenges of expanding access in secondary school are still pressing. Limitations in the availability of administrative data restrict a more granular analysis in terms of enrolment, but estimations from survey data show that, despite progress, gaps in school attendance are relevant both in lower secondary (third grade of *educación escolar básica*) and upper secondary (*educación media*). In particular, age-specific attendance ratios for lower secondary education reached a level of 92% in 2015, but net attendance ratios, i.e. the share of children aged 12-14 who attend lower secondary education, were at 78% for that same year. The gaps seem higher for upper secondary: age-specific attendance ratios remained relatively stable in recent years at around 70%, while net attendance ratios show that in 2015 only 57% of the population aged 15-17 were attending the level of education that corresponds to that age (i.e. upper secondary or *educación media*) (Figure 4.2).

Figure 4.2. Age-specific and net attendance ratios in Paraguay, by level of education

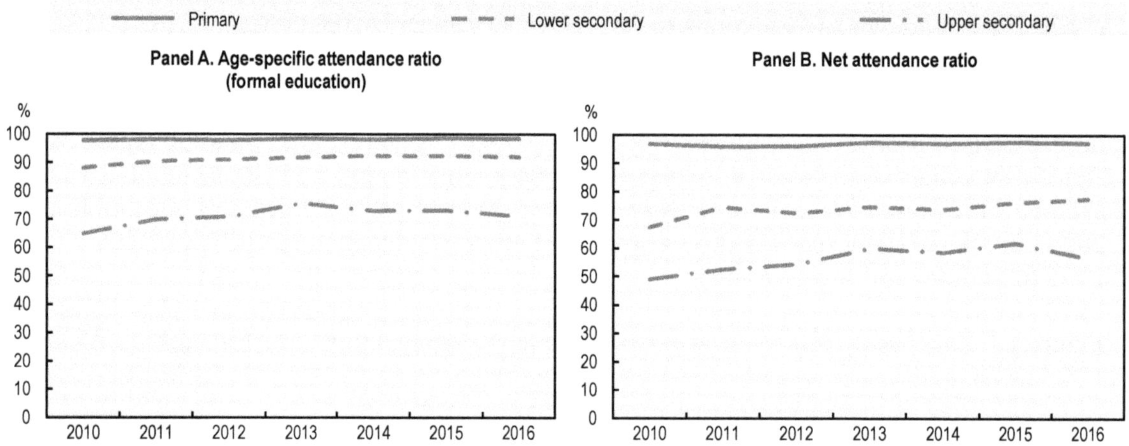

Note: Panel A represents the estimated share of children who are attending formal education (at any level and grade) grouped by the cycle that corresponds to their age as of 31 March on the year of the survey: primary (6 to 11), lower secondary (12 to 14) and upper secondary (15 to 17). Panel B represents the share of children who are attending the cycle corresponding to their age (irrespective of the grade).
Source: *Multi-dimensional Review of Paraguay. Vol I: Initial Assessment* (OECD, 2018). Authors' calculation based on the Permanent Household Survey of Paraguay (DGEEC, 2017).

StatLink https://doi.org/10.1787/888933823356

Access to pre-primary education (*educación inicial*) is also a challenge in the country. Though coverage is relatively large for pre-school (age 5), with a net enrolment rate of 77% in 2012 (Elías et al, 2014) access to pre-primary education in ages 0-4 is insufficient. Recent comparable data is scarce, but figures from 2012 present gross enrolment rates in pre-primary education (ages 0 to 5) of around 38% in Paraguay, well below the LAC average of 71% for that same year (World Bank, 2018a). Pre-primary education in Paraguay includes four levels: *maternal, pre jardín, jardín and preescolar*. The *Plan Nacional de Desarrollo Integral de la Primera Infancia 2011-2020* includes specific measures to support early childhood care that include participation in education programmes. In addition, the *Plan Nacional de Educacion 2024* sets the target of reaching universal pre-school coverage by 2024. However, progress has been limited in this respect, particularly in rural areas and indigenous communities. In fact, only around half of teachers in pre-primary education have the right qualifications. Lack of continuity in policies for early childhood, the predominance of a sectoral, non-integrated approach, scarce school and financial resources, weak infrastructure, and poor statistics can be highlighted as the main barriers to the expansion of quality pre-primary education in the country (Elias et al., 2014).

Striking inequalities persist in access to the education system, particularly at the secondary level, and mainly linked to socioeconomic status and geographical location. While access to primary education is widespread, inequalities appear at the secondary level around various dimensions. Income is a relevant predictor of access to secondary education: 96% of those in the richest quintile were enrolled in this education level in 2015, but only 67.7% of those belonging to the poorest quintile were. Likewise, net enrolment rates in urban areas are significantly larger (87% in 2015) than in rural areas (70%), and this has an impact on indigenous communities, which live largely on rural areas (Elías et al. 2016) (Figure 4.3). These disparities in access to the education system suggest that, instead of being a mechanism of social mobility, it can lead to a perpetuation of socioeconomic inequities in the country (PREAL, 2013).

Figure 4.3. Enrolment rates in secondary education by gender, income groups and geographic area

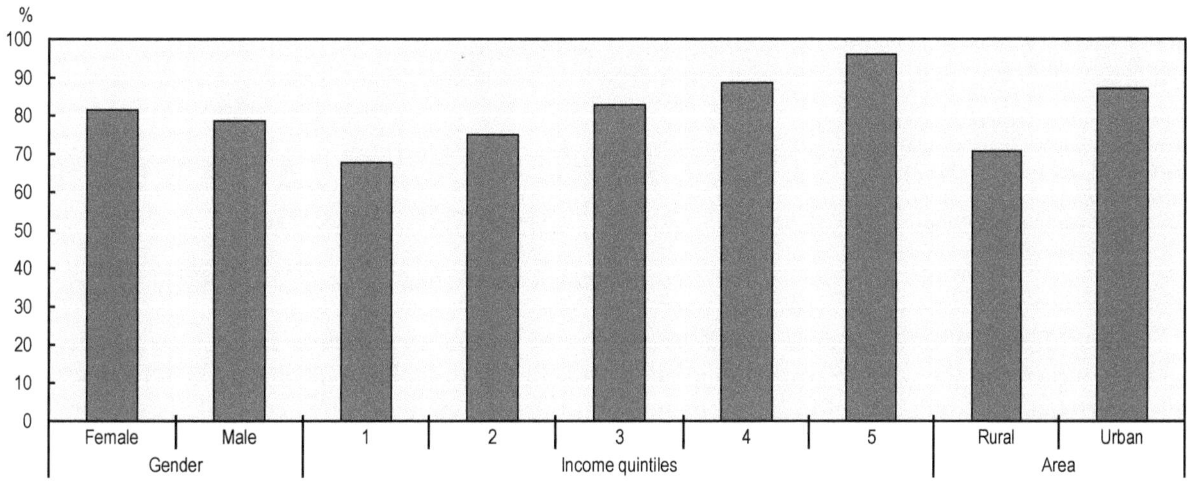

Source: Authors' elaboration based on CEDLAS and World Bank (2017).

StatLink https://doi.org/10.1787/888933823375

The large expansion in access must be accompanied by better progression within the education system, with higher completion rates across all levels of education

While more students enter the education system in Paraguay today, challenges remain regarding their progression once in it and their success in completing full grades. Students may stay in school longer now than a decade ago but many students drop out after the age of 11 (the official age for finalising primary education). Indeed, almost 99% of the population were attending school at age 11 in 2016. However, this figure starts to fall sharply after that age, when many begin to drop out of school. In 2016, 10% of 14-year-olds (the last official age of compulsory education) no longer attended school, and as many as 14%, 23% and 28% of those aged 15, 16 and 17, respectively, were not attending school. Overall, pupils tend to drop out during the transition from the second to the third cycle of "educación escolar básica" (i.e. the transition from primary to lower secondary, at ages around 12). However, drop-out rates accelerate during the transition from *educación escolar básica* to *educación media* (i.e. the transition from lower secondary to upper secondary, at ages around 15). After this level, at least half of the population aged 18 or older has left the education system (Figure 4.4).

Figure 4.4. Percentage of the population in the education system by age

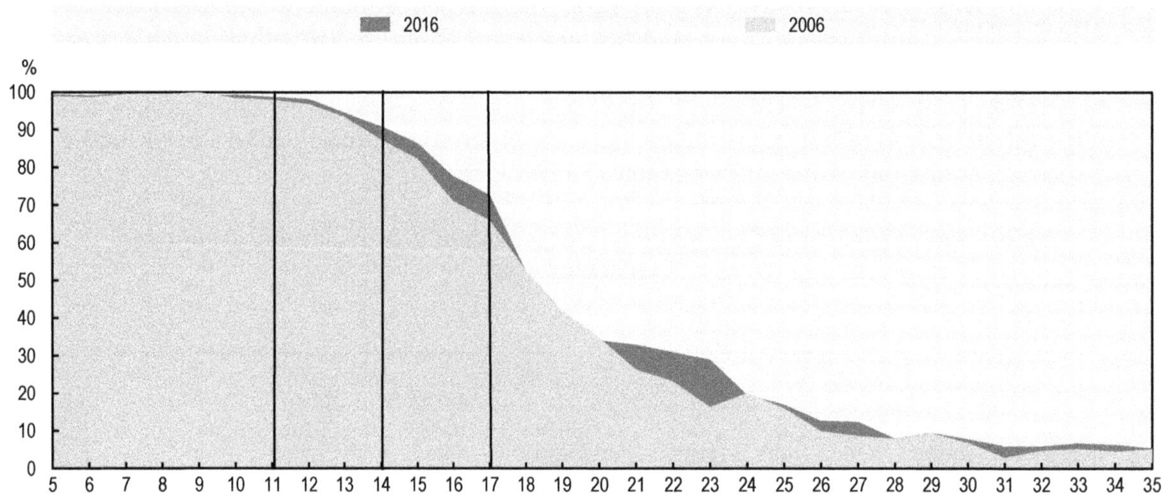

Source: Own elaboration based on household survey (EPH 2006 and 2016) (DGEEC, 2017).

StatLink https://doi.org/10.1787/888933823394

Most dropouts between ages 5 and 18 are linked to the household's lack of economic resources and the need to work. On average, two out of three Paraguayans aged 5-18 who were not attending school in 2016 claimed that this was explained by economic issues. In particular, 30% of drop-outs say they do not have enough resources at the household, while 31% declare that they must work. Geographical reasons (i.e. the lack of a local school) only explain around 5% of drop-outs, while family issues and lack of motivation were cited in 10% and 7% of dropouts respectively (DGEEC, 2017). What causes students to drop out of school varies across age and gender. Between ages 12-14 the main reason is the lack of resources in the family, while between ages 15-18 it is the need to work. Economic drivers are more prevalent among men than among women, with the latter dropping out also due to "family reasons" or household work (Figure 4.5). The drivers of drop-out and other forms of school exclusion (such as repetition and over-age schooling) are, however, more complex and rooted in the weaknesses of the education system, and usually go beyond the direct causes mentioned by families. In particular, in addition to economic barriers, there are social and cultural factors regarding the perception of the right to education, as well as material and pedagogic factors or political, financial and technical barriers that limit the inclusiveness of schools and of the education system overall (UNICEF, 2012).

These dropout results suggest that the journey across the education system is a tortuous one for many, and in fact over-age attendance is significant at some levels. In 2014, around 16% of students were attending primary education (first and second cycle of *educación escolar básica*) with two or more years of over-age, and more than 17% of students were attending secondary education (third cycle of *educación escolar básica*) with two or more years of over-age (Elias, Walder and Sosa, 2016). In particular, these phenomena affect rural areas and men, who are more likely to drop out when they are attending school with over-age.

Figure 4.5. Main reasons for dropout for different age groups, 2016

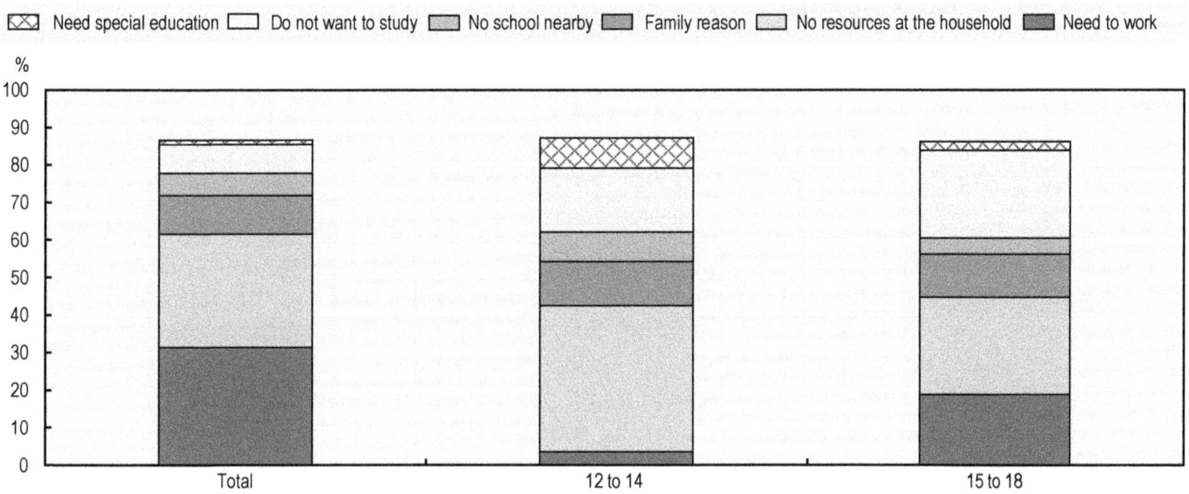

Source: Own elaboration based on household survey (EPH 2006) (DGEEC, 2017).

StatLink https://doi.org/10.1787/888933823413

Figure 4.6. Completion rates for primary, lower-secondary and upper secondary school in Paraguay

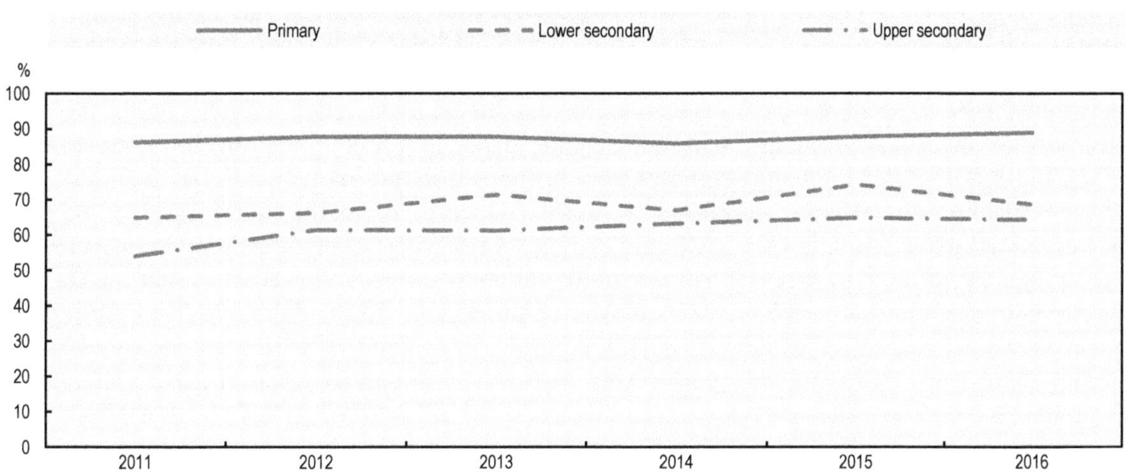

Note: Completion rates are calculated following UNESCO's definition (i.e. percentage of a cohort of children or young people aged 3-5 years above the intended age for the last grade of each level of education who have completed that grade).
Source: Own elaboration based on household surveys (EPH, 2011-2016) (DGEEC, 2017).

StatLink https://doi.org/10.1787/888933823432

The barriers faced by students to access the education system and to progress once in it translate into relatively unsatisfactory completion rates, despite progress in recent years. Completion rates reach levels of almost 90% for primary education, but around 32% and 35% do not complete lower-secondary and upper-secondary respectively, according to 2016 data (Figure 4.6). Inequalities in completion rates are also significant: only 84.4% of children from the poorest quintile complete primary education, relative to 99.2% of the richest quintile. And primary completion rates in urban areas reach a level of 96.2%, compared to 89.3% in rural areas (CEDLAS and World Bank, 2018).

Learning must be improved: more students spend longer periods at school, but their performance suggests they do not learn enough

Schooling has significantly improved in Paraguay but the quality of the education system remains a core challenge. More people access the education system today, and the average years of education of the population have increased. However, this has not been accompanied by more and better learning, and schooling without learning represents a failed promise and a waste of public resources (World Bank, 2018b). Efforts to bring children to school must be strengthened by policies to improve the quality of the education system and support better learning processes. This is true not only in Paraguay but in the LAC region as a whole. After decades where the emphasis was placed on expanding education coverage, the main challenge today is to turn the educational path into a meaningful experience that will improve social and economic inclusion.

Student performance faces significant challenges and has experienced little improvement in recent years, highlighting the gaps in quality of the Paraguayan education system. The *Sistema Nacional de Evaluación del Proceso Educativo* (SNEPE) is a sample based test that measures student performance in the areas of mathematics and communication in Spanish and in Guaraní. Results from the 2015 SNEPE show that almost a third of students in all the grades where the test is performed (3rd, 6th and 9th grade of *educación escolar básica* – i.e. primary and lower secondary; and the third grade of *educación media* - i.e. last level of upper secondary) have the most basic skill level (Level 1, which includes the recognition of concepts, objects, elements and basic calculations). Only between 7-9% of students had Level 4 skills, i.e. the highest level, which entails the solution of complex problems without explicit data. In communication in Spanish, including reading and linguistic comprehension, the results are as follows: between 29-31%, depending on the grade, had Level 1 results (which involves the literal, fragmented or superficial understanding of a text), and only between 6-8% of students, depending on the grade, performed to Level 4 (intertextual understanding of the text) (Figure 4.7). Relative to the previous SNEPE, which was conducted in 2010, there has been little improvement, and not for all levels. As an example, at the end of lower secondary (9th grade) there were more students performing at Level 1 of mathematics in 2015 (32%) than in 2010 (24%). The tests for communication for 6th and 9th grade show a slight improvement in results, while the test for communication in 3rd grade and for mathematics in 3rd and 6th grades experienced a more significant improvement (MEC, 2018).

Accumulating more years of education does not necessarily improve learning or test results. Results from LAC countries participating in the OECD Programme for International Student Assessment (PISA) 2015, namely Argentina, Brazil, Chile, Colombia, Costa Rica, the Dominican Republic, Mexico, Peru and Uruguay, illustrate this. Results from these countries vary significantly, but on average fifteen-year-olds performed 92 points lower than OECD students in mathematics, 69 points lower in reading and 78 points lower in science, which is equivalent to approximately two years of schooling, two-and-a-half years of schooling and three years of schooling lower than their OECD peers, respectively (OECD/CAF/ECLAC, 2018). That is, while the average years of education of a 15-year-old in these countries have come close to converging with the OECD average, it could be argued that a year of schooling at a school in a LAC country is still not the same as studying for one year at a school in an OECD country, as the knowledge transmitted or learned in one year in the former is less than in the latter.

Figure 4.7. Results of students in national evaluation tests, by grade and by level of performance, 2015

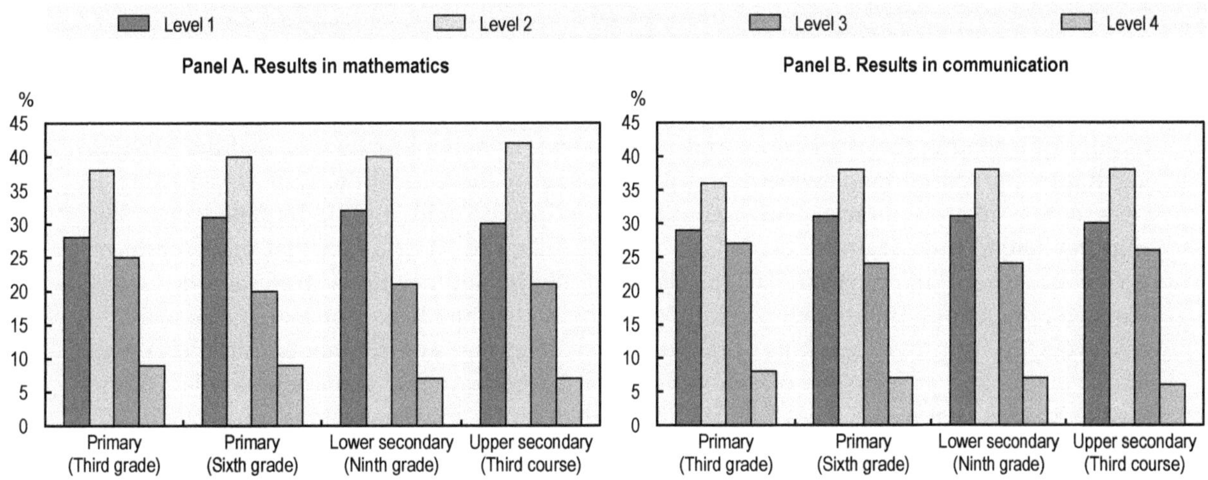

Source: Authors' elaboration based on MEC (2018).

StatLink https://doi.org/10.1787/888933823451

International evaluations confirm that learning in Paraguay faces significant challenges also when compared with countries of a similar level of development. UNESCO's Third Regional Comparative and Explanatory Study (TERCE) showed that 83% of Paraguayan children in grade 3 scored at level 2 or lower in mathematics, and 77% scored in level 2 or lower in reading (UNESCO, 2015). This is significantly worse than the best performer in the LAC region, Chile, where less than 40% of students performed at level 2 or lower in both tests. TERCE only covers LAC countries. Comparisons beyond the LAC region are difficult until the first results from the participation of Paraguay in PISA for development are released in late 2018. However, LAC countries participating in both tests are ranked in a similar order: the highest in PISA, Chile, scores 67 points below the OECD average (OECD, 2015). This gives an idea of the gap in students' performance between Paraguay and OECD countries. Altinok et al. (2018) developed a database of harmonised learning outcomes based on existing international and regional student assessments. This makes it possible to draw comparisons between countries and over time (1965-2015). This dataset shows that Paraguay has a mean score for primary education, for the average over 1960-2015, of 412 points, corresponding to a very low level of skills (meaning that students have very basic skills in mathematics, science and reading). This places the country well below Argentina (439), Brazil (441), Costa Rica (477), Chile (460), Colombia (432), Ecuador (435), Mexico (453), Panama (421), Peru (425) or

Uruguay (474), and only above Bolivia, the Dominican Republic or Venezuela among those LAC countries available in the dataset.

Disadvantaged groups or students in remote areas score lowest on learning outcomes. Results from the SNEPE show that in mathematics and communication in Spanish, students from private schools perform better than those in public schools, though the opposite occurs for the test in communication in Guarani, the main indigenous language in Paraguay and an official language of Paraguay along with Spanish. Likewise, students from urban areas tend to perform better than those in rural areas in mathematics and communication in Spanish (albeit to a lesser degree than the urban/rural difference in guaraní), while rural students perform better in the guaraní communication test (MEC, 2018).

Low quality of teaching drives the poor learning outcomes in the country

Learning outcomes are influenced by multiple school-related factors, mainly linked to the quality of teaching, the availability and effective use of school resources, and the existing capacities for school management and governance of the education system. Learning is poor across many countries, but mainly in low-income and middle-income ones. The reasons behind this "learning crisis" are mainly linked to: (i) the fact that many children arrive at school unprepared; (ii) the lack of skills and/or motivation among many teachers, preventing them from teaching effectively; (iii) the lack – or ineffective use of – resources to improve teaching practices and learning environments; and (iv) poor management and governance of schools and of the education system as a whole (World Bank, 2018b). Paraguay faces significant challenges in all these areas and, as already presented, many children arrive to school unprepared or in poor conditions for effective learning. Learning is ultimately determined by a complex array of factors that go beyond the boundaries of the school but, among the school-related factors, the quality of teaching is probably the single most important factor determining the quality of learning. Consequently, this section's focus is on exploring ways to improve teaching.

Teaching must be improved to achieve better learning outcomes

The overall number of teachers in Paraguay is relatively high, as shown by the comparatively low ratio of students per teacher, though with significant variations between regions. Pupil/teacher ratios for primary and secondary education are similar or below those of many LAC countries and other benchmark countries (Figure 4.8). While this is positive news, low ratios can also be the result of inefficiencies in the distribution of teaching resources (i.e. there can be schools with too few students in certain areas and a reallocation could make sense), and they can hide discrepancies between schools in rural areas and urban areas. This is the case in the Central department, where the ratio pupil/teacher remains above what is desirable (Elías et al. 2014).

Qualifications are low for a large share of teachers which represents a significant barrier to effective learning. In fact, in 2012 only 59% of teachers in pre-primary education (*educación inicial*) had the qualifications that are mandated to teach at that level (up from 49% in 2004), and only 49% had the qualifications to teach in pre-school (i.e. the last year of pre-primary education), up from 32% in 2004, with a big discrepancy between the urban (63%) and rural areas (39%). For primary education (first and second cycle of EEB), the picture is significantly brighter: 92% had the required qualifications in 2012 (up from 85% in 2004). The level of qualifications of teachers varies largely depending on the level of education where they teach, with most of the more qualified teachers in secondary education (Figure 4.9) (Elías et al., 2014).

Deficiencies in the design of teachers' careers provide few incentives for teachers to improve their performance. The teachers' career can be understood as the legal framework that regulates the conditions of the teaching profession, in aspects such as access to the profession, responsibilities, professional development, or remuneration. In Paraguay, the *Estatuto del Docente* approved in 2001 is the current legal framework, but there are many pending challenges that suggest that it is time to move towards a more modern teachers' career. In particular, current challenges demand actions at all the stages of the teachers' pathway. First, it is critical to improve incentives to attract talent and select the most suitable candidates to the teaching career. Second, prospective teachers must be equipped with relevant skills and the quality of the training offered by teachers' training institutions must be ensured, while the selection mechanisms to start teaching need to be improved. Third, new teachers must be supported, and the quality of continuous education must be guaranteed and accompanied by strong incentives and sound evaluation mechanisms to support constant professional development.

Competitive selection processes to become an educator are recent in Paraguay and reveal that the skills of candidates are low and that teaching does not attract talent. Evidence about the performance of teachers is scarce, but data from competitive selection processes to become a teacher show that in 2009 more than 75% of candidates did not pass the test or meet the minimum requirements to become a teacher. In 2010, more than 50% failed the tests to become a teacher or director (PREAL, 2013). More recently, preliminary results of the written test of the last public competition for teachers, carried out in February 2016, showed that around 53% had failed the exam. In addition, the framework for competitive entry into teaching (*Reglamento de Seleccion del Educador Profesional*) was only recently implemented (2009). Consequently, the training levels of teachers vary considerably, particularly among veteran teachers.

Figure 4.8. Pupil/teacher ratio in Paraguay and selected countries, by level of education

2015 or latest available

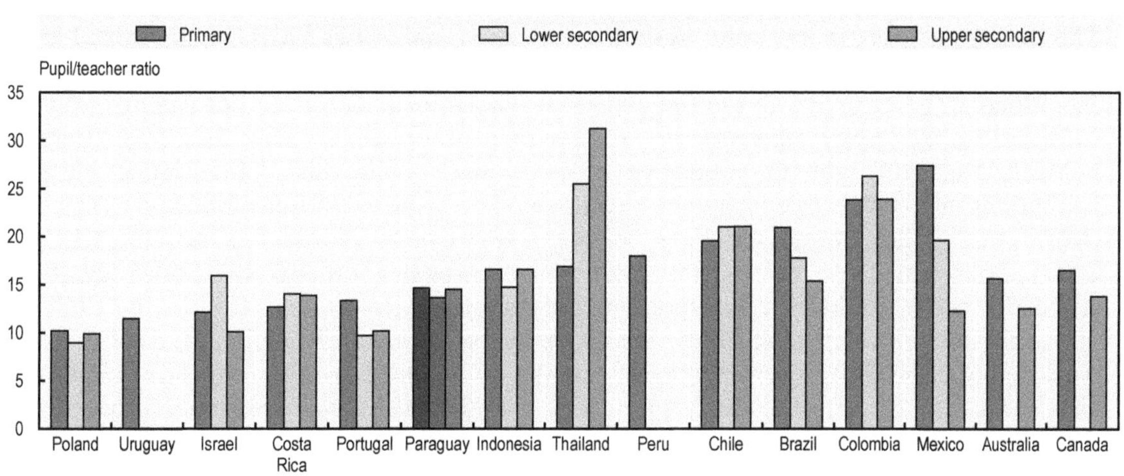

Source: Multi-dimensional Review of Paraguay. Vol I: Initial Assessment (OECD, 2018).

StatLink https://doi.org/10.1787/888933823470

Educators' qualifications and skills largely depend on the quality of teacher-training systems. The *Instituciones Formadoras de Docentes* include all higher education institutions that are entitled to train and certify teachers. They include universities, higher education institutes, and IFDs, i.e. *Institutos de Formación Docente* (institutes for teacher training). In particular, a majority of teachers have a training degree from these IFD, which fall under the responsibility of the Ministry of Education (Figure 4.9). This type of training corresponds to the non-university tertiary education level (ISCED 5), and includes degrees for teaching in pre-primary education, primary, lower secondary, with different levels of specialisation, and upper secondary, with different levels of specialisation (3-year degree).

Figure 4.9. Distribution of teachers according to their level of education and the level of education where they teach

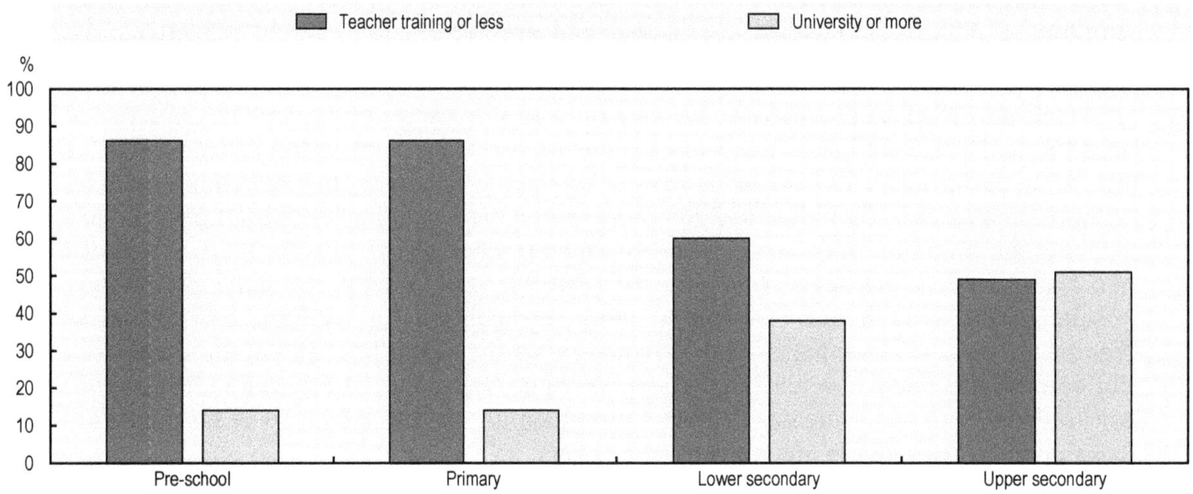

Source: Elías et al. (2014).

StatLink https://doi.org/10.1787/888933823489

The quality of IFDs is low, and while the education authorities have acknowledged in recent years the importance of improving them through mechanisms for licensing and accreditation, progress is still modest and slow. The guidelines for the licensing of IFDs (*Mecanismo de Licenciamiento de Instituciones Formadoras de Docentes*) were published in 2007 with the objective of improving quality and transforming these institutions into centres of educational excellence. The Ministry of Education and Science (MEC) must follow these guidelines before an IFD can be allowed to operate (MEC, 2007). Following these efforts, the creation and licensing of new IFDs was legally suspended between 2007-13, in response to the disorderly expansion of IFDs in the 1990s and early 2000s, which took place oftentimes at the expense of quality, and led to an over-supply of potential teachers (PREAL, 2013). This control over the supply of IFDs is an essential component of quality, but must be complemented by accreditation processes that help to ensure that the quality of the training provided by an institution meets the required standards. The accreditation process falls under the responsibility of the ANEAES (*Agencia Nacional de Evaluación y Acreditación de la Educación Superior*), created in 2003. This process is still in its early stages for IFDs. ANEAES is expected to publish the IFD accreditation guidelines in 2019. The urgency revealed by low performance of students and teachers in the country suggests that ANEAES should be given the institutional and financial capacity to carry out these demanding tasks and develop a robust IFD accreditation system.

Poor quality of teaching is directly linked to the weaknesses of evaluation mechanisms and the lack of incentives to improve performance. Evaluation mechanisms are crucial to improve information on teaching practices and identify main gaps and challenges. They should be the basis of developing tools and programmes to help teachers improve their performance. Teachers' evaluations have been traditionally weak in Paraguay. Since 2016, the Evaluation system to ensure quality based on a policy of holistic evaluation (*Sistema de Evaluacion para el Aseguramiento de la Calidad con base en una Política de Evaluación Integral*) intends to take an overarching approach to the evaluation of the education system, including education institutions, teachers, and students. Regarding teachers, the proposal is to have a pedagogical support system (*Sistema de Acompañamiento Pedagógico*), focusing on how the educator manages the curriculum, his professional development, and the link with social actors. The final objective is to establish a culture of evaluation that can support teachers in improving their performance and recognising their crucial role in societies. Evaluations should be complemented by incentives to improve performance. These incentives have been generally weak in Paraguay, where increases in teachers' salaries have been mostly linked to the accumulation of years of experience, accreditations, and training, instead of performance or merit (PREAL, 2013).

The limited and low quality options for continuous training represent an additional barrier to effective teaching and the improvement of performance throughout the teacher's career. In addition to the initial training, IFDs also provide continuing education, which is aimed at supporting teachers as they update or strengthen their knowledge and skills once they are already in service. Evidence on the quality and impact of this type of education is scarce in Paraguay, but the literature suggests that it is fragmented, of a small scale, and mostly unrelated to the needs of educators (UNESCO, 2015; World Bank, 2013). Also, incentives are low for acquiring this type of training, given the way in which the increases in the remuneration scale (*escalafón docente*) is designed.

Policies must continue to expand access to school as well as completion rates, particularly among the most disadvantaged groups

Policy design, implementation, monitoring and evaluation must be based on reliable statistics to be successful. Today, the administrative data needed to produce relevant education indicators are inaccurate in some cases. A good example is the overestimation of the population projections of the 2002 census, which has led to a lack of statistics for some key education dimensions in recent years such as enrolment. In this context, efforts are being made to build a system of education indicators that is more reliable. The launch in 2016 of a unified student registry (*Registro Único del Estudiante*) is a step in this direction. This is a way to centralise information of students that should favour the production of more reliable, easy-to-manage and comparable data on access, progression, and completion, among other things. Being able to produce sound education statistics is critical to support policymaking and to measure progress. The education goals included in the National Development Plan, as well as the more specific targets that will eventually be part of the PNTE 2030, will have to be based on sound statistics. Indeed, data-related capacities will have to be strengthened if those goals and targets are to be monitored correctly. Likewise, SDG 4 sets a number of targets in the field of education for 2030, and tracking progress towards them requires sound and internationally comparable statistics.

Policies to support access in remote areas and across most disadvantaged socioeconomic groups, particularly in some education levels, must be pursued to complete the universalisation of compulsory education. Access to early childhood education is still low and must be expanded, given its key role in improving well-being and learning outcomes across the life cycle (Heckman, 2006). Indeed, having attended pre-primary education raises PISA scores by the equivalent of one additional year of secondary schooling, according to the results of LAC countries participating in PISA 2012 (OECD/CAF/ECLAC, 2014).

Various areas for policy recommendations can be highlighted related to pre-primary education. First, families and children should be supported in overcoming their main barriers – economic and geographic – to access pre-primary education. The target is to reach universal pre-schooling (age 5) by 2024, as set in the *Plan Nacional de Educacion 2024*, and expand overall coverage for all levels of initial education. This entails placing particular efforts in rural areas and among indigenous communities. The conditional cash transfer programme, known as *Tekoporã*, must continue its support to most disadvantaged families, linking its disbursement to pre-school attendance. And the school kits (*kits escolares*) must be guaranteed, as they can mark the difference between attending pre-school or not among the most disadvantaged. To avoid geographical barriers, the *maestras mochileras* programme represents an interesting initiative of non-formal initial education that could be scaled-up. This consists of teachers visiting households with children aged 0 to 5, to support early childhood development. Second, it is important to raise awareness within communities about the importance of early childhood education and care. To this end, strengthening the role of the Childhood and adolescence councils (*Consejos de la Niñez y Adolescencia*) to raise awareness in communities should be considered. Third, expanding compulsory education to age four should be considered. This has already happened in countries like Argentina, Brazil and Uruguay. Finally, and in a more structural manner, the offer of pre-primary education must be enlarged, as it is scarce today. This goes together not only with having more schools, but also more – and better – teachers.

Access to lower secondary and upper secondary education can also be improved, mainly across some segments of society and regions where coverage is still insufficient. This is an area where the role of scholarships can be critical, but generally these focus on higher education levels, thus with a potentially regressive impact, as not many students from poor households reach tertiary education. Also, *Tekoporã* is a strong tool to support youth from the most disadvantaged backgrounds to access secondary school. Distance learning solutions and open education for educación media are a good mechanism to reach rural areas or students who cannot attend classes and follow a rigid schedule, and thus should be strengthened, but taking into account that blended learning, where students learn remotely but also benefit from in-person instruction, can be particularly effective (OECD, 2016). Finally, expanding access to secondary education could be supported by strengthening school transport in remote areas.

Policies to favour school retention and completion, avoiding repetition and drop-out, must be at the centre of all efforts. Most dropouts take place in the transitions between lower and upper secondary schools, and onwards. Hence policies must focus on reducing repetition and dropout, and favour a more successful progression within the education system. This would help lift completion rates. The main reasons behind dropout are economic, and thus scholarships are also an interesting tool to discourage students from leaving the education system. Mechanisms to identify and support students at risk of exclusion are also relevant, with flexibility in pedagogical methods to support those with higher difficulties. A gradual expansion of the school day could be considered, starting with a small sample of schools to assess the impact in the reduction of dropout (as well as in learning outcomes).

Policies to improve learning outcomes must focus on teachers, educational resources, and the management of schools

Improve evidence on learning outcomes to inform policy making. The SNEPE is currently the main tool for evaluation of student performance in the country, but its public availability has been irregular, and the use of its results to inform and support evidence-based policy-making very limited. To complement this, PISA will provide informative results and will help administrators develop policy actions. Notwithstanding this effort, the engagement in the next round of PISA should be considered as part of the ambitious commitment of the country to transform education. This will allow for a deeper analysis of learning outcomes, will inform policy and practice, and will be useful to establish a rigorous comparison with international standards, which should help to set the bar higher.

Improve teaching to achieve better learning outcomes. The quality of teaching is probably the single most important factor determining the quality of the broader education system (Hanushek and Rivkin, 2012). One of the core policy challenges to transform education and improve teaching in Paraguay is re-shaping teachers' career pathways, which demands strong political will. This will be crucial to:

- Attract talent and raise the status of teaching, to ensure that the best candidates enter and remain in the profession. This entails rethinking mechanisms for selection, but also incentives (salaries, social recognition, etc.) in the exercise of teaching, to make the profession attractive. Countries like Singapore or Finland have strong and competitive teacher selection processes that guarantee that candidates are top performers. In Paraguay, the move towards competitive selection processes goes in the right direction, but should probably be accompanied by probationary periods for teachers in the first steps in the teaching profession, with mentoring, support, and an induction programme to identify challenges, complement gaps and support the development of instructional practices;
- Strengthen incentives to develop and improve once in the teaching profession. This involves strengthening the link between performance and rewards (not just in terms of pay progression but also regarding access to higher responsibilities and different roles), and supporting good quality in-service training, to enable educators to update and improve their pedagogical skills. Given the existing gaps among current teachers, strengthening in-service training can be particularly effective in raising overall teaching quality in the short-to-mid-term;
- Establish a stronger, more systematic system for the evaluation of teachers' performance, which should be understood as a way to support teachers in identifying constraints, monitor progress in their career, and favour re-skilling and the development of new pedagogical methods. This should include not only the assessment of school principals and peers, but also external evaluations to ensure and independent and fair judgement.

Raise the quality of the *Instituciones de Formacion Docente.* The quality of teaching cannot be enhanced without a major improvement in the quality of training institutions. MEC's efforts to control the supply of these institutions and establish clear criteria for their licensing are a step in the right direction. Yet, these efforts should also include a process of accreditation of IFDs to be carried out by the ANEAES. The latter's budget and human resources should be augmented in order to secure the capacities needed to carry out these tasks effectively, which should include powers to close an institution if the standards are not met. The evaluations associated to this accreditation process should be a tool to identify areas of improvement, and one requirement of accreditation could be that institutions publish the proportion of graduates that gain permanent posts as teachers, to help prospective students make informed choices. Evaluations should also be used to provide support for IFDs in boosting overall quality, including for both initial and continuing education.

Improving the transition from school to work is critical to favour employability and access to good quality jobs

Education and skills can play a major role in enhancing job prospects and access to good quality jobs in Paraguay. Participation in labour markets with good job conditions constitutes a fundamental aspect of well-being. In this sense, improving the transition from school to work in Paraguay – through better education and skills for all – must be a priority for public policy.

Yet the transition throughout the education system in Paraguay still has many hurdles that stand in the way of successful inclusion in labour markets. A considerable share of students does not access the education system, particularly at the upper secondary level. And among those who access, there are many that leave school too early, as illustrated by high drop-out and low completion rates. In addition to this, learning outcomes are poor, and increased schooling does not provide good quality education and skills, making it difficult for workers to move beyond low-skilled occupations. An additional fundamental barrier to good quality employability is low relevance: the education and skills acquired in the education system are oftentimes distant from the ones that are more valued and that remain scarce in labour markets, which are keys to finding a better job. Demand-side issues – i.e. the capacity of the economy to provide good-quality job opportunities – are also critical to understand school-to-work transitions, but go beyond the scope of this analysis.

The transition from school to work is bumpy and many young people leave the education system to enter bad quality jobs

Transitions from school to work are difficult in Paraguay, with more than half of students leaving the education system to join inactivity, unemployment or informality. Yearly out-of-school transitions rates show that among urban youth (ages 15-29) in Paraguay, around 30% of males enter inactivity when they leave school, while almost 10% join informal jobs, and 25% become unemployed. The remaining percentage joins formal jobs. Young females show significantly worse transitions: only around 15% access formal jobs after leaving school, while as many as 40% become inactive, 12% join informal jobs, and above 35% become unemployed (Figure 4.10). The comparison with Argentina and Brazil shows that a larger share of students transition to employment in Paraguay, though this should be interpreted with caution, as only urban youth are considered in this analysis, and the share of rural population vary largely between Paraguay (40%) and Brazil (14%) and Argentina (8%), which may lead to biases (World Bank, 2018a).

The transition from school to work is particularly difficult for the most disadvantaged socioeconomic groups. After age 15, young people withdraw from school in large numbers, which has particularly adverse consequences for low-income households. At age 29, and among youth living in extreme poor households, around 6 out of 10 workers are not employed, nor in education or training (NEET), 3 out of 10 are informal workers, and only 1 out of 10 workers has a formal job. In vulnerable households, half of workers at age 29 are either NEET or informal. The picture is somewhat brighter for youth living in middle-class households, where only around 2 out of 10 workers are either NEET or informal at age 29 (Figure 4.11). Guarani-speaking households face greater risks of being informal, as most formal jobs are located in Asuncion (Ruppert Bulmer et al., 2017).

Inactivity is widespread and affects women the most, with negative consequences on well-being. Around 25% of young females and almost 8% of young males were NEET in Paraguay in 2014. The larger share of NEET among females is usually associated to work in the household: indeed, many women working in the household are productive and contribute to the economy, as they are engaged in unpaid domestic work and caregiving (OECD/CAF/ECLAC, 2016). The consequences of such large shares of inactivity among young people are straightforward: not only do they face a stigma and difficulties to participate in various dimensions of society (thus increasing the risk of engaging in risky behaviour) they also lack a fundamental source of income and social protection. In addition, they struggle to acquire new – or maintain existing – skills that would be crucial for their future integration into labour markets.

Figure 4.10. Transitions from school to the labour market among youth (ages 15-29) in Paraguay and other selected Latin American countries (2005-2015)

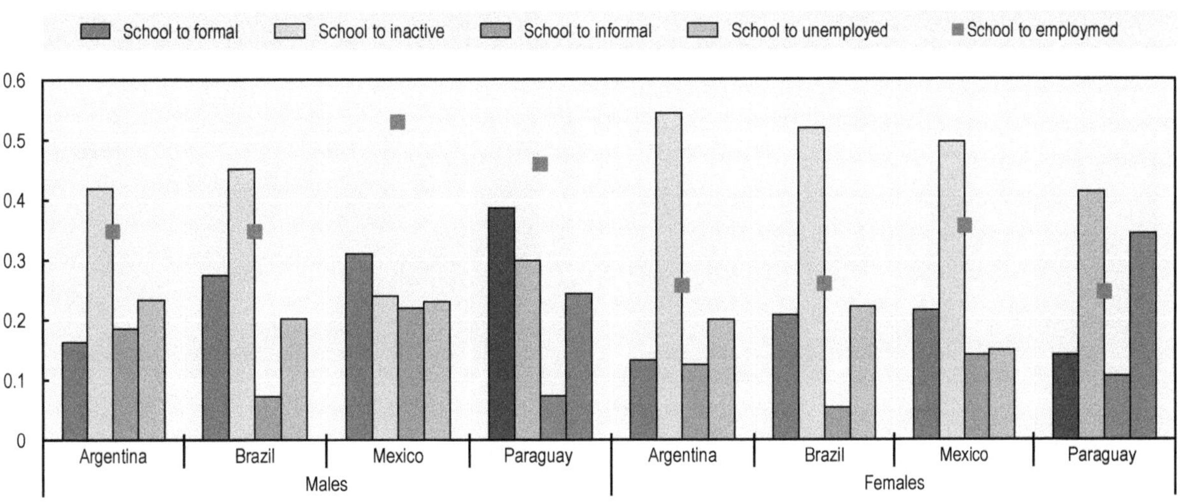

Note: Results show yearly transition rates out of school for the period 2005-15. These are calculated as the ratio between the flow of people transitioning from Condition 1 (school) to Condition 2 between time 0 and 1, over the total stock of people in Condition 1 in time 0. Transitions are year to year (from year t to year t + 1). Only the urban population is covered due to data limitations.
Source: *Latin American Economic Outlook 2017: Youth, Skills and Entrepreneurship* (OECD/CAF/ECLAC, 2016).

StatLink https://doi.org/10.1787/888933823508

Informality is a widespread phenomenon in Paraguay, with heavy consequences for workers and the wider economy. Labour informality affected 64% of workers outside the agriculture sector in 2015 (OECD, 2018). Informal jobs tend to be associated to low quality job conditions, lower earnings, higher levels of insecurity, a poorer quality of the working environment, and no access to social protection and other benefits associated to formal jobs. While informality sometimes represents a first step on a labour trajectory that can improve at later stages, it acts in many cases as a trap, leading to poor labour market outcomes in the future. Evidence from Argentina, Brazil, Chile and Mexico shows that, of all urban adults (ages 30-55) transitioning each year from an informal job, 70% move to another informal job (OECD/CAF/ECLAC, 2016). Informality also limits the development of skills, as it usually entails working at low-skilled professions performing low value-added tasks, frequently leading to a deterioration of workers' skill sets. Workers in the informal sector are more difficult to identify and thus they are difficult to reach with training and active labour market policies, while training at informal workplaces is almost non-existent.

Figure 4.11. Activity status of youth by single year of age and socio-economic group in Paraguay, 2014

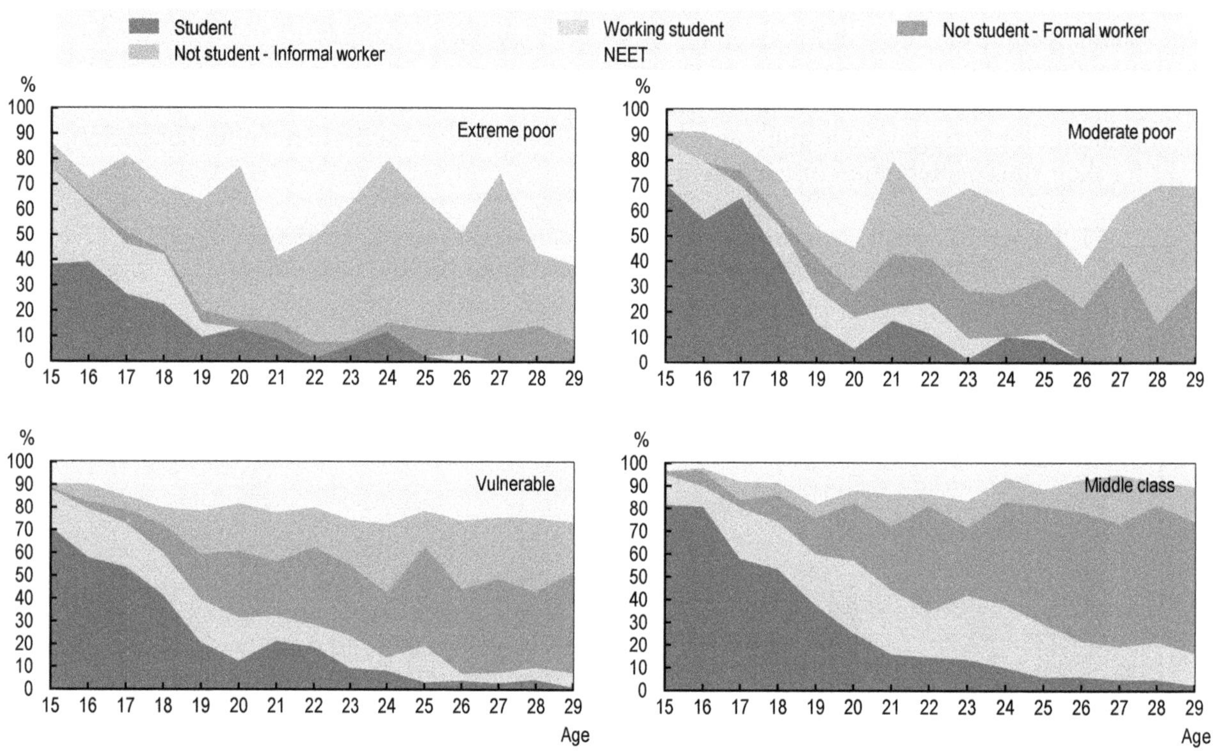

Note: Socio-economic classes are defined using World Bank classification: "Extreme poor" = youth belonging to households with a daily per capita income lower than USD 2.50. "Moderate poor" = youth belonging to households with a daily per capita income of USD 2.50-4.00. "Vulnerable" = individuals with a daily per capita income of USD 4.00-10.00 "Middle class" = youth from households with a daily per capita income between USD 10.00-50.00. Poverty lines and incomes are expressed in 2005 USD PPP per day (PPP = purchasing power parity). LAC weighted average of 16 countries: Argentina, Bolivia, Brazil, Chile, Colombia, Costa Rica, Dominican Republic, Ecuador, El Salvador, Guatemala, Honduras, Mexico, Panama, Paraguay, Peru and Uruguay.

Source: *Latin American Economic Outlook 2017: Youth, Skills and Entrepreneurship* (OECD/CAF/ECLAC, 2016).

StatLink https://doi.org/10.1787/888933823527

The education system does not provide the right skills to favour access to good quality jobs

Low levels of education and skills are a direct cause of poor school-to-work transitions in Paraguay. In particular, there are many complex and diverse causes of informality in the country including: (i) the low-skill labour force, (ii) an economic structure where subsistence micro, small enterprises dominate, (iii) the relatively high cost of formalisation (with little incentive to become formal), (iv) the deficiencies in the design of social protection programmes and (v) the weaknesses in terms of workers' representation (Ayala, 2016).

Informality decreases with the level of education among Paraguayans. While informal work remains above 80% for those with no education or with just a lower secondary education, it affects around 70% of those who have completed upper secondary education, and only 30% of those who have completed higher education (Figure 4.12). The fact that informality remains high even for workers who have completed significant levels of education – i.e. upper secondary – could be explained by two phenomena, which can be at play simultaneously: first, the skills acquired in the education system are not relevant for the demands and requirements of existing formal jobs; and second, there are few formal job opportunities due to an economic structure that is not conducive to their creation.

Figure 4.12. Labour informality by level of education, 2016

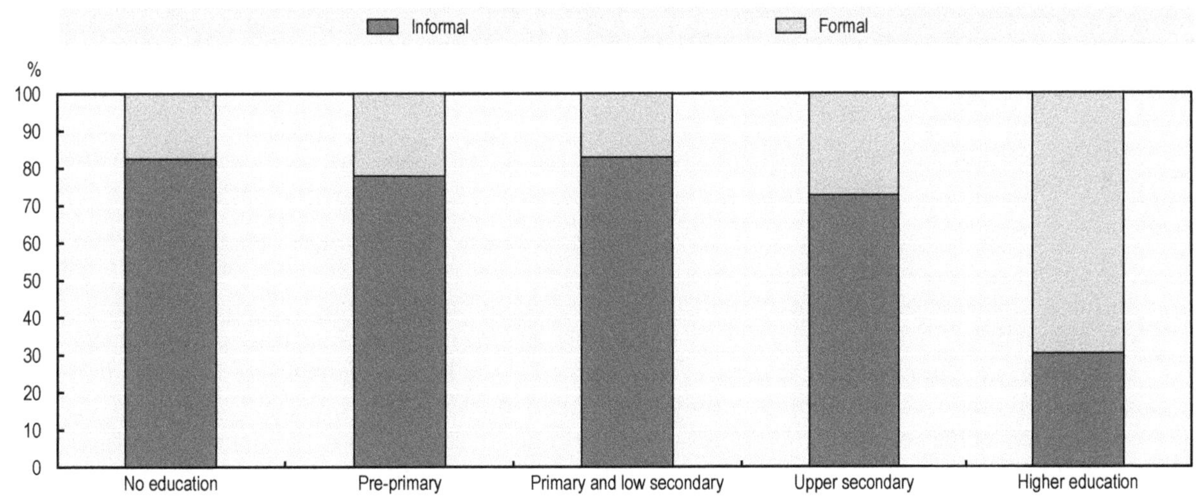

Note: Workers with no health insurance of any type are assumed to be informal.
Source: Own elaboration based on EPH 2016 (DGEEC, 2017).

StatLink https://doi.org/10.1787/888933823546

Low relevance of skills limits the opportunities to access formal jobs, as illustrated by the substantial difficulties faced by formal firms to find the workers with the skills they need. Around 80% of formal firms in the country claim that they face difficulties to fill their vacancies. This is significantly above the already high LAC average of 65%. The skills that are more difficult to find are mainly related to emotional intelligence, communication skills and critical thinking, all part of a group of generic, soft skills that are scarce among

Paraguayan workers. Also, other more specific, technical skills related to budget, financial or computing skills appear as particularly relevant given the unmet demand (Figure 4.13).

Figure 4.13. Percentage of formal firms with difficulties to fill vacancies, by country, sector and type of skills

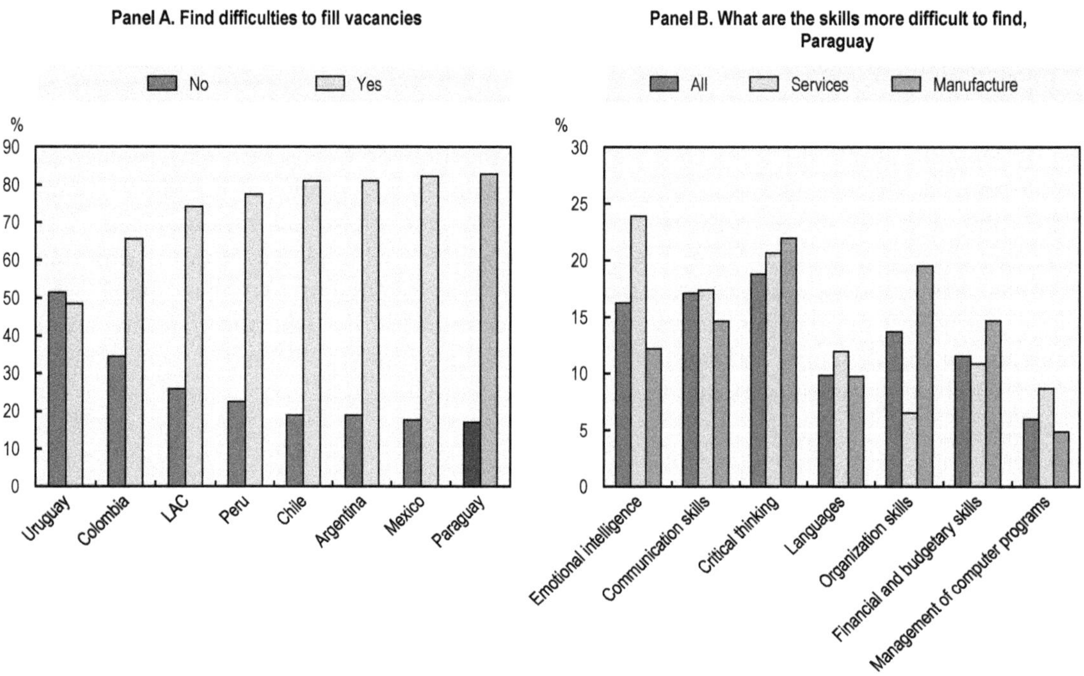

Source: Authors' elaboration based on *Survey on skill demand and shortages in Latin America* (OECD/Manpower, forthcoming).

StatLink https://doi.org/10.1787/888933823565

Returns to education have increased for skilled occupations, pointing to a relative scarcity of high-skilled workers. Since the beginning of the century, returns to university education, i.e. the monetary returns of reaching a higher level of education, have not had a uniform trend. Most recently, they have been on the rise, however. This can be interpreted as the result of a relative scarcity of high-level skills (i.e. the demand for high skills has grown faster than the supply). Returns on mid-and-low-level skills, associated to secondary and primary education respectively, have decreased in recent years (Figure 4.14). Factors driving these trends can be related to demand or supply. The expansion of access to primary and secondary education, which has taken place in some cases at the expense of quality, could be a driver of these declining returns. But demand-side dynamics leading to a shift towards higher-level skills could also be driving these trends. Changes in returns to education is similar to that of most LAC countries, where there has been a pattern of expansion of the relative supply of skilled and semi-skilled workers (i.e. higher and secondary education). This led to a fall of returns to secondary education, but returns to higher education have been more volatile, with a significant increase in the 1990s, a decline and relative stability in the 2000s, and an upsurge after 2012. Recent evidence suggests that this can be better explained by looking at demand-side factors (i.e. the change in the demand for skilled workers) rather than the supply side (Galiani et al., 2017).

Figure 4.14. Returns to education in Paraguay, 1995-2014

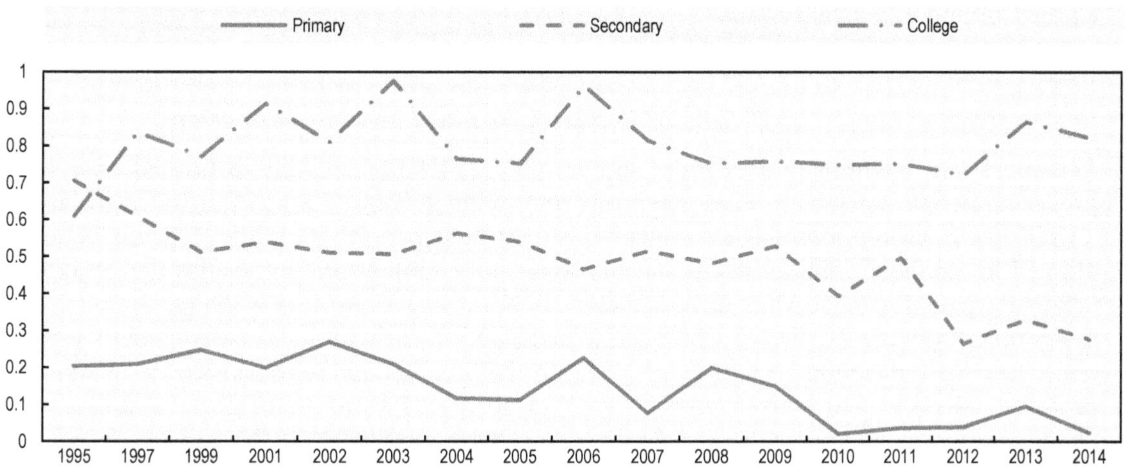

Note: The figure presents the coefficients of educational dummies on a Mincer equation regression.
Source: Authors' elaboration based on CEDLAS and World Bank (2017).

StatLink https://doi.org/10.1787/888933823584

Upper secondary education must be modernised to provide more relevant skills

The *educación media* (upper secondary education) is perceived as not preparing students to access labour markets or enter higher education with the right skills. The *educacion media* in Paraguay has two main paths. First, the scientific baccalaureate (*bachillerato científico*), which is usually more associated to the preparation of students for university education, and has three different options depending on the focus of the curriculum: social sciences, basic sciences, and arts and literature. Second, the technical baccalaureate (*bachillerato técnico*), or upper-secondary technical and vocational education and training (TVET), which is more oriented towards labour market insertion or to prepare for post-secondary TVET, and has more than 25 types of training in agriculture, industry and services. Three out of four students of *educación media* were enrolled in the *bachillerato científico* in 2011 (MEC, 2012). Existing evidence, though very limited, suggests that students find that the skills acquired in *educación media* are not sufficiently relevant in the workplace, a view shared by firms, while higher education institutions claim that students reach this level with insufficient levels of skills.

The curriculum of *educación media* must be redesigned so that it favours labour market insertion and provides a more solid basis for accessing higher education. The curriculum of *educación media* must be oriented towards training students with skills for the 21st century. In increasingly knowledge-based economies, and in a context where manufacturing and certain low-skill tasks are increasingly becoming automated, the demand for repetitive manual skills is declining, while the demand for information-processing and other high-level cognitive and interpersonal skills is growing. In addition to mastering occupation-specific skills, workers in the 21st century must also have information-processing skills and various "generic" skills, including interpersonal communication, self-management, and the ability to learn, to help them weather the uncertainties of rapidly changing labour markets (OECD, 2013). Recent efforts to transform the curriculum of *educación media* were a move in the right direction, with a skills-based approach that promotes more workplace learning. However, institutional turnover and fragmentation have limited the success of these initiatives. Now, a more co-ordinated effort should be started in the aim of building on the findings and lessons learned from previous initiatives.

Strengthening technical and vocational education and training could support the improvement of school-to-work transitions and life-long education

Technical and vocational education and training (TVET) can play a critical role in preparing people for jobs in Paraguay, thus improving school-to-work transitions for all. TVET has a strong potential as a mechanism to help people get skills that are better aligned to the labour market needs. In this sense, it is another option besides the general academic path for those who have a technical vocation, as well as a viable option for many other individuals: people who wish to access a job early in their careers, adults who once left the education system and want to have a second opportunity to acquire professional skills, and individuals who want or need – as a way to adapt or re-skill – to change professional paths (OECD/CAF/ECLAC, 2016; UNESCO, 2016).

TVET is highly fragmented in Paraguay, with many providers and multiple modalities that limit its potential as a strong, integrated system of professional training. The main pillars of TVET in Paraguay are broadly organised as follows. First, there is formal TVET, which falls under the responsibility of the Ministry of Education. At the level of *educación media* it is provided through *bachilleratos técnicos* as well as by the *formación profesional media* (professional training), which is more clearly oriented towards direct labour market insertion. At the level of higher, non-university education, TVET is provided in the *Institutos Técnicos Superiores*. In addition to this, there are modalities of permanent education for young people and adults. Historical data shows that traditionally around 25% of students following a *bachillerato* enrol in *bachillerato técnico*. And recent data from MEC shows that only a small fraction enrol in *formación profesional media*, while around a third of students enrolled in *educación permanente* are following a TVET programme in one of its modalities. Second, there is non-formal TVET, which is usually under the supervision of the Ministry of Labour and is mainly provided through the *Sistema Nacional de Promoción Profesional* (SNPP) and the *Sistema Nacional de Formación y Capacitación Laboral* (SINAFOCAL). Finally, there are many other forms of TVET offered by other ministries and bodies in specific areas like agriculture, health or construction. In sum, TVET in Paraguay is highly fragmented, with multiple training options being offered by a plethora of actors. While there have been successful TVET experiences and programmes in Paraguay, they have grown in a dispersed and uncoordinated manner. They are usually planned by different bodies with a focus on specific groups or very specific needs (MEC et al., 2011; UNESCO, 2013).

Paraguay lacks an integrated system of technical and vocational education and training. In recent years, efforts to better co-ordinate TVET programmes and communicate about them to the general public at the national level have been ineffective in establishing an integrated national TVET system. *The Plan Nacional de Mejoramiento de la Educación Técnica y Profesional 2011-2013* represented an effort to expand the TVET offer and improve its quality by strengthening public-private collaboration and raising funds. The law that was discussed in 2012 to regulate and articulate TVET did not come to fruition. The new statutes of the Ministry of Education, approved in 2017, establish the functions of an advisory body called *Consejo Nacional de Educación y Trabajo* (CNET), which operates in a tripartite scheme where one of its objectives is to propose and approve a strategic plan for TVET, fostering co-ordination with the various sectors involved in the execution of public policies related to education and work. Among the functions of the CNET, an inter-ministerial technical unit is created, which is responsible for installing and keeping updated the *Sistema Nacional de Cualificaciones Profesionales*, whose activities have been carried out since 2014 with a working team of both ministries of education and labour. This should be a relevant stepping stone to move towards an integrated TVET, which demands broad, ambitious efforts, that must be complemented with specific actions that deal with the main challenges of TVET at different levels (upper-secondary, post-secondary, permanent and non-formal education) and in different areas: quality, relevance, and coherence/efficiency of the system.

Upper-secondary TVET must be supported to be an effective gateway to the labour market but also to post-secondary TVET. Given the dropout rate after age 15, making TVET more useful at the upper-secondary education level can be an effective mechanism to keep students in school and improve transitions to jobs. In addition to the aforementioned measures to support better learning in *educación media*, which are related to teachers and teaching practices, school resources and school management, particular focus must be placed on upper-secondary TVET as a way to favour better school-to-work transitions. To this end, it is critical to design vocational programmes adapted to economic changes and needs, with more mechanisms to facilitate dialogue between educators, unions and firm associations and adapt curricula to these evolving needs. It is also fundamental to focus not only on specific skills, but also on foundation and generic skills that are transferable and prepare workers to adapt to changing skill demands and to build vocational training pathways. Career guidance to deliver active orientation and feedback to young learners is also essential, in order to identify vocations and inform them about labour market prospects. Finally, making significant use of the workplace as a quality learning environment is a critical element to train in the practical aspects of the specific profession and favour a smoother transition to jobs (OECD, 2010). These actions, together with specific communication efforts, must be effective in raising the reputation of initial TVET in Paraguay as a mechanism to effectively transition from school to work. In this respect, anecdotal evidence suggests that *bachillerato técnico* is well regarded by Paraguayans, and contrary to most countries in the LAC region, it is seen as being a more solid training platform from which to access higher education than the *bachillerato científico*. However, the perception it has as a mechanism to access jobs or to start a vocational pathway can be significantly improved.

The quality and relevance of post-secondary TVET must be improved. While initial TVET at the upper secondary level can provide useful skills, such training is sometimes – and increasingly so – insufficient for certain jobs and must be complemented with post-secondary TVET of the highest quality and relevance (OECD, 2014). Post-secondary TVET is mainly provided in Paraguay through the *Institutos Técnicos Superiores* (ITS), which fall under the responsibility of the Ministry of Education, as set out in the Law of Higher Education 4995/13. To improve their quality and relevance, three elements appear critical. First, integrating work-based learning in TVET programmes, as this represents a strong learning environment that also facilitates subsequent recruitment. This should be made compulsory, and funding for public ITS should be associated to compliance with this. Second, teachers should have strong teaching skills and up-to-date industry knowledge and experience. This entails promoting flexible arrangements to facilitate the hiring of practitioners directly from industry or to establish part-time arrangements. Also, qualification requirements for teaching at this level should be adapted to reflect the desired mix of requirements: academic, pedagogical and practical skills. Third, the curriculum must reflect a mix of technical and job-specific skills as well as basic skills. In fact, international evidence shows that many adults, even with post-secondary education, have weak basic skills, while firms claim these abilities are particularly difficult to find (OECD/Manpower, forthcoming; OECD, 2014). These dimensions should be incorporated into criteria used by the *Consejo Nacional de Educación Superior* and the Ministry of Education to determine the suitability of ITS. In the LAC region, some best practices can be transposed to future reform. As an example, in Brazil and Colombia there is an obligation for workplace training or traineeship after TVET that has had positive results for labour market insertion. And Jamaica is a good example of training for TVET teachers, through its Vocational Training Development Institute (UNESCO, 2016).

Non-formal TVET needs to be better co-ordinated and supported. The role of SINAFOCAL, created in 2001, is more related to the definition of the strategy for professional training, with a clear responsibility to supervise the quality of non-formal TVET, including the certification and accreditation of skills, as well as a research role involving the analysis of skills demands of the productive sector. The SNPP, operational since 1971, focuses on the actual provision of training. In practice, both bodies provide training and the distribution of attributions is still somewhat unclear. While progress is being made in this direction, the objective should be to have a co-ordinated, complementary functioning of these two institutions where the role of SINAFOCAL to strengthen the quality of the non-formal TVET system is supported financially. The recent development of a registry of institutions of professional training (REIFOCAL) is a step in the right direction. On the other hand, the SNPP can be an effective tool to favour labour market insertion, but challenges related to outdated or insufficient infrastructure to provide good quality training suggest that its financial resources need to be increased.

Paraguay must move towards a national, integrated TVET system that supports quality and relevance, favours the transparency of learning outcomes and the transferability of qualifications, and provides clear career pathways. The multiple modalities of TVET represent a challenge to guarantee its quality and relevance across the country. Thus, a national policy for TVET must be designed to co-ordinate the existing offer, enhance the transparency of learning outcomes, and set qualifications that are easy to interpret both for students and employers, uniform across the country and accompanied by rigorous assessments. It can also facilitate transitions from non-formal training to formal options. In this respect, developing a National Qualifications Framework should be considered: while this can be costly, it can also be enormously beneficial. Discussions around this should be part of the agenda towards the definition of the PNTE 2030. The recognition of prior skills can also be critical in a country where learning often takes place outside formal education such as within the family, at the workplace and through self-directed individual activity. Finally, building clear career pathways can make the TVET system more attractive.

The match between the supply and demand of skills must be improved to support better employability

Improving the transition from school to work and fostering better employability demands efforts that go beyond the education and skills system and include mechanisms to better match these skills with the actual demands from the economy. Policy emphasis placed on improving the relevance of skills should thus be complemented by more information and better programmes to effectively make the match between workers and job vacancies.

The reach of active labour market policies (ALMPs) must be extended in order to support training and intermediation programmes that favour access to job vacancies. ALMPs and Public Employment Services can facilitate a better transition from school to work through programmes for training and intermediation, but their coverage is limited in Paraguay (ILO, 2014). In 2009, more than 90% of job search in the country took place through informal channels (Mazza, 2011). This suggests that the potential to improve the efficiency in the match between job supply and demand is large. Public employment services can be strengthened not only by expanding them and making them more present at the local level, but also by introducing performance management frameworks, more tailored job search assistance, and by increasing the use of digital technologies to expand their reach and effectiveness. Regarding training services, and beyond the role of SNPP and SINAFOCAL, there have been valuable public-private partnerships to provide training to disadvantaged youth, such as *Sape'a* and *Nuevas Oportunidades de Empleo para Jóvenes,* but their small scale has limited their impact (OECD/CAF/ECLAC, 2016).

Improving labour market information can be an effective tool to support better education and career choices. Providing information to students about available options and professional career paths after graduation can support them in making informed choices about their field of study and future professional career. This can be an effective way of signalling sectors where skills are scarcer and help in closing skills gaps. An interesting example in this direction is the web service called *Ponte en Carrera* in Peru, which collects information on educational offerings and labour market demands and makes it public for the use of all prospective students.

Setting up institutional mechanisms to foster dialogue between educators, private sector and workers will be critical to anticipate and identify skills needs. Skills councils for particular economic sectors, involving various stakeholders, can support a better identification of skills needs, and can be informative to develop specific training programs to respond to those gaps. The role of the *Observatorio Laboral* of the Ministry of Labour should be strengthened, as a critical body to provide information about skills needs, including specific data on gaps at the regional level. The *Consejo Nacional de Educación y Trabajo* is a step in the right direction to promote interministerial cooperation to search for policy responses to bride existing gaps between the demand and supply of skills.

Policy recommendations

Box 4.2. Main recommendations to promote an education and skills system that fosters inclusiveness and employability

1. Policies to support a better education system for all

1.1. Adopt a national pact on education – the PNTE 2030 – built on a consensus reached in a consultative process:

- Set specific targets and milestones for the different areas of action.
- Establish specific financial commitments.
- Mobilise international expertise to learn from best practices.

1.2. Strengthen efforts to expand coverage and foster completion, particularly in pre-primary and secondary, and among the most disadvantaged groups:

- Produce better education statistics to evaluate future challenges, monitor progress, and inform education policy.
  - Use the Registro Unico del Estudiante as a way to centralise student information and favour the production of more reliable, easy-to-manage and comparable data.
  - Overcome the current challenges for the production of basic education metrics regarding access, enrolment, progression and completion.
- Support access in remote areas and across the most disadvantaged socioeconomic groups.
  - Support access to pre-primary education, helping families to overcome main barriers:
    - Economic: strengthen the conditionality of CCT Tekoporã with preschool attendance.
    - Geographical: scale-up the non-formal, initial education programme maestras mochileras.
  - Raise awareness within communities of the importance of early childhood education:
    - Strengthen – or establish when non-existent – the role of the Consejos de Ninez y Adolescencia.
  - Expand the offer of pre-primary education:
    - More and better school and teachers, and developing modalities to address special needs.
    - Consider expanding compulsory education to age 4.
  - Expand coverage in secondary education:
    - Scholarships earmarked for students from disadvantaged groups and/or with special needs.
    - Reinforce "educación media abierta y a distancia".
    - Strengthen school transport for secondary education in remote areas.
- Policies to favour school retention and completion, avoiding repetition and dropout:
  - Consider a gradual expansion of the school day, starting with a pilot to measure impact on the dropout reduction (and learning outcomes).
  - Develop mechanisms to identify and support students at risk of exclusion, with flexibility in pedagogical methods to support those with greater difficulties.

1.3. Policies to improve learning and the overall quality of the education system:

- Improve evidence on learning outcomes to inform policy-making.

- Strengthen the SNEPE as the main tool for evaluation of student performance, improving its use and the public-availability of results to favour analysis and evidence-based policy-making.

- Improve teaching to achieve better learning outcomes.
  - Re-shape teachers' career pathways to:
    - Attract talent and raise the status of teaching to ensure that the best candidates enter and remain in the profession. This entails rethinking mechanisms for selection, but also incentives (salaries, social recognition, etc.).
    - Strengthen incentives to develop and improve, with a stronger link between rewards and performance.
    - Reinforce and systematise teachers' evaluations, to monitor progress and assess weaknesses to support improvement.
  - Raise quality of the Instituciones de Formacion Docente:
    - Initiate the process of accreditation of IFDs, and strengthen ANEAES to guarantee capacity to carry out this task effectively.
    - Improve the quality of both initial and continuing education.

2. Policies to improve access to better quality jobs

2.1. Transform and modernise the curriculum of educación media técnica:

- Reform curricula to prioritise 21st century skills.
- Develop mechanisms to adapt the curriculum of bachilleratos técnicos to the fast-changing demands of industry, involving private sector and other stakeholders.
- Provide a mix of technical, job-specific skills with soft and basic skills.

2.2. Strengthen the TVET system:

- Improve the quality of VET: strengthen accreditation efforts of Institutos Superiores Técnico-Profesionales.
- Make it more relevant: modernise curriculum and connection with private sector.
- Build VET pathways to support students' transition to the workplace.
- Support VET for adults and establish a system for the recognition of skills acquired in the labour market, to give adults a second chance.

2.3. Improve the match between labour supply and demand:

- Strengthen active labour market policies to favour employability in formal jobs: training and intermediation systems.
- Set up an information system to attract students to sectors with higher demand.
- Consider establishing skills councils in dynamic sectors (e.g. a pilot in some segment of agroindustry) and establishing an observatory to anticipate demand for certain skills Consider establishing a qualifications framework to facilitate the recognition of skills.

References

Altinok, N., N. Angrist, and H. A. Patrinos (2018), Global Data Set on Education Quality (1965-2015), Policy Research Working Paper 8314, World Bank Group, Washington D.C.

Ayala, D. (2016), *Ocupación Informal en Paraguay: Evolución, Características y Acciones de Políticas Públicas*, Observatorio Laboral.

CEDLAS and World Bank (2017), *Socio-Economic Database for Latin America and the Caribbean,* CEDLAS [Centre for Distributive, Labour and Social Issues in Latin America], Universidad Nacional de La Plata (Argentina) and World Bank, http://sedlac.econo.unlp.edu.ar/eng (accessed on February 2018).

DGEEC (2017), *Encuesta Permanente de Hogares* [Permanent Household Survey] (database), Dirección General de Estadística, Encuestas y Censos de Paraguay, Fernando de la Mora, www.dgeec.gov.py/datos/encuestas/eph (accessed on February 2018).

Elías, R., G. Walder and D. Sosa (2016), "Perfiles de la exclusión educativa en la República de Paraguay" in *Informe integrante de la Iniciativa Global por los Niños Fuera de la Escuela*, OOESCI, Unicef-UIS, UNESCO.

Elías, R., N. Briet, C. Spinzi and B. Aquino (2014), *Revisión Nacional 2015 de la Educación para Todos: Paraguay*, Ministerio de Educación y Cultura, Asunción.

Galiani, S. et al. (2017), *Educational Upgrading and Returns to Skills in Latin America: Evidence from a Supply-Demand Framework*, NBER Working Paper No. 24015.

Hanushek, E. and S, Rivkin (2012), "Boosting teacher effectiveness" in *What lies ahead for America's children and their school*, Stanford: Hoover Institution Press, 23-35.

Heckman, J. (2006), *Skill formation and the economics of investing in disadvantaged children*, Science, Vol. 312, pages 1900-1902, http://jenni.uchicago.edu/papers/Heckman_Science_v312_2006.pdf.

ILO (2014), *Paraguay: Mesa de Dialogo Social. Políticas de Empleo*, International Labour Organization, Asunción, www.oit.org/wcmsp5/groups/public/---americas/---ro-lima/---sro-santiago/documents/genericdocument/wcms_248872.pdf.

MEC (2018), *Presentación de Resultados de la Evaluación Nacional de los Aprendizajes, Aplicación Censal 2015*, Ministerio de Educación y Ciencias de Paraguay, Asunción.

MEC (2012), *Estadística Educativa 2011, Datos e Indicadores de la Educación*, Ministerio de Educación y Ciencias de Paraguay, Asunción.

MEC et al. (2011), *Plan Nacional de Mejoramiento de la Educación Técnica y Profesional en el Paraguay 2011-2013*, Ministerio de Educación y Ciencias de Paraguay, Asunción.

MEC (2007), *Mecanismo de Licenciamiento de Instituciones Formadoras de Docentes*, Ministerio de Educación y Ciencias de Paraguay, Asunción, www.mec.gov.py/cms_v2/adjuntos/14692?1506353855.

MH (2017), *Diseño de la Estrategia de Transformación Educativa del Paraguay 2030*, Ministerio de Educación y Ciencias de Paraguay, Asunción.

OECD (2018), *Multi-dimensional Review of Paraguay: Volume I. Initial Assessment*, OECD Development Pathways, OECD Publishing, Paris, https://doi.org/10.1787/9789264301900-en.

OECD (2015), *PISA 2015 Results (Volume I): Excellence and Equity in Education*, OECD Publishing, Paris, http://dx.doi.org/10.1787/9789264266490-en.

OECD/CAF/UN ECLAC (2018), *Latin American Economic Outlook 2018: Rethinking Institutions for Development*, OECD Publishing, Paris, http://dx.doi.org/10.1787/leo-2018-en.

OECD/CAF/UN ECLAC (2016), *Latin American Economic Outlook 2017: Youth, Skills and Entrepreneurship*, OECD Publishing, Paris, https://doi.org/10.1787/leo-2017-en.

OECD/CAF/UN ECLAC (2014), *Latin American Economic Outlook 2015: Education, Skills and Innovation for Development*, OECD Publishing, Paris, https://doi.org/10.1787/leo-2015-en.

OECD/ E. Hanushek / L. Woessmann (2015), *Universal Basic Skills: What Countries Stand to Gain*, OECD Publishing, Paris, http://dx.doi.org/10.1787/9789264234833-en.

OECD (2014), *Skills Beyond School: Synthesis Report, OECD Reviews of Vocational Education and Training*, OECD Publishing, Paris, http://dx.doi.org/10.1787/9789264214682-en.

OECD (2013), *OECD Skills Outlook 2013: First Results from the Survey of Adult Skills*, OECD Publishing, Paris, http://dx.doi.org/10.1787/9789264204256-en.

OECD (2010), *Learning for Jobs, Synthesis Report of the OECD Reviews of Vocational Education and Training, Series: OECD Reviews of Vocational Education and Training*, OECD Publishing, Paris, http://dx.doi.org/10.1787/9789264087460-en.

PREAL (2013), *El Desafío es la equidad: Informe de Progreso Educativo. Paraguay* [The challenge is equity: Educational progress report. Paraguay], Programa de Promoción de la Reforma Educativa en América Latina y el Caribe and Instituto Desarrollo.

Ruppert Bulmer, E., S.M. Watson, and D. De Padua (2017), *Paraguay Jobs Diagnostic: the dynamic transformation of employment*, Working Paper, Jobs Series N° 9, World Bank, Washington, D.C., http://documents.worldbank.org/curated/en/500641499411206696/Paraguay-jobs-diagnostic-the-dynamic-transformation-of-employment.

UNESCO (2016), *La enseñanza y formación técnico profesional en América Latina y el Caribe: una perspectiva regional hacia 2030*, Oficina Regional de la UNESCO para América Latina y el Caribe, OREALC/UNESCO, Santiago.

UNESCO (2015), *Informe de resultados: Tercer Estudio Regional Comparativo y Explicativo* [Third Regional Comparative and Explanatory Study], Laboratorio Latinoamericano de evaluación de la calidad de la educación, UNESCO, Santiago.

UNESCO (2013), *World TVET Database: Paraguay* (database), UNESCO-UNEVOC International Centre for Technical and Vocational Education and Training.

UNICEF (2012), *Finishing school. A right for Children's Development: a joint effort*, Global Initiative on Out-of-School Children, UNICEF Regional Office for Latin America and the Caribbean.

World Bank (2018a), World Development Indicators (database), Washington D.C.

World Bank (2018b), *World Development Report 2018: Learning to Realize Education's Promise*, World Bank, Washington D.C., https://openknowledge.worldbank.org/handle/10986/28340.

World Bank (2013), *Estado del Arte de la Profesión Docente en Paraguay. Ideas Inspiradoras para la Elaboración de Políticas Educativas*, World Bank, Asunción.

ORGANISATION FOR ECONOMIC CO-OPERATION AND DEVELOPMENT

The OECD is a unique forum where governments work together to address the economic, social and environmental challenges of globalisation. The OECD is also at the forefront of efforts to understand and to help governments respond to new developments and concerns, such as corporate governance, the information economy and the challenges of an ageing population. The Organisation provides a setting where governments can compare policy experiences, seek answers to common problems, identify good practice and work to co-ordinate domestic and international policies.

The OECD member countries are: Australia, Austria, Belgium, Canada, Chile, the Czech Republic, Denmark, Estonia, Finland, France, Germany, Greece, Hungary, Iceland, Ireland, Israel, Italy, Japan, Korea, Latvia, Lithuania, Luxembourg, Mexico, the Netherlands, New Zealand, Norway, Poland, Portugal, the Slovak Republic, Slovenia, Spain, Sweden, Switzerland, Turkey, the United Kingdom and the United States. The European Union takes part in the work of the OECD.

OECD Publishing disseminates widely the results of the Organisation's statistics gathering and research on economic, social and environmental issues, as well as the conventions, guidelines and standards agreed by its members.

OECD DEVELOPMENT CENTRE

The OECD Development Centre was established in 1962 as an independent platform for knowledge sharing and policy dialogue between OECD member countries and developing economies, allowing these countries to interact on an equal footing. Today, 27 OECD countries and 25 non-OECD countries are members of the Centre. The Centre draws attention to emerging systemic issues likely to have an impact on global development and more specific development challenges faced by today's developing and emerging economies. It uses evidence-based analysis and strategic partnerships to help countries formulate innovative policy solutions to the global challenges of development.

For more information on the Centre and its members, please see *www.oecd.org/dev*.

OECD PUBLISHING, 2, rue André-Pascal, 75775 PARIS CEDEX 16
(41 2018 27 1 P) ISBN 978-92-64-30619-6 – 2018

www.ingramcontent.com/pod-product-compliance
Ingram Content Group UK Ltd.
Pitfield, Milton Keynes, MK11 3LW, UK
UKHW051502290926
15471UKWH00008B/1361

9 789264 306196